ISSUES AND RESPONSES IN STATE POLITICAL EXPERIENCE

ISSUES AND RESPONSES IN STATE POLITICAL EXPERIENCE

EDWARD W. CHESTER
University of Texas at Arlington

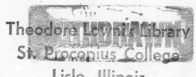
1968

LITTLEFIELD, ADAMS & CO.
Totowa, New Jersey

Preface

This volume consists mainly of a series of detailed investigations of various political issues which have played a key role in state history since 1876, examined both in isolation and in conjunction with each other, as in constitutional revisions, statehood drives, and gubernatorial programs. It is especially fitted to serve as a supplementary text or as outside reading in courses in state politics or state government. Since the overwhelming majority of general works in the field of political science deal with theories and generalizations rather than concrete facts, there often is a need to supplement these with additional historical data. Unfortunately, there is no place for the scholar to go if he wishes to obtain detailed background information in the area of state politics or state government other than the histories of the various states; a satisfactory collection of such histories, moreover, usually is available only in the larger libraries. It is true that specialized studies on certain topics exist, but as a rule these minimize the historical element in their emphasis on abstractions. In addition, because of the defeat of the states' rights doctrine in the Civil War, since the Reconstruction period of that war many historians have concentrated excessively on national developments.

Although one might read this book with profit solely for the historical data it contains, the conclusion not only explains at length how various factors have molded state politics and government, but also attempts to contrast state history with national history. The theory set forth herein stresses the fact that there is a greater imbalance in the histories of most states than there is nationally, and that this imbalance has led at times to political behavior of an extremist variety at the state level. This interpretation serves as an effective device for contrasting state political history with national political history. The question of how political behavior at the state level differs from that at the national level is one which merits far more study than it has received to date, since it is impossible to understand many of the dissimilarities between state government and national government without taking this question into consideration. Consequently, this book not only calls attention to this question, but also provides some tentative answers to it; the Annotated Bibliography at the end of the book suggests additional material for those who might care to pursue the matter further.

Among those who have read this manuscript and offered criticisms the author especially wishes to thank Dr. Frank Munger of Syracuse University, who made some valuable suggestions as to the condensation and elimination of otherwise unwieldy material, but he assumes complete responsibility for the final version as presented here.

EDWARD W. CHESTER

Contents

Chapter 1

Character Sketches of Five
Political Eras

Each historical period has its own special features and characteristics. To set the stage for the chapters that follow we will attempt here to draw brief portraits of the five major subdivisions of American political history since the end of the Reconstruction period, these being 1876-1901, 1901-1919, 1919-1931, 1931-1945, and the post-World War II era. Each incident, of course, must be identified with a particular historical epoch and its unique intellectual atmosphere before it is fully understood. Unfortunately, there are few readily available sources of detailed background information in the areas of state politics and state government. One must constantly keep in mind that there are many differences between state political history and national political history; we shall develop this theme at length in the conclusion, where a comparative analysis is set forth based on the topics emphasized in this volume, pointing out that there is more of a political imbalance statewise than nationally. Nevertheless, even the most superficial examination reveals that similar trends were present at both the national and the state levels during each of the historical periods under consideration.

1876–1901

Most historians would agree that the outstanding feature of state politics during the period from the end of Reconstruction to the coming of the Progressive era was its basic conservatism. There was no sharp division between the two major parties on issues. Far from being their own masters, state governments were dominated by powerful economic interests such as the Southern Pacific Railroad in California and Anaconda Copper in Montana. It was during this era that lingering memories of the Civil War and subsequent Reconstruction led to the emergence of a number of Democratic one-party states in the South and Republican one-party states in the upper New England and upper Great Plains states. Despite the successes of the Workingmen's Party in California between 1877 and 1883, no third party was able to achieve a noteworthy series of victories at the polls prior to the emergence in the 1890's of the agrarian-oriented Populists in the West and in the South. Among its leaders were Benjamin Tillman of South Carolina, Tom Watson of Georgia, James Weaver (the 1892 Presidential nominee) of Iowa, Ignatius Donnelly of Minnesota, Jerry Simpson and Mary Lease of Kansas, and William Jennings Bryan (the 1896 Presidential nominee) of Nebraska. Unfortunately for the Southern wing of the party, the attempt by white Populists to ally themselves with the Negro element there led not only to the rejection of their ideas, but also to the disenfranchisement of the Negro by white conservatives. Because of the prevalent atmosphere of *laissez faire,* state governments limited their activities severely, even in such vital areas as schools and roads; nevertheless, states such as Ohio, Connecticut, and Mississippi suffered from debt problems during this era. Perhaps surprisingly, this basically conservative age witnessed the adoption of a number of new state constitutions, thanks in part to eight territories becoming states.

The most powerful of all the economic interests during this era were the railroads. Despite the combined efforts of the Grangers, the Farmers' Alliances, and the Populists, attempts to check the power of this group never proved to be overly effective. The Supreme Court did uphold state regulation in *Munn v. Illinois* (1877), but then reversed itself in the Wabash case nine years later. It is true that Texas (as well as Florida) repealed certain land grants for building railroads, canals, and ditches during this period, while Texas and Arkansas also initiated a large-scale series of prosecutions against various trusts by the end of the century. But drastic measures of this sort were not common; far more frequent was the granting of wholesale privileges, bounties, and favors to economic interests. Typical was the measure passed in 1899 by Delaware, providing liberal terms for the chartering of corporations. As far as labor is concerned, the United States Supreme Court did uphold hours regulation for child labor in 1894, but it had yet to rule affirmatively on the bulk of state labor legislation. Since it was unable to obtain most of its goals peacefully, despite the founding of the American Federation of Labor (A.F.L.) in 1886, labor frequently resorted to violence; the Homestead Strike is a prominent example, as is the nation-wide railroad strike of 1877. New York and Massachusetts, though, did set up boards of arbitration and mediation in 1886.

1901–1919

In contrast to the reforms of the Populist era, those of the Progressive period were characterized by a broader base (urban as well as rural) and by a broader scope (regulating business in general as well as the railroads). Actually, Progressivism was more of a concept than a party, since one found Progressives in both the Republican and the Democratic Parties, although the Progressive wing of the Republican Party did offer its own Presidential candidate in 1912 (Theodore Roosevelt). Among its other leaders were Tom Johnson of Ohio, William U'Ren of Oregon, George Norris of Nebraska, William Allen White of Kansas, Albert Beveridge of Indiana, and a number of governors. As for third parties at the state level, perhaps the most significant new one that emerged during these years was the Nonpartisan League of North Dakota, a semi-Socialist organization that favored a system of state-owned elevators, mills, packing plants, banks, insurance companies, and credit associations. The Progressive era witnessed an increase in governmental spending as well as in government regulation; thanks in part to the various educational drives and good road movements, the states began to expand their programs in these areas. As agencies and departments proliferated, the need for governmental reorganization became obvious for the first time. Perhaps the most perplexing question with which one must deal in analyzing this era is the reason why the urban middle class, which largely viewed the Populist program with alarm during the 1890's, accepted many of their ideas a decade later. Richard Hofstadter has analyzed this phenomenon in terms of a reaction on the part of this class to a decline in status, although not every historian accepts his sociological theorizing.

One of the most significant developments of the Progressive

era was the attempt by reformers to lessen the influence of the various pressure groups that dominated many state governments. In some cases, these efforts were successful, as the Southern Pacific Railroad officially retired from California politics in 1911; in other cases, they bore less fruit, as the inept attacks on Anaconda Copper in Montana during this period demonstrate. Relative to the governmental regulation of business, an examination of the records of the more outstanding governors reveals the scope and variety of the measures which many state legislatures passed at this time. One prominent example was the Kansas "blue-sky" securities law of 1911; another was the restrictions which Governor James Vardaman of Mississippi placed on outside capital. Many significant acts were also passed protecting the rights of labor, including the first effective maximum hours law for children (Illinois, 1903) and the first minimum wage law for women and children (Massachusetts, 1912). But the United States Supreme Court, which was still thwarting the efforts of the states to regulate the railroads (Shreveport Case, 1914), likewise was hindering their attempts to protect labor (*Lochner v. New York,* 1908; *Coppage v. Kansas,* 1915) despite its decisions in *New York Central Railroad Co. v. White* (1917), *Muller v. Oregon* (1908), and *Bunting v. Oregon* (1917). Politically, labor remained largely ineffective, its efforts to obtain its demands through strikes at times reasonably successful (Anthracite Coal Strike, Pennsylvania, 1902), at times dismal failures (Boston Police Strike, Massachusetts, 1919).

1919–1931

The twelve years of Republican rule, which one might date either from the Congressional election of 1918 to that of 1930, or from the Presidential election of 1920 to that of 1932, marked a retreat from the crusading efforts on behalf of reform of the previous two decades. At the national level, the Republican Party dominated politics, although at the state level the Democratic Party showed considerable strength. It was during this era that many of the great political bosses (such as Tom Pendergast, Edward Crump, Frank Hague, and Harry Byrd) first solidified their hold on their states, while the Ku Klux Klan enjoyed a few years of ascendancy in Indiana under D. C. Stephenson. No new third party which appeared on the scene enjoyed much immediate success; the Farmer-Labor Party of Minnesota did elect Floyd Olson governor in 1930. With few exceptions, state governments made few attempts to expand their scope of operations, and in many cases they actually reduced their range of activities. Business was pampered more than it was regulated, while labor was given little additional protection. It was not a period when the conditions were such that one could easily make an outstanding political contribution, although it did witness the inception of the interstate compact and authority movement with the setting up of the Port of New York Authority (1921) and the signing of the Santa Fe Compact vis-a-vis the Colorado River (1922).

Despite the fact that business interests were politically ascendant, an occasional attempt at reform did take place. The voters of Montana, for example, passed a measure in 1924 increasing the tax burden on Anaconda Copper. In addition, Georgia, Maryland, and North Carolina enacted the first state anti-chain store taxation laws in 1926, while California approved the first state fair-trade measure in 1930. But these episodes were the exception rather than the rule. More common were the attempts by various states to restrict labor, the most extreme of which was the Kansas anti-strike law of 1920; the United States Supreme Court invalidated this several years later in the Wolff Packing Company Case. In general, however, that body did more to retard than to advance the cause of labor during this period, as attested by its decisions in *Truax v. Corrigan* (1921) attacking the failure of the Arizona courts to issue an anti-labor injunction, and in *Adkins v. Children's Hospital* (1923) invalidating a measure establishing minimum hours for women. It is noteworthy that, aside from infrequent episodes such as the Gastonia textile workers' strike, the era of Normalcy witnessed few significant labor walkouts, an indication of the relatively weak position of the unions. The A.F.L. did support the Progressive candidate, Robert La Follette, for President in 1924, but this was its only significant excursion into politics prior to 1952.

1931–1945

Together with the Progressive epoch, the New Deal period stands at the pinnacle of reform eras during the last century. One of the most significant characteristics of these years was a drastic expansion of federal regulatory activities; another was a sharp increase in federal spending. Politically, no new major party emerged, but the states' rights Democrats lost control of their party to the proponents of national planning; correspondingly, the anti-Progressive elements of the Republican Party came forward to challenge the New Deal, generally ignoring its liberal wing except on those occasions every four years when that party chose its Presidential candidate. Third parties, moreover, thrived at the state level as they had not done since the Populist days of the 1890's; Wisconsin, for example, chose the Progressive Party nominee (Philip La Follette) chief executive in 1934. Perhaps the most radically oriented state during the 1930's, though, was California. Upton Sinclair ran a strong race for governor on the Socialist Party ticket in 1934, while Dr. Francis Townsend mobilized considerable public sentiment on behalf of his welfare proposals a number of years later. Other important political developments of this period included the fall from power of the Republican machine that had directed the affairs of Pennsylvania since the Civil War, and the break-up of the Pendergast machine in Missouri following the jailing of its leader on vote fraud and income tax evasion charges in 1938. Former governor Huey Long of Louisiana, who was on the way to becoming dictator of his state, was assassinated in 1935, thus cutting short a career unparalleled in the history of American politics.

Although such a generalization invites criticism, it is still reasonably apparent that the impetus for reform at this time came from the national government more than it did during the Progressive era. For this reason, certain state administrations of the period have been labeled "Little New Deals." Various new regulations were applied to business, but it must be remembered that many states were no longer dominated by one or two economic interests to the extent that they once had been, and for this reason it was more difficult to single out a particular scapegoat for punishment. On the other hand, the United States Supreme Court took a more liberal attitude toward governmental regulation of business, as one notices in its 1931 decision upholding anti-chain store taxes at the state level, and in its 1936 decision finding for constitutional state laws allowing resale price maintenance contracts. Still, in many ways the measures that many states passed to protect labor were more significant. Following the creation in 1935 of the Congress (originally

Committee) of Industrial Organization (C.I.O.), labor began to capitalize on government's favorable attitude toward it by increasingly involving itself in state politics, but it enjoyed little real success except in the large industrial states. New York did enact the first fair employment practices act in 1945, but Florida and Arkansas also passed the first right-to-work measure in 1944. Fortunately for labor, by 1937 the United States Supreme Court finally had come around to a position where it was upholding state laws designed to protect labor; for example, it found constitutional a Washington minimum wage law in *West Coast Hotel Co. v. Parrish* (1937) and invalidated an Alabama anti-picketing statute in the Thornhill Case (1940). It also sidestepped the legality of sitdown strikes in *Apex Hosiery Co. v. Leader* (1940) by leaving their policing to the states. Nevertheless, despite the gains which it was winning legislatively, politically, and judicially, labor did not respond by taking a more conciliatory attitude toward management in the years prior to World War II, instead sponsoring such crippling walkouts as the general strikes in San Francisco and Terre Haute, the prolonged walkout in the Harlan County, Kentucky coal fields, and the Flint sitdown strike.

The Post-World War II Era

As one comes closer and closer to the present, it becomes increasingly difficult to generalize about state politics, because one lacks perspective and because one must overcome prejudices. Nevertheless, it is obvious that two of the major developments of this era have been the slow growth of the two-party system in a number of states (both Northern Republican and Southern Democratic) where one party once predominated, and, more recently, the increasing role that the Negro voter has assumed. The ultimate implications of the latter is not measurable at the present moment, as it is difficult to determine for how long a period Negroes will continue to vote as a bloc. In contrast, the decline of the political boss, which had begun during the 1930's, reached considerable proportions by 1948; during these elections, Edward Crump of Tennessee and Frank Hague of New Jersey suffered crushing defeats. Third parties, too, have not prospered recently, as the Farmer-Labor Party of Minnesota fused with the Democrats in 1944, while the Progressive Party of Wisconsin joined the Republicans in 1946. One exception would be New York, where both a Liberal Party and a Conservative Party have been active in recent years. Summarizing the period, one might observe that nationally its conservative phase lasted from the Republican Congressional victory in 1946 to the election of John F. Kennedy as President in 1960, or perhaps more accurately, to the elevation of Lyndon Johnson to the Presidency in 1963. Only from that date have liberals enjoyed the power to push such domestic reforms as civil rights and Medicare through Congress. As for the state level, it is more difficult to generalize, since some states did enact liberal legislation during the 1950's. Governmental spending at all levels has progressively increased during the past twenty years, but this in itself is no indication that true qualitative change has taken place, because this rise in expenditures has been partly attributable to inflation.

One of the most remarkable aspects of governmental policy at the state level in recent years has been a sharp reversal of attitude toward those economic interests that once dominated many state governments. Following the period of New Deal reforms, the states began to realize that they were penalizing themselves economically by discriminating against business in general, and for this reason they not only began to assist those concerns already present in a state, but also to attract outside capital. This movement has flowered into full bloom since World War II. Actually, further regulation of business (at least on an extensive basis) may not be desirable, since most of the needed laws are already on the statute books, while increased competition among business units has served as an additional safeguard against monopoly. In contrast, the political position of labor currently varies widely from state to state, as does the legislation designed to benefit it or restrict it. Despite the victories it won in a number of states in 1958 in its campaign against right-to-work laws, labor really has played a dominant role politically in only two states (Michigan and Hawaii) in recent years. Thus, it is not surprising that just as many states have adopted right-to-work laws as fair employment practices laws, while just as many state labor relations measures imitate the Taft-Hartley Act as copy the Wagner Act. There seems to be no doubt, though, that strikes and walkouts everywhere lack the violence that once characterized them; the marathon strike that took place at Kohler, Wisconsin, between 1954 and 1960 was decidedly the exception rather than the rule. Few path-breaking United States Supreme Court decisions relative to the regulation of business or the protection of labor have occurred in recent years, at least in comparison with those of earlier epochs.

The Future Prospects of States' Rights

As everyone knows, the growing power of the national government has been viewed by advocates of states' rights as a threat to their survival; United States Supreme Court decisions have progressively widened the scope of federal authority, while, beginning with the New Deal, Congress has spent increasingly large sums for a veritable galaxy of projects. As a result, the states have been politically overshadowed to the point where a few commentators have even suggested that they be eliminated. Confronted with this situation, supporters of states' rights might well examine the material presented in this volume, because it reveals that the states themselves have been at least partially responsible for their decline in power, and that it is still possible for them to recover some of their lost prestige. This truth is one which is far too often overlooked by those apologists who write sadly of the impending political death of the states.

The key to an understanding of how the states themselves have contributed to their downfall politically is to be found in an analysis of the extent to which reforms have originated at state and national levels, especially during the great eras of protest. Populism, with its lengthy program of proposed innovations, was essentially a grass roots movement that spread over rural America, and in its heyday (the 1890's) it was more successful statewise (the West and the South in particular) than nationally. The Progressive epoch, too, featured a number of notable developments locally, despite the emergence of such strong national leaders as Theodore Roosevelt and Woodrow Wilson and the enactment of many reform measures by Congress. By the time of the New Deal, however, political reform had become something that was imposed downward from above; one recalls that several state administrations were referred to as "Little New Deals," as they were imitations rather than innovations. Occasional experiments originated at the state level, such as the Nebraska unicameral legislature (1935) and the Minnesota commissioner of administration (1939), but these were decidedly the exception, not the rule. Politically speaking, reform sentiment which once had crystallized state-wise in the Populist Party and the Progressive movement, at least partially independent of the two major parties, now operated mainly through the predominant Democratic Party, aside from such isolated third parties as the Progressive Party of Wisconsin and the Farmer-Labor Party of Minnesota. If Franklin Roosevelt was influenced by political developments at the state level, it was by the ideas of such isolated extremists as Huey Long and Dr. Francis Townsend, not by the general reform movement that was going on there.

Today, we appear to be entering another major reform era. It is significant that the two developments which have had the greatest impact on the states politically have been the United States Supreme Court decisions relative to the Negro, accompanied by a series of national civil rights acts, and the United States Supreme Court decisions commanding the reapportionment of state legislatures. In both cases, moreover, one finds not cooperative acquiescence statewise, but rather active opposition, as it is now the states that lag behind in instituting reforms. It is difficult, if not impossible, to point out one widespread innovation that the states themselves have sponsored in recent years that the national government has copied. The argument that the states have been deprived of their opportunity to institute reforms by large-scale federal spending does not stand up under close scrutiny; the initiative, referendum, and recall did not entail large expenditures of money, and they rank among the key reforms of American political history. In addition, the theory that United States Supreme Court decisions expanding the scope of federal authority have correspondingly reduced that of the states, while obviously true to a degree, ignores such undisputed facts as the increasing judicial acceptance over the last generation or so of state legislation regulating business and protecting labor. Thus, it is not entirely accurate to picture the states as innocent victims caught in a squeeze involving a free-spending Congress on the one hand and a centralization-minded highest tribunal on the other. Nevertheless, it is apparent that, during reform periods, the national government has increasingly seized the initiative and assumed for itself numerous powers that the states themselves might exercise. What occurs during the *status quo* phase has far less impact on the redistribution of power governmentally; the Eisenhower Administration, to cite the most recent example, at least gave lip service to states' rights.

Turning to the future, there is no simple answer to the question of whether the states will eventually disappear as governmental units, as it is impossible to predict what developments the years ahead will bring. Admittedly, the state governments are not able to compete with their counterpart in Washington in playing the role of Santa Claus, and for this reason mayors of large cities (such as John Lindsay of New York) are turning to federal authorities for massive financial assistance. Yet, there is no reason why states may not experiment along numerous lines which do not require lavish expenditures and consolidate their authority in these areas if such innovations prove to be fruitful; such developments as the various interstate compacts may bring about a far more satisfactory solution to regional problems than would federal intervention—no reason, of course, except a lack of enlightened leadership. If the states continue to decline as political units, then, it will be as much attributable to a failure to counteract the dry rot within rather than to failure to outflank the frontal attack from without, since no iron-clad law of historical development has decreed their inevitable passing from the political scene.

Chapter 2

Sectional Rivalries and
Capital Transfers

Sectionalism, in the opinion of most commentators, is one of the key themes of American history. Inspired by the example set by Frederick Jackson Turner, numerous analysts have examined our past in an effort to determine to what extent sectional rivalry has affected the historical process. Their conclusion that its impact has been considerable is unquestionably justified. As sectionalism exists nationally, so it flourishes statewise; the separation of West Virginia from its mother state during the Civil War is perhaps the most extreme example of this phemomenon that one might cite. (Today, however, only the eastern panhandle of the former markedly resembles the latter.) In general, chroniclers of state history do not emphasize sectional rivalry to the degree that they should, and this chapter constitutes an attempt to remedy this neglect. It is obviously impossible to cover every state here, but we do offer representative examples in the following pages of the major varieties of sectionalism, touching as well on separatism and city rivalries.

One might begin a discussion of the impact of sectionalism on various states by examining its relationship to geography. Among the more notable instances of the impact of the latter on the former is Alaska. Isolated from continental United States by a two-thousand-mile stretch of land, the Forty-Ninth State has a set of interests somewhat different from those of the mainland. Moreover, it is split into two parts, since the narrow coastal fringe which joins the panhandle to the main body of central and western Alaska is often impassable because of the glaciers which sweep across it, and this militates against its unity. Idaho affords another instance of virtual bifurcation. The Salmon

River, which cuts across central Idaho, runs through a deep gorge which even today hampers travel and communication between the northern and the southern parts, and the resulting division has played a key role in both the territorial and the state history of Idaho. The south has tended to dominate the state politically, C. E. Robins (1947–1951) being only the second governor from the north. As for culture, Spokane is the focal point of the panhandle, while Salt Lake City is that for the remainder of the state; the opposition of northern Idaho to the establishment of a four-year branch of the University at Pocatello, in the south, is a significant aspect of sectional antagonism here. Still another example is Hawaii, where rivalry among the islands exists.

If one is to attribute sectionalism in Idaho to the Salmon River, in the cases of Washington and Oregon he must cite the Cascades Mountains as the divisive factor. As a result of this barrier, the settlers of western Washington and Oregon turned to cattle and sheep raising, mining, and dry farming, while those of the eastern half of the two states became lumbermen, dairymen, fishermen, and farmers. The suggestion has been made that the parts of these two states west of the mountains be united as one state, and those east of the Cascades as another, but the consummation of such a project is no longer feasible. As for politics, one might point out that, in the case of Washington, the western part tends to be Democratic, the eastern, Republican. Turning our attention momentarily to an eastern state, the Green Mountains divide Vermont north and south in much the same manner; Vermonters preserved political harmony up to 1928 by selecting senators and governors from alternate sides of the barrier. Burlington is the center of the western half, while the east really lacks a focal point—perhaps because its population is more diversified. Since 1928, however, legislative members have begun to regard themselves as northerners or southerners, so that the former sectional division here apparently is undergoing a metamorphosis.

Aside from the instances of sectionalism rendered inevitable by geography, one could mention several other case histories from the West. Eastern Montana, for example, has much in common with western North Dakota, but the more populous western part of the state's interests largely coincide with those of northern Idaho and eastern Washington. Admittedly, there is much to censure in the record of the Anaconda Copper Company which dominates the state, but one wonders whether Montana would possess the unity that it does have were it not for this monolithic organization. There is an east-west cleavage in North Dakota similar to that in Montana; here the eastern portion of the state inclines toward conservatism because of the rich soil and plentiful rainfall, while the western sector tends toward liberalism since the climate there is more arid and the soil less productive. The most influential segment of North Dakota's population is located in the Red River Valley and is oriented toward the Twin Cities (Minneapolis and St. Paul) of Minnesota. Instead of allowing a monolithic corporation to bring order to chaos as Montanans have, North Dakotans have developed one of the most unusual political organizations (the Nonpartisan League) ever to function in a state. If the nature of sectionalism varies from one state to another, so does the response to this challenge.

In the case of Oklahoma, the sectional character of the state is more complex. White settlers did not enter the territory until 1889, so that, apart from the Indian element, Oklahoma has had a relatively brief history. Nevertheless, pronounced differences do exist here. The farmers of the state, many of whom came from Texas, Mississippi, and Arkansas, are divided into the wheat growers of the north central and northwestern parts, and the cotton raisers of the southwestern and central sections. Then there are the mining regions, whose population is largely drawn from elements descended from European miners. As for the Indian population, it has been traditionally centered in the eastern half of the state, and it was this half which was slated to become the independent state of Sequoyah shortly after the turn of the century. Politically, it might be added, the northern part of Oklahoma is traditionally Republican, although the state usually votes Democratic; Oklahoma elected its first Republican governor in 1962. Another instance of racial sectionalism is New Mexico, with its "Anglos" in the east and its Spanish-Americans in the west.

There have been instances, moreover, in which sectional control of a state has shifted. This is especially evident in the case of Nevada, where Virginia City held the ascendancy during the first score of years following the state's (territory's) separation from Utah. The flowering of the rich mining camps in the eastern part of Nevada witnessed a subsequent shift of power to that area, after which Tonopah and Goldfield had their day in the sun. In more recent times, however, Reno has gained dominance over the state, although Boulder (Hoover) Dam and various mining centers challenge its ascendancy now and then. As the history of Nevada parallels a series of mining cycles, frequent shifts in the center of power in the state were only natural. Politically speaking, southern Nevada usually votes Democratic and western Nevada, Republican.

Two examples west of the Mississippi of a fundamentally urban-rural division have been Arizona and Nebraska. In the case of the former, Phoenix (Maricopa County) is in perpetual contention with the remainder of the state (formerly a single congressional district, but now two); Tucson, the state's second largest city, once allied itself with Phoenix, but now lines up with the rural areas more and more frequently. During recent years, Phoenix has controlled the executive branch of the state government, while the rest of Arizona has dominated the legislative arm. As for Nebraska, the initial rivalry between the north-of-Platte and south-of-Platte sections has been complicated by two developments: the continuing growth of two major cities, Omaha and Lincoln, and the increasing schism between the Sand Hill and Panhandle regions of the west on the one hand, and the more populous eastern counties on the other. The result has been that westerners and urbanites have taken turns in aligning themselves with the eastern rural majority so as to enact legislation favorable to them. It is against this background that the unicameral legislature operates.

Turning now to the South, one might cite the conflict between northern and western Florida and southern Florida as another example of one section losing its ascendant position statewise. In the days before the Civil War, the majority of Florida's population was centered in the north above the Suwannee River; most of the tax money and political leaders were drawn from this area during this period, and the Constitution of 1887 was designed to preserve its leadership. Over the past century, however, southern Florida has developed from a quasi-tropical wilderness into a thriving paradise, and it is now this region that is the dominant one. Legislative reapportionment, though, is encountering rough sledding in this state for the reason that the northern counties are hesitant to allow a reduction in their no longer justified bloc of seats. Many proposals have appeared over the years advocating the division of this state into two independent parts, but nothing has ever materialized out of any of these schemes.

There also has been a shift in population and wealth in South Carolina, but here the movement has been from the coast toward the northwest. The latter region is more democratic than the seaboard, but its civilization is less mature; low-country men and Virginians have introduced much of the culture there. In recent years, up-country support of candidates from Charleston in various elections indicates that the antagonism between the two regions (which was once manifest in the question of the cancelling of the state debt) is lessening. A somewhat similar situation exists in North Carolina, where the leadership of the state has passed largely from the old rural plantation aristocracy of the east into the hands of the new urban, industrial element of the Piedmont. Over the years, the east more or less dominated the legislature and various important offices through political acumen, but a westerner, Kerr Scott, broke the policy of rotating the governorship between the east and the west by successfully running for the office of chief executive in 1948. Consequently, the east's ascendancy may be nearing the end.

While in coastal Southern states the sectional struggle takes the form of a rivalry between the Tidewater and the Piedmont, it assumes other patterns elsewhere in Dixie. In Arkansas, for example, the people of the Ozark and Ouachita Mountain regions frequently are aligned against those of the cotton- and rice-growing lowlands. The rivalry between independents and conservatives in Arkansas is typified by such episodes as the expulsion of now-Senator William Fulbright as President of the University. In neighboring Louisiana, on the other hand, north and south Louisiana fought against New Orleans prior to 1900, while groups from these two sections joined forces with the city after that date to effect their desires. An awareness of this fact is essential to anyone who is attempting to explain the Long era in Louisiana politics. French and Catholic influences, of course, are more prevalent in the southern half of the state.

Likewise, one requires a knowledge of sectional patterns in Mississippi if he is to understand the careers of such demagogues as James Vardaman and Theodore Bilbo. Here the hill counties, mainly populated by whites, have traditionally been in conflict with the Delta, where the Negroes predominate. For years after Reconstruction, the whites of the Delta were in the ironical position of suppressing the rights of the colored man on the one hand, yet dominating the legislature by counting him when determining the apportionment of seats. Such was the fear at one time that the Negroes might attempt to recover control of the state that the legislature reorganized Mississippi's Congressional districts so as to create one of the most famous examples of gerrymandering in American history. The emergence of southeastern Mississippi as a political force has somewhat complicated the old struggle between the hill counties and the Delta, as the two white sections (northeast and southwest) do not always vote together; the northeast, for example, once combined forces with the Delta to pass an apportionment measure over the objections of the southeast.

Still other patterns of sectional cleavage are evident in the South. In the case of Kentucky, the rural people of the western part of the state have been trying throughout its history to wrest control of the government from the urban people and Bourbons of the east, but by and large their attempts have been a dismal failure. As for Tennessee, the eastern third is a focal point of discontent; this region is the home of the mountain folk. Here, however, instead of working within the dominant Democratic Party, the rebels have allied themselves with the Republicans, but with no more over-all success than that enjoyed by the western Kentuckians. The other two sections are the west, focused on Memphis, and the middle, focused on Nashville. Then there is Alabama, where the northern and southeastern parts of the state often join forces against the Black Belt, a strip cutting across the south central portion that most closely resembles the stereotyped image of the Deep South. The farmers of this area, which contains many Negroes, in turn often throw in their lot with the "big mules" (i.e., steel, coal, iron, insurance, and utilities interests) of Birmingham and Mobile.

As far as Maryland and Delaware are concerned, sectionalism in these two states frequently takes the form of a battle between a single city and the remainder of the state. There has been a long tradition of antagonism between the agricultural counties of Maryland and Baltimore, which is the commercial and industrial center, although improved communication and transportation, extended commuting areas, and rural electrification all have tended to break down this barrier. Likewise, there is friction in Delaware between the agrarian area outside of Wilmington and that city, a center for manufacturing and corporate administration. The fact that the Chesapeake Canal separates most of the state from the extreme north aggravates rather than lessens the division here, which was a factor at the constitutional convention in 1897.

We find a slight variation on this pattern in Massachusetts, which is essentially urban, where a coalition of the outlying towns perpetually challenges the authority of Boston. The latter is not always victorious, as is demonstrated by the success of the maneuver which put the Boston police force under the control of a commissioner appointed by the governor. Political commentators often cite the schism between Democratic New York City and Republican upstate New York as a typical example of the urban-rural bifurcation of a state, but there are many industrial centers strung across the state east to west, some of which vote Democratic just as New York City does. Thus, one must question the selection of this particular case as the most representative of its type. More clear-cut is the dichotomy between Chicago and downstate Illinois, or between Detroit and the remainder of Michigan.

As our final example, we might note the only American state which nature has divided into two widely separate parts, Michigan, so as to determine what effect this "apartness" has had on its vis-a-vis the development of sectionalism. As for economic ramifications, the mines of the Upper Peninsula are owned by corporations financed by Easterners, while the railway lines of this section are linked with Milwaukee and Chicago rather than with Detroit, the focal point of the Lower Peninsula. The Lower Peninsula, though, has dominated state politics over the years; it was not until 1910 that a resident of the northern country was elected governor, and the repetition of this event was a rarity. This was Chase S. Osborn, a Sault Ste. Marie publisher and a liberal Republican. Over the years, the two parts of Michigan probably have drawn closer together, but the Upper Peninsula is too deficient in resources and population to challenge the ascendancy of the southern portion, at least in the immediate future.

Separatist sentiment, of course, is the most pronounced form of sectionalism at the state level, while the secessionist movement in the South before the Civil War was its most violent manifestation nationally. There have been several instances of this phenomenon in the period since the end of Reconstruction, especially in the West. Southwestern Dakotans, for example, were so dissatisfied with the Dakotan territorial government that in 1876 they requested Congress to create an independent territory out of the mineral region. A bill establishing the Territory of the Black Hills was introduced in Congress later that year. This Dakotan separatist movement was headed mostly by Deadwood men, who as zealous Democrats were opposed to Republican domination in political matters, as well as being out of sympathy with the non-mining areas. Needless to say, this maneuver was unsuccessful, although Congress did split Dakota Territory into two parts (North and South) when that body finally granted it statehood.

Another abortive attempt to set up an independent territory involved the Oklahoma panhandle; at one time, this area was more or less a "no man's land." Settlers organized this strip as the Territory of Cimarron in 1887, although Congress never recognized the action. Not only did a provisional legislature pass a series of laws, but it also placed restrictions on non-residents gathering buffalo bones, cow manure, wood, or grapes, an action which is an early example of state or territorial opposition to outside domination. Upon the opening of the Oklahoma Territory to white settlement in 1889, however, many of the squatters left "Cimarron" for greener pastures, and the area eventually became a part of the state of Oklahoma.

In contrast, in 1891 a movement to transfer part of Idaho to Wyoming arose when the Idaho legislature passed a measure (the Idaho Australian Ballot Law) which permanently excluded Mormons from voting. The Mormons of Idaho thereupon petitioned Congress to alter the Idaho-Wyoming boundary so as to make Bear Lake and Bingham Counties a part of the other state, but this action became unnecessary when a jury brought in a verdict of innocent in a test case which arose in the aftermath of the passage of this law. Unlike their ancestors of several generations ago, these Mormons lacked the migratory urge which had led their forefathers to establish Utah as a sanctuary for those who adhered to the teachings of Joseph Smith; the relatively tame nature of their reaction, coupled with the shortly-to-come self-imposed restriction on polygamy in Utah, reveals that this religious group had lost some of its primitive élan by that date.

Of more recent vintage was the agitation in west Texas for separation from the remainder of the state; this section, which was not settled until after 1875 because of the Indian menace, is less conservative than the eastern half, where the influence of the old South still exists. It might be recalled here that the act under which Texas joined the Union as a state provided that up to five states could be created out of the original entity, so that any proposed division would have a legal precedent. There have been two noteworthy instances since 1876 when separatist sentiment flared up. The first ensued when "drys" in west Texas and "wets" in east Texas became involved in a bitter dispute over the prohibition issue; the second occurred when many individuals in west Texas became dissatisfied because that section was not receiving its due share of educational institutions. The location of the Technological College at Lubbock, however, terminated this later group of protests. This sectional bifurcation of Texas is complicated by the existence of such areas as the Mexican border and the northern panhandle.

As a final example of attempted division, one might cite several episodes from California history. Here a group of malcontents circulated petitions in 1915 calling for the separation of this state into a North California and a South California. The Nevada legislature, not to be outdone, countered by passing a resolution proposing a lengthwise rendering of their neighbor along the Sierra divide, with the eastern strip (which contained the headwaters of various Nevada rivers) going to that state. Neither proposal, of course, was ever adopted. The California election of 1890 had likewise involved a possible bifurcation, but no steps were taken in this direction despite the fact that the southern candidate won. Even as late as 1941, the four northernmost counties of this state attempted to join with the southernmost county of Oregon so as to form a new state of Jefferson, but this scheme collapsed with the death of its originator and the advent of Pearl Harbor. Still, there exist such issues as the control of surplus water which threaten to divide California, and thus division schemes will continue to arise.

Another manifestation of sectionalism at the state level is the rivalry between two or more cities. Although quite a few instances exist, we shall analyze three cases as particularly representative, beginning our survey with an examination of the struggle between Minneapolis and St. Paul.

It would seem that nature itself decreed that St. Paul, located as it is at the head of river navigation, was to become a commercial town, while Minneapolis, situated close to the water power at the Falls of St. Anthony, was to become a manufacturing center. Rivalry was so sharp at one time (1890) that both cities padded their census figures, since each was determined to be listed as the more populous. As for religion and politics, in St. Paul the Irish Catholics are a pillar of the Democratic Party, while in Minneapolis the Scandinavians and the Lutherans bolster Republicanism. It is true that in recent years those cities have drawn closer together, but each still retains many of its original features. A curious sidelight on this rivalry is that the American League baseball expansion of 1961 involved the unprecedented (at least for the major leagues) move of admitting an entry from a state (Minnesota) rather than from a city (Minneapolis or St. Paul) so as to forestall an inevitable howl from the city which failed to receive the franchise.

In regard to the competition between San Francisco and Los Angeles, the ascendancy here has passed from the former to the latter during this century, although the Bay City, which developed much earlier, was once very much the dominant metropolis. Consequently, an analysis of the factors retarding the growth of San Francisco, built by gold, railways, and the port, and stimulating that of Los Angeles, founded an oil, climate, and real estate, is in order. In the first place, San Francisco has failed to advertise itself to the extent that Los Angeles has, while the topography of the San Francisco area is not so propitious to expansion as is that of Los Angeles. San Francisco, moreover, was hurt by the labor unrest and the graft trials of the first decade of this century, as well as by the great earthquake-fire of 1906. On the other hand, Los Angeles has enjoyed an unprecedented boom in agriculture, petroleum, hydroelectric power, and motion pictures over the past half century, while the Owens River aqueduct and the San Pedro deep water harbor, a relative absence of labor controversies, and an abundance of good roads and automobiles have aided the growth of the city. San Franciscans, though, tend to rationalize this situation by claiming that their city represents quality and Los Angeles, quantity.

Still another noted rivalry of this type has been that between Kansas City and St. Louis. These two Missouri cities are dissimilar in many ways. Kansas City, a great center of the cattle trade, has had a reputation for wildness and lawlessness; St. Louis, on the other hand, concentrates on manufacturing and finance, and is more conservative that its competitor. In addition, Kansas City has a western orientation and is basically

Protestant, while St. Louis has ties with the South and is more heavily Catholic. As for politics, at one time Kansas City was the Democratic stronghold in the state, but, since the eclipse of the Pendergast machine, the focal point of Democratic power has shifted to St. Louis, where the Republicans at times have been strong. Admittedly, this rivalry is not so well known as the other two cases just discussed, but the two cities do furnish many significant points of contrast.

It is true that instances do exist of states in which a group of cities are locked in a struggle with each other, but such a situation is a rarity, as almost invariably one or two metropolises will dominate a state. Two exceptions to this rule are Ohio and Connecticut. In Ohio, Cleveland, Columbus, Cincinnati, Toledo, Youngstown, Dayton, Canton-Massilon, and Akron are rivals, while in Connecticut Bridgeport, Hartford, New Britain, New Haven, Stamford, and Waterbury are in contention with each other. Connecticut, however, is almost totally urban, while Ohio does contain many rural areas; agriculture consequently plays a much more important role in Ohio than it does in Connecticut. The cities of the former state, moreover, are larger than those of the latter, as Ohio itself surpasses Connecticut in size. Still another difference between the two states which one might point out is in the psychological atmosphere, as the New England tradition of Connecticut is quite distinct from the Midwestern *Weltanschauung* of Ohio. Still, both states are multi-metropolitan, and thus we should consider them in conjunction here.

The material herein presented demonstrates that a state is often just as much an illogical abstraction as a nation frequently is, since each may be an amalgam of contradictory political, social, economic, and geographic forces. It is these rivalries within a state (or nation), however, such as those between various cities which may act as the leaven of progress. The relative importance of the four above-mentioned varieties of sectional friction does vary from state to state; in many cases, the balance among them has changed within a particular state over the years, and the future doubtless will bring new adjustments. Any definite study of state sectionalism, of course, would involve a thorough examination of this historical evolution. On the other hand, separatist sentiment appears to be on the decline, although it does crop up now and then in such a state as California. We shall refer again to the political consequences of sectionalism in the conclusion, where we shall show that it has been a key factor in the development of one-party states.

Those conversant with early American history will recall that the nation's capital migrated from Annapolis to Philadelphia to New York to Washington within the space of a few short years late in the eighteenth century. A similar transfer, albeit usually of a one-step character, has taken place in quite a few states, even in the era since Reconstruction; the struggles between various cities for the honor of being the site of the government of a state frequently have been of a rather agitated nature. They are, moreover, a significant aspect of sectional rivalry. The examples presented in the following pages will demonstrate, among other things, that in many cases more than two cities will contend with each other, that the pressure groups involved may be economic, and even religious as well as political, and that agitation for capital removal is in some cases episodic, in others, chronic. As mere incidents in the historical process, however, these cases are quite fascinating.

An instance of the more routine variety of capital contest was that which led to the selection of Denver as the permanent capital of Colorado. That city had served as the site of state government on a temporary basis, but the legislature refused to appropriate the money for a capitol building until the people selected a permanent location. An election was held in 1881 for this purpose, and Denver received an absolute majority of the votes cast, so that a run-off contest was not necessary. A law, moreover, was passed at this time which stated that the electorate might not move the capital of Colorado from Denver except by a two-thirds vote; in the days before government became so complex that now it is almost impossible to transfer it, it frequently was necessary to adopt such a provision to guarantee that the capital would stay in one place. Today, of course, no choice other than Denver seems logical.

The case of Rhode Island, in contrast, merits attention because it exemplifies the gradual abandonment of a multiple-capital system. Up to 1854, there had been five capitals of the state—Providence, Newport, East Greenwich, Bristol, and South Kingstown; during its sessions, the General Assembly moved around from one town to another. After this date, though, the number of capital cities was reduced to two (Newport and Providence), while it was narrowed to one (Providence) by a constitutional amendment adopted in 1900. This multiple-capital system of Rhode Island is undoubtedly one of the neglected curiosities of American history, and such a precedent provides food for thought for those who object to the increasing centralization of political power in Washington. On the other hand, the fact that such a system arose in our smallest state is highly ironic.

Attempts to transfer the capital of a state from one city to another, of course, are not always successful. One might cite as a typical instance of this variety of thwarted ambition the efforts of Macon to supplant Atlanta as the capital of Georgia through the years to about 1916; Atlanta itself had obtained this honor over Milledgeville in 1877. Macon, which was expanding during this period, carried her request for capitalhood to the state legislature every year, arguing that she was more geographically suited capitalwise than was Atlanta. This claim was not unjustified. Macon's arguments, however, fell on deaf ears, thanks largely to some clever counter-lobbying on the part of Atlanta. A similar effort to remove the capital of Kentucky from Frankfort around 1891 failed when a committee appointed by the legislature to study the question endorsed the present capital, as well as selecting a location there for a new state house. In Florida, the previously discussed shift in the sectional balance of power almost deprived Tallahassee of the privilege of being the site of the state government. In 1900, only 52 per cent of the voters of Florida cast ballots in favor of keeping the capital there, the remainder of the electorate preferring it to be removed to a more central geographic location; Jacksonville, Ocala, and St. Augustine were suggested as alternate possibilities. Perhaps the main reason that the capital was kept at Tallahassee was the distinctive charm of the metropolis and the hospitality of her people.

Quite naturally, the selection of a city as the site of state government carries with it a considerable economic advantage as well as considerable prestige. Thus, it is only natural that vote-buying and other forms of corruption would accompany many of the elections held for this purpose. One would presume that a large number of these capital contests were tainted, but it is doubtful whether all of the others in conjunction could rival dirt-wise the fight in Montana between Helena and Anaconda. Tied in as it was with the great Clark-Daly political feud, it is not surprising that both sides spent a total of one million, five hundred thousand dollars during the 1894 capital election; Helena was the victor on this occasion, as it had been in 1892. Governmental policies, though, afterward continued to originate in the offices of the Anaconda Copper Company rather than at the statehouse, since the history of this state is one of the prime instances of an economic group dictating the policies of state government.

As we have pointed out, pressure groups are not always of the political or economic variety; the capital fight between the Alaskan cities of Sitka and Juneau demonstrates that they may take other forms as well. For a long time there had been ill feelings between the Presbyterian missionary groups of Sitka, which supported prohibition, and certain business interests in Juneau (and Skagway) which were in favor of licensing. In this particular case, the squabble was settled by Congress rather than by popular vote; Juneau was awarded the capital through a piece of legislation passed in 1901. As is noted elsewhere, however, authorities in Washington have often ignored the wishes of the people of Alaska, since throughout history they have more or less blindly imposed their will on our northernmost state.

Turning now to Oklahoma, we encounter an instance of the people of a territory rejecting a capital which Congress had selected. Here the main rivals were Oklahoma City, Guthrie, and Shawnee; a fourth town, Frisco, stood by in case the main contenders failed. Actually, Guthrie had an advantage, as the Organic Act had designated it as the temporary capital, and it was also more populous than either of the other two contenders at the time of the first state legislature. Yet, Oklahoma City won an easy victory in a special election held in 1910, and the capital was immediately moved to that city, despite the fact that Congress had designated Guthrie as the site of state government at least until 1913. The United States Supreme Court upheld this action in *Coyle v. Smith* in 1911, ruling that Congress had illegally sought to regulate a matter of internal and domestic concern. It should be added that Governor Steele vetoed a bill in 1890 which would have moved the territorial capital to Kingfisher, while the "new Jerusalem" plan to locate it at the geographic center of the state failed in the election of 1908.

Regarding Arizona Territory, the migration of its capital from Tucson to Prescott to Phoenix is more similar to the transfer of the national capital in the early days of American history from Annapolis to Philadelphia to New York to Washington than any of the other cases discussed herein. Tucson was the site of the territorial government between 1867 and 1877, while Prescott was its location between 1877 and 1889; it was not until the latter year that the capital was moved to Phoenix. Phoenix, moreover, at this time was a metropolis in its birth pangs, not an old, established town, although today it is the largest city in the state. One interesting sidelight of the final transfer was that members of the legislature traveled *en masse* from Prescott to Phoenix by way of Los Angeles; a group of citizens in Phoenix allegedly raised a fund to pay all the expenses of this junket.

Involved as some of the above examples may be, in no way do they match in complexity the struggle between eleven contenders for the privilege of serving as the territorial capital of the Dakotas. Unlike most of the other cases, here there was no logical choice, and the result was a free-for-all in which eleven towns took part. Although the cities of Yankton (then the territorial capital) and Huron figured prominently during the early stages of discussion, Bismarck (the present capital of the state of North Dakota) won out in the 1883 voting, mainly for the reason that the southern counties could not agree on a common choice. This selection was made by the legislature rather than by the electorate. Admittedly, the lawmakers later passed a bill removing the capital from Bismarck to Pierre (which was in the southern portion of the territory), but the governor vetoed the measure, partly because Pierre lobbyists had been guilty of bribery. After they had obtained separate statehood, South Dakotans chose Pierre as their capital; this city defeated Huron for this honor by forty-one thousand votes to thirty-four thousand votes in an election held in 1890. (Huron, though, had won a referendum five years previously.) In 1901 and 1903, a legislative caucus endorsed Mitchell as the state capital, but an election held in 1904, in which the Milwaukee Railroad backed Mitchell and the Northwestern backed Pierre, resulted in a victory for the latter.

One might cite other examples of fights over the location of the site of state government as well, including the attempt made in 1888 to move the capital of Kansas from Topeka to the center of the state, and the effort made in 1889 to transfer the capital of Washington from Olympia to North Yakima or Ellensburg. Both, of course, were unsuccessful. Significantly, neither these two struggles nor any of the others discussed herein post-dates World War I. While at one time cities may have built new capitol buildings so as to encourage the transfer of the state capital to that place, today the administrative bureaucracy of state government is so vast that its removal from one site to another would be almost impossible. (This generalization ignores the recent creation of a new Brazilian capital city in the wilderness.) Still, there probably are instances where such a move would be desirable at the state level from the point of view of efficient government, as the fast tempo of modern life necessitates a capital site favorably located from the point of view of both communication and transportation.

Chapter 3

Business Interests and
Governmental Action

The relationship which exists between the business interests of a state or a nation and its government is of great significance, even though that school of thought which interprets history in economic terms often distorts this truth through overemphasis. On the one hand, if the government adopts policies detrimental to business interests, the state or nation suffers economically as a result; on the other hand, the business interests may become so powerful that they dominate the government, and such a set of circumstances thwarts the democratic process. Aside from this problem there is the dilemma of outside capital. In many cases, a state or a nation has been so lacking financially that it has had to look elsewhere for funds with which to develop its resources; yet, after outsiders had moved into the state or nation and bolstered economic growth, malcontents have charged that they were milking its wealth. Nationally, these dilemmas have assumed a different form than they have in the case of the states; it is the object of this chapter to analyze its manifestations at the latter level.

We set the stage for our analysis with a few general comments concerning United States economic history. Prior to the Civil War, America was basically agricultural, but that conflict gave a stimulus to industrial growth which changed the nature of American society. Whether the Great Entrepreneurs of the post-Civil War period (Carnegie, Rockefeller, et al.) were robber barons who exploited the people or captains of industry who set this country on the road to economic progress is a question scholars are still debating. The fact remains that, at least up to the Populist and Progressive eras, a majority of the American people, almost every leader of the Republican Party, and every national administration were sympathetic to their cause. No single individual or economic interest, though, has ever dictated policies to Washington; both Grover Cleveland and Theodore Roosevelt did turn to J. P. Morgan for assistance during financial crises, but the latter individual's role was hardly that of a boss.

The United States government, of course, has aided business in many ways, with the protective tariff and the land grant being two of the more important techniques. Both of these pre-date the Civil War. When it finally did initiate a notable piece of regulatory legislation (the Interstate Commerce Act of 1887), it was the railroads who were the primary target; the more sweeping Sherman Anti-Trust Act of 1890 proved to be rather ineffectual because of its vague terminology. The Progressive era, however, ushered in a stricter governmental attitude toward business in general. Both Theodore Roosevelt and William Howard Taft conducted campaigns against the trusts (with varying success), and Congress passed such notable regulatory measures as the Elkins Act of 1903, the Hepburn Act of 1906, the Pure Food and Drug Act of 1906, the Meat Inspection Act of 1906, and the Mann-Elkins Act of 1910. The first, second, and fifth of these pertained to the railroads.

With the inauguration of Woodrow Wilson as President, reform received a new impetus, and both a new anti-trust law with teeth in it (the Clayton Anti-Trust Act) and the Federal Trade Commission Act became law in 1924. Twelve years of Republican rule (1920–1932) witnessed little additional regulation, although Herbert Hoover did set up the Reconstruction Finance Corporation in 1932 to aid business. The arrival of the New Deal, though, brought with it a deluge of regulatory statutes, of which the most famous are the Federal Securities Act of 1933, the Securities Exchange Act of 1934, the Wheeler-Rayburn Public Utility Holding Company Act of 1935, and the Robinson-Patman Federal Anti-Price Discrimination Act of 1936. When the United States Supreme Court declared the National Industrial Recovery Act to be unconstitutional, it invalidated the most far-reaching law of all. The regulatory measures which Congress has passed in the last twenty-five years, with a few exceptions, have merely expanded or modified these and earlier pieces of legislation.

As for American economic dependence on other countries, World War I is the critical date, as prior to that holocaust we were a debtor nation; after it, a creditor one. It has been estimated that in 1914 foreigners had seven billion dollars invested in the United States; the British had a greater stake than did any other European nation, although the Dutch and the Germans also had extensive holdings. This amount, however, represented only a small percentage of total American investments. Still, there had been several occasions in the past when European panics or depressions had precipitated similar catastrophes here, and our economic ties with England were an important factor in our decision to wage war on the British side during World War I. Since that date, there has been relatively little concern in regard to European or other foreign investments in this country, as generally speaking it has been American investments abroad which have been the bone of contention. The Mexican expropriation of American oil properties in 1938 was one extreme reaction to this economic invasion.

Having sketched in this broad background, let us turn now to various examples of one or more business interests dictating policies to a state government. One of the most notorious cases which one might cite was the Southern Pacific Railroad's domination of California politics down into the twentieth century. It is true that the Southern Pacific did suffer two major setbacks (an unsuccessful three years' fight in Congress to scale down the railroad's obligations to the federal government and a futile six years' struggle to have a deep-water harbor constructed at the railroad-controlled Santa Monica waterfront), but as late as 1906 it was determining policies and candidates at the Republican state convention. The Southern Pacific, though, officially retired from politics in 1911. This machine is particularly noteworthy because it is a typical case of the most common form of business domination of politics in the late nineteenth century— that of the railroads.

Montana furnishes another flagrant instance of business interests controlling a state government, as for many years Amalgamated (now Anaconda) Copper has charted its affairs. Perhaps Anaconda's most noteworthy display of power came in 1903 when it steamrollered a "Fair Trials Bill" through the legislature; the company wanted a law enacted at this time providing for a change of venue in case either party to a civil suit regarded the judge to be corrupt or prejudiced. In order to force the governor's hand (who was anti-company), Anaconda Copper instituted a general shut-down affecting the entire state, and the chief executive (Joseph K. Toole) consequently called a special session of the legislature at which this body passed such a measure. Six hundred fifty delegates converged on the capital to protest in behalf of a new anti-trust party, but their action was futile.

Another instance of how Anaconda has silenced its critics was its attack on an obscure young university professor named Louis Levine, who had the courage to publish a book in 1920 entitled *The Taxation of Mines in Montana*. The most offensive feature of this volume (in the eyes of Anaconda) was that it pointed out that a discrepancy existed between the taxes which Montana imposed on the farmers and those which it levied on the company. Enraged by Levine's findings, J. Bruce Kremer not only demanded that the president and the chancellor of the University of Montana prevent the publication of this work, but also brought charges against Levine before the Board of Education which led to his being fired. It is true that a special faculty committee investigation forced Levine's eventual reinstatement, but he left Montana shortly thereafter, charging that the intellectual atmosphere of the state was not conducive to independent inquiry. Today, Anaconda still more or less runs the state through the press and the legislature, although its domination is not so openly brazen as it once was; very little liberal legislation goes on the law books there even now, as the company desires to preserve the *status quo* and keep taxes down.

As for Nevada, both railroad and mining interests have dominated this state at various times. The influence of the Central Pacific was so strong in 1879 that it was able to buy the votes of the entire legislature, forcing one of its leading critics, F. E. Fisk, to leave the state for Oregon. The railroads eventually declined in power, but, by the end of World War I, George Wingfield, Vice President of the Goldfield Consolidated Mining Company, had emerged as the political boss of Nevada. Operating a bi-partisan machine, Wingfield secured the cooperation of most of the major interests, but he met his Waterloo in 1934 when the Sacramento *Bee* published a Pulitzer Prize winning series of articles about him. About this time, too, all of his banks were liquidated through various receiverships. On the other hand, the situation in Hawaii has been more complex. Here the Big Five—Alexander and Baldwin Ltd., American

Factors Ltd., C. Brewer and Company Ltd., Castle and Cooke Ltd., and Theo. H. Davies Company Ltd.—serve as buying and selling agents for the state's sugar and pineapple industries, as well as take part in politics. Their influence has been the greatest in the legislature, as an examination of Hawaii's statutes reveals. Whether statehood over the long run will tend to have an adverse effect on the political power of the Big Five remains to be seen.

Returning to the railroads, most authorities agree that the two major railroads serving Nebraska, the Union Pacific and the Burlington, wielded considerable power in the period following Reconstruction as to the selection of state officials. This is borne out by the fact that, during the late nineteenth century, no individual was ever elected to the Senate there who was opposed by the railroads. A similar situation existed in Iowa in the 1880's when Judge N. M. Hubbard, who represented the Chicago and Northwestern Railway, acquired such political influence that he was the dominating figure behind the scenes at all state conventions. During the same era in North Dakota, Judson Le Moure and Alexander McKenzie, both advocating the cause of the railroads, came to be the protector of other business interests as well (including banks, insurance companies, line elevators, and lumber companies). Even the now largely obsolete canals played a key role in at least one state, as Arthur P. Gorman, president of the Chesapeake and Ohio Canal Company, directed the political fortunes of Maryland from 1869 to 1895. Gorman, moreover, won election to the Senate in 1891 and narrowly missed his party's Presidential nomination in 1892.

The situation in New Jersey is somewhat different in that control of this state has shifted from one business interest to another over the years. At first the railroads (in particular the Pennsylvania) directed the affairs of New Jersey, but the public utilities and insurance companies eventually wormed their way into a favored position. Their ascendancy persisted regardless of whether the Republicans or the Democrats were in control, and it was through their influence that the legislature passed laws such as the measure under which so many corporations have chartered in the state. The only two serious challenges that business interests have been faced with were those of the Progressives early in this century and organized labor in recent years; although some important reforms were enacted as a result of the efforts of the former (especially during the governor-ship of Woodrow Wilson), the latter must be regarded as more of a long-term threat.

While the fortunes of Montana are determined to a large extent by Anaconda Copper, those of Arkansas are controlled to a lesser degree by the Arkansas Power and Light Company. Perhaps nowhere else in this country does a utility wield such power in a state; to make matters worse, the company is absentee-owned, and this fact has caused even more discontent. So influential is the Arkansas Power and Light Company that at one time it was able to block a proposed scheme to create an Arkansas Valley Authority. Senator Joseph Robinson, who was the majority leader of the upper house at this time and who was also a close friend of Harvey Couch, the company's director, persuaded President Franklin D. Roosevelt that Arkansas did not desire a project similar to the T.V.A. At least one governor, however, has been elected here as a result of opposition to the A. P. & L., although many chief executives of the state must be regarded as its pawns. As we know, Arkansas has been heavily Democratic since Reconstruction, as have the other states in Dixie.

Railroads, too, have dominated Southern states just as they have Western ones. Following Reconstruction, the Louisville and Nashville Railroad largely controlled the state government of Kentucky; when agricultural prices began to fall during the eighties, increased freight charges led to the calling of a consti-tutional convention in 1890. Finally, in 1893, the legislature passed a law regulating railroads, and shortly thereafter, William Goebel rose to the governor's chair as a critic of the L. & N. (It was at this time that a new railroad commission was established.) Perhaps of a more esoteric character was the Louisiana State Lottery Company, which operation controlled the politics of that state during the latter part of the nineteenth century. Using the name of Confederate hero Pierre G. T. Beauregard to further ticket sales, Democrats allied with this concern were able to dominate the state through the governor's extensive appointive power. Here, as in Kentucky, it was the farmers who led the opposition, but seemingly with less success. Following the turn of the century, though, the large oil com-panies forged to the front, dominating Louisiana until the time of Huey Long.

Even New England has not escaped untouched. In the case of

Maine, the timber companies and the power interests in conjunction with the textile and shoe manufacturers dominate politics. More than three-fourths of Maine is wooded, and most of this acreage is owned by a few timber companies and paper manufacturers; these groups have left behind them a long record of corruption, especially in the period when they were acquiring land. As for water power, this state's potential is as great as that of almost any other state east of the Rocky Mountains, and businessmen in this field naturally invaded politics both to secure rights and to protect themselves. Turning to New Hampshire, it may be true that the race track which is located here does not dictate every policy that the government adopts, but no less than forty-four legislators worked at Rockingham in 1955, so that this lobby is unique among special interests at the state level. Thanks to its efforts, New Hampshire receives a smaller percentage of pari-mutuel receipts than does any other New England state; the mere existence of the track is an incitement to corruption, as dishonest bookmakers are likely to attempt to bribe governmental officials. Both of these states, of course, have been strongly Republican down to the last few years. Then there is Vermont, where four Proctors have served as governor; all of these individuals were simultaneously president of the Vermont Marble Company. This era of rule extended all the way from the end of Reconstruction to the end of World War II, but may not recur again because of increasing Democratic strength. The railroads also have been powerful here, while Fred Howland of the National Life Insurance Company once exerted great influence as well.

Citing some other contemporary examples of business control, until labor became a major force politically the automobile manufacturers largely dominated governmental policies in Michigan, along with the Dow Chemical Company and Gerber Baby Foods. Then there is Arizona, where the electric utilities have replaced such copper interests as Phelps Dodge as the state's most active lobby. As for Pennsylvania, the Pennsylvania Manufacturers Association, a highly conservative organization once led by Joseph Grundy, has played a key role at Harrisburg along with the Mellon interests of Pittsburgh. In the case of Texas, the petroleum industry has predictably been a major force in government and politics, but so, too, has been the Texas Life Convention, an association of insurance companies. Finally, one might cite Ohio, where the business lobby at Columbus is dominated by a triumvirate composed of the Chamber of Commerce, the Manufacturers Association, and the Council of Retail Merchants; electric utilities are also active here. Perhaps the influence of none of the above is so extensive and so obvious as that of the Southern Pacific in California or Anaconda in Montana once was, but on numerous occasions they have been able to secure the passage of, or defeat, a piece of legislation. Curiously, Du Pont has not exerted the direct influence on Delaware's politics and government that one might expect, partly because it has more important preoccupations, partly because state officials more or less leave it alone.

Now that we have examined the histories of various states where certain economic groups have dominated the government, let us shift our attention to a consideration of the various measures which state legislatures have enacted for the benefit of private enterprise. As the most popular place to go when one desired a divorce was once Nevada, the Mecca for those who wanted to charter a corporation was once New Jersey. Standard Oil, for example, successfully applied here after the Supreme Court had dissolved it as a trust in 1892. It is true that Woodrow Wilson did put a damper on corporate expansion in New Jersey during his governorship, but things have more or less returned to normal since then. Encouragement of trusts, protection of monopolies, and non-regulation of holding companies have characterized this state's attitude toward business over much of its history, although on occasion New Jersey has clamped down on abuses. Doubtless influenced by the example of its larger neighbor, Delaware passed a Corporation Law in 1899 in an effort to attract enterprises seeking a charter into the state. This measure proved to be highly successful. On the whole, Delaware has made even less of an attempt to hamstring industry than New Jersey has; until recently there was little governmental control over public utilities other than the railroads, while the regulation of working conditions was rather perfunctory. In regard to holding companies, along with West Virginia and Maine these two states have been the ones that have done the most to encourage their growth over the years.

Perhaps the favorite technique which states have used to stimulate business is to exempt it from certain taxes. For our first example we might cite Florida; as outside interest in this state's economic potentialities had developed by that time, the legislature successfully proposed a constitutional amendment in

1923 which forbade the levying of state income and inheritance taxes. It is true that this law-making body did institute a tax of the latter type in 1931 so that Florida could share in such levies with the federal government, but there has been a pronounced tendency here in recent years to shift taxation for business and property to luxuries. In the case of Colorado, its Constitution of 1876 included a provision that mines would not be taxable for the next decade, and this exemption proved to be most welcome in a state which then drew and still draws much of its income from the earth. As for Mississippi, a law was adopted by this state in 1882 by which new industries were excused from taxation for the first ten years of operation. This act, which was extended on the basis of a five-year holiday from state taxes and a ten-year period of grace from local imposts, was largely responsible for the increased textile activity here. (With the elevation of James K. Vardaman to the governor's chair, as will be pointed out shortly, economic development suffered a severe setback in Mississippi.) Perhaps the most extreme case that one might cite is Alaska, where, prior to 1949, many industries paid no taxes whatsoever; when the legislature finally did pass a comprehensive tax program in that year, the Alaska Steamship Company and other interests fought a two-year delaying action in the courts. Significantly, a measure was enacted in 1957 providing tax relief for up to ten years for new business firms desiring to locate there.

Another device which state governments have employed to aid business is that of the land grant, although most of these had been made by the date at which this monograph technically begins. The railroads were the main recipient of these. No less than nine states made substantial land grants to various business interests, but, with the exception of Texas and Maine, most of these consisted of swamplands that they had previously received from the United States government. Texas, though, granted these interests no less than thirty-five million acres, this being approximately 70 per cent of the total state donation of forty-eight plus million. As we shall see later, Texas and other states made attempts to reacquire a portion of these grants at a later date. The overwhelming majority of the federal grants were made between 1850 and 1871, with the last such donation occurring in the latter year; most of the state grants were also made during the same period.

Despite the fact that an intensive campaign against business in general did not take place at the state level until the Progressive era, limited regulation did pre-date many of the liberal charters, tax exemptions, and land grants with which the states aided private enterprise. Rhode Island, for example, created a commission as early as 1836 to which it gave the power to examine railroad transactions and proceedings. Similar groups were set up in New Hampshire, Connecticut, Vermont, New York, and Maine before 1860; it was here rather than in the Midwest, then, that the inception of railroad regulation is to be found. But it is the laws relative to railroads and grain elevators that the latter group of states, beginning with Illinois in 1871, passed as a result of the crusading spirit of the Granger Movement that historians have singled out for special attention. (Minnesota, Wisconsin, and Iowa enacted similar laws in the same decade.)

In 1877, in *Munn v. Illinois,* the United States Supreme Court upheld an Illinois law fixing maximum rates for grain storage, and it was thought at the time that this decision might open the gates to further state regulation in other sectors of business. But in 1886, in *Wabash, St. Louis, and Pacific R. R. Co. v. Illinois,* this same tribunal rejected an Illinois law prohibiting long-and-short-haul clauses in transportation contracts, and this action placed a damper on measures of this type. Later court decisions in *Chicago, Milwaukee and St. Paul R. R. Co. v. Minnesota* (invalidating a Minnesota act) in 1890 and in *Smith v. Ames* (invalidating a Nebraska act) in 1898 dealt severe blows to railroad regulation at the state level. The federal government, however, began to play a more important role in this area with the passage of the Interstate Commerce Act in 1887. With the arrival of the Progressive era, several states (in particular Iowa, California, and Wisconsin) made a renewed attempt to crush the political power of the railroads through new legislation. Nevertheless, in 1914, the United States Supreme Court again sabotaged state efforts by its decision in the Shreveport case, in which it upheld federal control over intrastate rates in an instance where the latter interfered with control of interstate rates. Perhaps even more important than any of these decisions was the fact that the highest tribunal accepted the 1882 argument of Roscoe Conkling that the due process of law clause of the Fourteenth Amendment protected corporations against the states' police power.

State anti-trust laws have enjoyed much kinder treatment in

the courts, but whether they have been overly successful is open to question. The first law of this nature was passed by Kansas in 1889, although similar legislation had been enacted by eighteen other states by 1891. The Sherman Anti-Trust Act, of course, dates from 1890, but its numerous loopholes force one to regard the Clayton Anti-Trust Act of 1914 as the first really effective piece of federal legislation. Two important cases at the state level which resulted in the dissolution of a trust were those involving the North River Sugar Refining Company (New York, 1890) and the Standard Oil Trust (Ohio, 1892). Standard Oil, though, later reorganized as a group of interlocking directorates and then as a holding company, and a subsequent attempt to cite the organization for contempt (1899) found the state supreme court unable to reach a decision. Statewise, these two cases are the counterparts of *Northern Securities Co. v. U. S.* *(1904), Standard Oil Co. of New Jersey, et al. v. U. S. (1911),* and *U. S. v. American Tobacco Co. (1911)* at the federal level.

Probably the most famous series of anti-trust prosecutions that occurred statewise was that of Arkansas. Here the actions of Attorney General Jefferson Davis launched a notable political career, although they were largely doomed to failure. Just prior to the turn of the century, in 1899, the Arkansas legislature passed the Rector Anti-Trust Law, a measure which stipulated that persons or corporations involved in any agreement to control prices could not operate in the state; upon its enactment, Davis immediately initiated over one hundred suits against insurance and express companies. Governor Dan Jones, who was a conservative, attempted to restrain Davis, but the legislature supported him, appropriating five thousand dollars so that he could employ additional help. As Davis filed more suits, businessmen began to hint that companies would begin a mass exodus from Arkansas unless he halted these prosecutions, but the state supreme court saved the day by handing down a decision adverse to Davis. The attorney general thereupon dropped all pending suits, declaring that he would not institute a suit against another trust "even if it organized in the State House yard with a brass band." Soon thereafter, though, Davis was elected governor of Arkansas, and one of his last acts before leaving office was to sign an ironclad anti-trust measure which forbade any pool or combination to do business in the state; as no prosecuting attorney dared to take action under it, this law remained a dead letter, and the legislature eventually repealed it in 1911.

If Arkansas history provides the most prominent example of concentrated trust-busting, Texas history furnishes the most noteworthy instance of prolonged trust-busting. Like Kansas, the Lone Star State passed its first anti-trust act in 1889, but it also supplemented this with related measures in 1895, 1899, and 1903, as well as by additional amendments in 1907. The individual most responsible for the placing of anti-trust legislation on the Texas statute books was James Hogg, who served as attorney general before becoming governor in 1891. Among the "trust-busting" attorney generals who followed Hogg were T. S. Smith, C. K. Bell, R. V. Davidson, Jewel P. Lightfoot, and B. F. Looney, each of whom filed a number of suits. Perhaps the most famous prosecution under the Texas anti-trust acts was the one which Attorney General M. M. Crane instituted against the Waters-Pierce Oil Company in 1897. Waters-Pierce did reorganize after the United States Supreme Court upheld the state against the company in 1900, but a later Texas attorney general (R. V. Davidson) obtained a judgment of over one and a half million dollars against it in 1906, dealing Waters-Pierce a further blow. In all, no less than 119 prosecutions were brought under the Texas statutes up to 1915.

A body of legislation which has grown to considerable proportions in the last generation is that of state fair-trade and loss-limitation acts. The first measure of the former type was passed in California in 1931, and this form of legislation was soon thereafter mirrored in the codes of fair competition that the National Industrial Recovery Act of 1933 set up, although the latter was invalidated by the United States Supreme Court in 1935. Loss-limitation laws won favor less slowly than their fair-trade counterparts, but half the states nevertheless had adopted them by 1940, as compared with forty-four states that had enacted fair-trade measures. As for the courts, our highest tribunal held in 1936 by a unanimous vote that state laws which allowed resale price maintenance contracts were valid (*Old Dearborn Distributing Co. v. Seagram Distillers Corporation*). (Loss-limitation laws, on the other hand, have received a mixed reaction in the courts.) The federal government, moreover, gave a boost to fair-trade laws at the state level by enacting the Tydings-Miller Act in 1937, which exempted the making of resale price maintenance contracts from restrictions imposed by anti-trust legislation. It must be said in fairness, though, that President Franklin D. Roosevelt may not have signed this measure had it not been attached to an appropriations bill.

Of related interest is anti-chain store taxation at the state level. State legislatures passed measures embodying this principle in Georgia, Maryland, and North Carolina in 1927, as well as in many other states since that date; their object is to even up some of the advantages that the chains enjoy, although they differ markedly in detail. Most such laws are based on that of Indiana, which establishes a tax graduated vis-a-vis the number of stores within the state, although in Louisiana the criterion is the number of stores within the chain system. As for the question of constitutionality, the first case to reach the United States Supreme Court saw that body upholding the Indiana law by a five to four vote (*State Board of Tax Commissioners v. Jackson,* 1931). It would appear, however, that chain stores do not arouse the animosity today that they once did, although they do still have their critics.

Another aspect of the stiffening attitude of state government toward business has been the discontinuing of tax exemptions; this has been particularly true in the case of the railroads. But it is an episode from Montana history involving an attempt to force Anaconda Copper to pay its just share of taxes which we will analyze here instead, as this crackdown marks one of the few times when a single individual was able to thwart the designs of this monolithic concern. Incensed because the production of Montana metal mines had reached more than twenty million dollars in 1922, while the state had collected only thirteen thousand dollars on a net proceeds tax, Governor Joseph Dixon called on the legislature to remedy the situation by equalizing the tax burden. When this Anaconda-dominated body failed to act, Dixon had Initiative No. 28 drawn up and placed on the ballot in 1924; this measure exempted from taxation mines with an annual gross production of less than one hundred thousand dollars, but subjected to taxation those with an annual gross production in excess of that figure. Dixon lost out in his attempt at re-election as chief executive, but Initiative No. 28 was victorious at the polls. Regardless of protests from the company that the tax was confiscatory, its profits sharply increased rather than decreased in the years that followed, while the tax structure of the state obtained a long-needed alteration.

As distasteful as subjection to taxation may have been to various business enterprises, the surrendering of land grants was an even more bitter pill for them to swallow. In Texas, for example, the legislature enacted a measure in 1882 which repealed grants to persons for the "construction of railroads, canals, and ditches." Although the railroads had patented thirty-five million plus acres here (far more than in any other state, as we have previously pointed out), they had to forfeit several million acres because they had failed to build sufficient mileage so as to be legally entitled to the land. As for Florida, the question of reclamation was a complicating factor in that state. Anxious for improved transportation facilities, the legislature of this state made land grant after land grant to the railways, but fifteen million acres of these were swamp and overflowed lands which the United States Swamp Land Act of 1850 had set aside for reclamation. It must be remembered that the land which Texas gave to the railroads was largely her own, that which Florida gave them largely that of the federal government. Since Florida had actually deeded only nine million acres to the railways, Governor William S. Jennings decided that the remaining land should be used for reclamation as had been originally intended; after the courts upheld him the state and the railroads reached a compromise settlement. One might cite examples involving other states as well.

In regard to the state "blue-sky" (securities) laws, perhaps their most noteworthy feature is that they preceded the parallel federal measures (the Securities Act of 1933 and the Securities Exchange Act of 1934), and Congress referred to them when it was drawing up these two statutes. The first such law that a state enacted was that of Kansas in 1911, and when our highest tribunal upheld this in *Hall v. Geiger-Jones* in 1917, other states followed suit, until by 1933 only Nevada had failed to pass such an act. The court argued in this particular case that the police power of the states encompassed the prevention of deception. It is not easy, though, to pass judgment on the exact value of this legislation statewise, as, despite its beneficial effects, it has left much to be desired.

Moving on to a quick survey of state governmental regulation in other fields, law-making bodies have passed pure food and drug laws in every state; despite the fact that they exhibit considerable variation as to detail, these measures tend in general to follow the federal laws, the first of which was the Pure Food and Drug Act of 1906. Those of North Dakota are particularly outstanding, as are those of Illinois vis-a-vis meats and Florida vis-a-vis citrus fruits. As for state regulation of public utility holding companies, most of it dates from 1930 and after, although a few states had such legislation on their law books prior to that date. The federal parallel in this instance is the Public Utility Holding Company Act of 1935. Then there is the fixing of prices by the state; in this connection, a New York measure relative to milk is significant, since by upholding it in the Nebbia case (1934), the United States Supreme Court disregarded the Conkling interpretation of the Fourteenth Amendment. In regard to state motor transport regulation, at one time these measures were highly diverse, but the national Motor Carrier Act of 1935 has stimulated a movement toward uniformity. State regulation of insurance also has resulted in much confusion; in this instance, however, there is no comparable federal law to serve as a model. State insurance systems exist in Wisconsin (life), in North Dakota, South Dakota, and Oklahoma (crops), and in Massachusetts (bank deposits).

Although some commentators have charged that such a move is a prelude to socialism, there have been instances where a state not only has regulated private enterprise, but also has actually gone into business for itself. In this connection, we might cite several examples from the history of the Dakotas. As for coal mining, South Dakota did buy a mine at Haynes, North Dakota, in 1919, but it sold this in 1936, while another attempt to open a strip coal operation at Firesteel failed when it became known that coal could be purchased elsewhere for less than it could be mined here. On the other hand, a state-owned cement plant at Rapid City which began operating in 1925 is still runnng; this enterprise has been something of a success. South Dakota also went into the retail gasoline business in 1923, but it did so for the sole purpose of keeping the price down. Then there is North Dakota, which currently maintains the only state-owned flour mill and the only state-owned grain mill in America; a scheme for a state-owned wheat elevator failed during the depression of 1893. In general, though, state ownership of business is usually not very extensive, despite such grandiose federal schemes as the Alaska Railroad Company, the Panama Canal, and the Tennessee Valley Authority.

Turning our attention to another important topic, there are those states whose enterprises have evolved without the aid of outside capital, but many others have not enjoyed this form of economic self-sufficiency. The capital used in the financing of Montana furs, cattle, silver, lumber, and copper, for example, almost invariably came from the outside rather than from within that state; Montanans at one time made regular pilgrimages to such cities as St. Louis, Chicago, San Francisco, New York, and Boston, seeking the assistance of entrepreneurs. For this reason, no one should claim that Montana has been the innocent victim of ruthless exploiters. In the case of North Dakota, the control of its state government once resided in St. Paul and Minneapolis rather than in Bismarck, while Eastern wealth furnished a good deal of the money used to build the railroads of the state. The North Dakota farmer, moreover, had to sell his crops in the East and buy his supplies there. Minnesota presents a slightly different picture in that local interests have largely run the lumbering and flour milling industries, despite the fact that such non-Minnesotans as Charlemagne Tower, John D. Rockefeller, and Henry W. Oliver have dominated the iron mining industry. The example of Minnesota demonstrates that outside economic control of a state is not always total, but instead may center on specific key industries.

As for Vermont, it is true that natives founded the basic enterprises of this state, but there has been a tendency in recent years for large national organizations to set up branch plants here; among these are the Bell Aircraft concern in Burlington, the National Carbon office in St. Albans, and the American Optical Company outlet at Brattleboro. Two factors attracting outside interests to the state are a low overhead and a reliable labor force. It is true that during the 1930's and 1940's an attempt was made to reactivate back country towns with small craft industries, but even some of the old established firms have fallen into out-of-state hands. The E. & T. Fairbanks Company is one example of this phenomenon. Nevertheless, Vermont remains more basically agrarian than any of its New England neighbors.

Numerous other examples of powerful economic interests residing outside a state charting its destiny might also be mentioned. One of the most notorious instances was the stranglehold which the Guggenheim-Morgan syndicate held earlier in this century over the Alaskan economy. Having organized the Alaska Syndicate, this group gained control not only of copper mines and gold properties, but also salmon canneries, a railroad, and a steamship line. Another case of absentee domination is Nevada. Most of the public utilities, mines, and land and range animals of the state, as well as two-thirds of the taxable property, are in the hands of non-Nevadans. In Utah, outside capital rather than the Mormons controls the mining industry, which provides a large number of people with jobs. In the case of Wyoming, coal was acquired by the Union Pacific as a subsidy for building that railroad, while iron ore is shipped to Colorado and crude oil to Utah for processing. To date, no satisfactory system of taxation for minerals has been secured here. As for Texas, although one Dallas firm controls one-sixth of its cotton factories, non-Texan entrepreneurs own the other textile mills. Electric Bond & Share, moreover, handles about two-thirds of the state's electric power, the two most important sulfur companies until recently did not have a Texan on their board of directors, and Standard of New Jersey owns three-fourths of Humble Oil. These miniature case studies by no means exhaust the examples that one might draw from the West, which long has been an economic colony of the North.

Vermont, moreover, is not the only Eastern state where outside capital has played a key role. In West Virginia, for example, ownership of the Chesapeake and Ohio Railroad shifted many times between 1873, when the line to Huntington reached completion, and 1888, when the firm of Drexel, Morgan and Company gained control of it. As for the Norfolk and Western Railway, its owners also held leases on extensive coal properties in the state; much of West Virginia's wealth is still in the hands of outsiders. Then there is Delaware, where aside from the Du Pont Company and two or three other organizations, industry was once largely locally owned and managed. After around 1900, though, consolidation in the leather firms, the iron foundries, and the castings mills initiated a more widespread movement in the direction of absentee landlordism. We have already referred to this state's liberal chartering laws for corporations and its encouragement of holding companies.

Although most of our examples thus far have come from the West, one could list equally significant ones from the South, as that section too became something of an economic colony of the North following the Civil War. The American Tobacco Company, for instance, did begin its operations in North Carolina, but afterward moved its headquarters to New York, from which place it established one of the nation's most prominent trusts. Outside capital, too, has played a major role in the development of Florida; in this connection, one might mention Henry Flagler, who constructed railroad lines down the eastern coast all the way to Key West, and then built resort hotels and sold lands along these. As for the Alabama iron and steel industry, this was under the control of the Tennessee Coal, Iron and Railroad Company down to 1907, but in that year the United States Steel Corporation, under the leadership of J. P. Morgan, purchased the Tennessee operation at a bargain price. Then there is the bauxite industry of Arkansas, which is mostly in the hands of the Aluminum Corporation of America, a Pittsburgh firm. These, moreover, are by no means the only instances of Southern industries the control of which resides in the North, as the charges that Walter Prescott Webb set forth in his controversial *Divided We Stand* do have a substantial basis in fact.

At this point in the narrative, one might cite perhaps the most extreme adverse reaction of all to the presence of outside capital in a state—that of Mississippi following the turn of the century. Incensed by the fact that the lumber industry, which Northern investors largely controlled, was prospering without the citizens of his state benefiting, Governor James Vardaman clamped down on the lumber trust along with the other corporate interests, pushing several harsh bills through the legislature. The long-range effect of this move was to deal industrialization in Mississippi a blow from which it did not recover for a third of a century; critics of Vardaman have justly charged that he burned down the barn to kill the rats, but most of the people of Mississippi were behind him. Thus, the law limiting the captial stock of corporations doing business in Mississippi to one million dollars was not repealed until 1924, a statistic which reveals how long-lived this animosity was.

Considering the widespread opposition which out-of-state capital once aroused when it removed wealth from a state and in-state wealth when it attempted to dominate the government, it is perhaps one of the greatest ironies of state history that in recent years many states have passed laws establishing boards, commissions, departments, and councils for the express purpose not only of assisting already existing industries, but also of attracting out-of-state ones. Even Mississippi instituted a BAWI (Balance Agriculture with Industry) Plan in the late 1930's which brought twenty industries into the state. A mere listing of these boards, etc., would not be very edifying, although a close analysis reveals that their functions do vary slightly from state to state. A sample might include the South Carolina Research, Planning and Development Board (1933), the Kansas Industrial Development Commission (1939), the Pennsylvania Department of Commerce (1939), the Utah Department of Publicity and Industrial Development (1941), the Michigan Economic Development Commission (1947), the New Jersey Division of Planning and Development (1948), the Massachusetts Division of Development (1953), and the South Dakota Industrial Development and Expansion Agency (1955). It is obvious, of course, that whatever the letter of the law may be, such legislation will not be a success unless the state government promotes a general atmosphere favorable to business, as was the case in North Carolina during the administration of Governor Luther Hodges (D, 1957–1961).

In conclusion, most commentators agree that wholesale crackdowns on private enterprise at the state level are a thing of the past, a relic of Populist and Progressive days long gone. There is not a single state today which is not aware of the fact that such a program of harassment would result only in the wholesale departure of various business concerns for greener pastures elsewhere, thus creating a severe economic crisis. Still, one must remember that economic interests do not dominate state governments today to the extent that they once did, and for this reason the necessity of "putting them in their place" is not so great as it once was. Outside capital still presents a problem, but without its assistance in some states there is not going to be any economic growth or development of any consequence; those who continually agitate against out-of-state financing must learn to live with this bitter fact. This is not to say that states make no effort to regulate business, as the numerous fair-trade, loss-limitation, and chain store measures that have been passed in recent years prove that the contrary is true. But it is beyond question that the general trend today at the state level is in the direction of encouraging economic activity, not only through the repeal of discriminatory legislation, but also through the establishment of boards and commissions to further this end. We will examine other aspects of this topic in the conclusion, in particular the different roles that economic interests have played in state and national history.

Chapter 4

Labor's Struggle:
Legislation and Strikes

No discussion of state history would be complete without an analysis of the role that labor has played in it. Organizationally speaking, during the period under consideration unions have been national in scope, but particular states differ markedly as to the extent of unionization since some have been more favorably disposed to labor activity than have others. In the case of labor legislation, an uneven pattern likewise exists, but in general the states have anticipated the federal government in enacting measures of this nature; prior to the coming of the New Deal, labor lacked the political power to pressure Congress into passing a comprehensive act favorable to its cause. As for strikes, laborers in a specific industry will on occasion walk off their jobs across the country, but there has been no nationwide general strike in American history. Surprisingly, the states where strikes take place most frequently are not always the site of the most memorable walkouts. From the point of view of politics, the American Federation of Labor long had a tradition of refraining from endorsing a Presidential candidate, unlike the Congress of Industrial Organizations; at the state level, labor has been able to assume a dominant role politically in only a handful of states, as we shall demonstrate later. Admittedly, the history of American labor is a topic on which others have written much, but there do remain a number of areas which need further study.

Prior to the Civil War, labor unions were essentially local in character, but immediately following the close of that conflict two nationwide unions were founded: the National Labor

Union (1866) and the Knights of Labor (1869). Both of these eventually failed, but the American Federation of Labor from its birth in 1881 successfully championed the cause of the workingman. Several other labor unions emerged over the years, including the Railway Brotherhoods and the radical but short-lived Industrial Workers of the World, but it was not until the formation of the Committee for Industrial Organization (now the Congress of Industrial Organizations) in 1935 that a real rival emerged to challenge the American Federation of Labor. The merger of these two labor unions in 1955 has not resulted in the creation of the invincible pressure bloc that some critics had envisaged, partly because such groups within the ranks of labor as the Teamsters and the Longshoremen constantly are sniping at it. From the standpoint of geography, unionization is most common today in the East, in the Midwest (aside from the farm states), and on the Pacific Coast. Unions naturally are stronger in industrial cities than elsewhere; non-organized workers are more common in non-manufacturing than in manufacturing industries, and are more likely to be found in the South than anywhere else, especially in textiles and lumber.

From the point of view of national legislation, labor made little progress prior to the present century. The Clayton Anti-Trust Act of 1914 did exempt labor from the scope of such legislation, thus freeing it from the danger that some "trust-buster" might wreck the union movement, while the Norris-La Guardia Act of 1932 did outlaw the yellow-dog contract and limited the use of injunctions in labor disputes. Aside from Section 7a of the later invalidated National Industrial Recovery Act of 1933 and certain provisions of the Clayton Anti-Trust Act, though, there was no sweeping piece of federal labor legislation prior to the Wagner-Connery Labor Relations Act of 1935, which strengthened the rights of labor and created the National Labor Relations Board. The federal government had made a handful of attempts to regulate hours in certain industries (railroads, coal), but the Fair Labor Standards Act of 1938 marked the first comprehensive regulation of hours (and wages) in industries engaging in interstate commerce. In contrast, the national child labor amendment has failed to win support in enough states to become part of the Constitution. Over the years, however, many persons came to feel that labor, which had fought so long against the abuses of management, was itself not above reproach, and these sentiments found expression in the Taft-Hartley Act of 1947; among other things, this measure reduced the powers of the National Labor Relations Board; outlawed the closed shop, secondary boycotts, and featherbedding; permitted damage suits against unions; and placed limits on union expenditures in political campaigns. Threats to repeal this act proved to be of no avail, and the Landrum-Griffin Act of 1959 actually strengthened some of its provisions.

The history of labor legislation at the state level is much more complex, as some states have compiled a much more progressive record in this regard than have others. This, though, is not surprising when one takes into consideration the fact that industrialization and unionization are more typical of some states than of others; it is the former rather than the latter which are more likely to be in the vanguard of advanced labor legislation, as the need is greater there. It would be possible to devote an entire book to this topic, but we must confine ourselves to a survey of maximum hours regulation, minimum wage regulation, workmen's compensation laws, unemployment insurance laws, right-to-work measures, fair-employment practices, and anti-yellow-dog contract measures. In the course of this discussion, it will be necessary to refer to a number of court decisions, as on more than one occasion the judiciary has thrown out legislative acts at the state level affecting labor.

Turning first to maximum hours regulation, in the case of children acts of this type date from 1842, when Massachusetts and Connecticut legislation effected certain restrictions; by the time of the Civil War, five other states had followed suit. It was not until after the turn of the century, however, that really effective laws were written onto the books, beginning with the Illinois law of 1903. As for women, five states (New Hampshire was the first of these) passed acts limiting their hours of employment to ten a day prior to the Civil War, but as a whole these were rather ineffective because of a common provision which enabled employers to contract for longer hours. The first piece of legislation of this nature with any real teeth in it was the measure which Massachusetts adopted in 1874 and amended in 1879; since that date, there has been steady progress vis-a-vis the passage of laws regulating the number of hours that women are to work. On the other hand, state legislatures have been somewhat reluctant to limit the hours of employment for men, partly for the reason that they are stronger than women and thus are capable of working longer hours, partly for the reason that, unlike women and children, they are invariably their own masters. A campaign for the eight-hour day for men did begin as early as Reconstruction, but the acts designed to effect this end which some states adopted proved to be unenforceable; true progress in this direction statewise dates from after the turn of the century. Many of these laws, moreover, are largely confined to workers in transportation, mining, and occupations where tasks are executed under air pressure.

In regard to the matter of constitutionality, the courts have posed no threat to the limitation of hours of employment for children by a state, mainly because a minor has no legal right to enter into a free contract. Perhaps the leading case that one might cite in this connection is *People v. Ewer,* 1894. Maximum hours regulation for women in the courts has encountered greater opposition; some state courts have upheld such laws (*Commonwealth v. Hamilton,* Massachusetts, 1876), while others have not (*Ritchie v. People,* Illinois, 1895). In 1908, though, the United States Supreme Court declared constitutional an Oregon act limiting hours of employment for women to ten hours a day (*Muller v. Oregon*). Three years earlier, that body had dealt a severe blow to state regulation when it found unconstitutional a New York measure establishing an eight-hour day for bakers (*Lochner v. New York*), but the decision there had been on a closely split vote. In 1917 (in *Bunting v. Oregon*), our highest tribunal upheld an act permitting Oregon to enforce a ten-hour day for all factory workers, and this action marked still another step in the establishment of a judicial tradition favorable to laws of this type. Still, some maximum hour laws have been found unconstitutional, including those of Pennsylvania (1938) and South Carolina (1939).

The development of minimum wage regulation has been a more recent phenomenon, and it has met with much stiffer opposition in the courts. Massachusetts passed the first such law for women and children in 1912, and fourteen other states, Puerto Rico, and the District ot Columbia enacted similar legislation between that date and 1923. The United States Supreme Court, though, dealt a death blow in 1923 to this variety of measure, at least as far as women are concerned, when it found a District of Columbia measure unconstitutional (*Adkins v. Children's Hospital*). The result was that these state laws as applied to women were either repealed or no longer enforced.

Our highest tribunal, however, has shown a marked tendency in recent years to reverse itself, and in 1937 it held a Washington minimum wage measure constitutional by a bare majority in the case of *West Coast Hotel Co. v. Parrish.*

As for workmen's compensation laws, the United States Supreme Court upheld state action in this field as early as 1917 (*New York Central Railroad Co. v. White*). Maryland had passed a measure embodying this principle in 1902, as did Montana and New York in 1910, but state courts had found these to be unconstitutional. Nevertheless, twenty states had enacted compensation laws by 1913, and ten more by 1915, despite the fact that several state courts had adopted an unfavorable attitude toward them. (The Ohio act was used as a model for similar pieces of legislation by certain other states.) In regard to the reasoning in the various decisions, the New York Court of Appeals held in *Ives v. South Buffalo Railway Co.* (1911) that is was a deprivation of an employer's property to force him to assume liability for an accident for which he might not have been responsible; on the other hand, the United States Supreme Court ruled in the 1917 decision mentioned above that it was not unreasonable for the state to require an employer to contribute a limited sum to compensate a worker for the loss of earning power. It is the latter point of view, of course, which now holds sway.

On the other and, in the case of unemployment insurance, it was not until 1932 that Wisconsin enacted the first law at the state level providing for this service. Many other states seriously considered following suit at this time, but none did so until 1935 because of the fear that the cost would be so great that industry within that state would be placed at a disadvantage vis-a-vis other states. The federal Social Security Act of 1935 offered a stimulus to the passage of such legislation statewise, however, as it made it highly unwise for a state to refrain from adopting a measure of this sort. Judicial reaction to these laws has been uniformly favorable, partly for the reason that the United States Supreme Court had undergone its ideological metamorphosis by the date that the relevant case reached it, although state courts had previously adopted a positive attitude toward them. (See in this connection *Chamberlain v. Andrews,* New York, 1936; *Gillum v. Johnson,* California, 1936; and *Carmichael v. Southern Coal and Coke Co.,* U.S., 1937.)

Despite the furor which they caused when they were first

introduced, it is not maximum hour, minimum wage, workmen's compensation, or unemployment insurance laws which arouse the most discussion today laborwise, but rather right-to-work acts. This type of measure, which outlaws the closed shop and the union shop, first appeared on the law books of a state in 1944, both in Florida and in Arkansas. Perhaps the most active year in regard to such legislation was 1947; since that date, however, five states (Louisiana, Delaware, Hawaii, Maine, and New Hampshire) have repealed acts of this or of a related nature. Nevertheless, a recent survey revealed that nineteen states currently have right-to-work laws. The year which witnessed the greatest number of fruitless attempts to enact legislation of this type was 1958, as during the election taking place that year nine of ten states rejected new proposals embodying the right-to-work principle. The one state that was the exception, Kansas, thereby became the sixth state to pass a constitutional amendment effecting this end.

While the right-to-work laws may be typical of conservative labor legislation at the state level today, fair-employment practice measures may be cited as representative of the liberal trend. Perhaps significantly, the first right-to-work act was passed in 1944, the first fair-employment practice act in 1945 (in New York). This Ives-Quinn Anti-Discrimination Bill not only prohibited employers from discriminating in the hiring or discharging of employees, but also prohibited labor unions from discriminating in the granting of full membership rights. Within five years, by 1950, such legislation was on the statute books in Connecticut, Massachusetts, New Jersey, New Mexico, Oregon, Rhode Island, and Washington, and by 1960, in Alaska, California, Colorado, Delaware, Michigan, Minnesota, Ohio, Pennsylvania, and Wisconsin as well. There also are voluntary laws of this nature in Indiana and Kansas. President Franklin D. Roosevelt, one might add, first set up a national Fair Employment Practice Committee in 1941, taking this action just prior to the appointed hour for a mass march on Washington led by the president of the Brotherhood of Sleeping Car Porters.

Let us next examine attitudes at the state level toward that *bête noire* of labor unions, the yellow-dog contract. In 1903, Kansas made it a criminal offense for an employer to require a worker not to join a union while laboring for that firm, being one of a dozen or so states to enact such legislation prior to World War I. Our highest tribunal, though, in 1915 declared the Kansas statute to be unconstitutional (*Coppage v. Kansas*), affirming that the law deprived persons of their property without due process of law, and it further upheld the principle underlying the yellow-dog contract two years later in the case of *Hitchman Coal Co. v. Mitchell*. As for the state courts, their reaction was more ambivalent; the courts of Massachusetts found an anti-yellow-dog contract law void in 1930 (*In re Opinion of the Justices*), but both the Ohio Supreme Court (in 1923) and the New York Court of Appeals (in 1927) refused to base an injunction on inducement to break yellow-dog contracts. Despite the decision in *Coppage v. Kansas,* Wisconsin did enact a measure outlawing yellow-dog contracts in 1929, although it was not until the passage of the Norris-La Guardia Act in 1932 that other states began to follow suit *en masse*. Section 3 of this law rendered yellow-dog contracts unenforceable in federal courts.

Of a more specialized character has been labor legislation vis-a-vis strikes; some of this has been pro-labor in character, while some has been anti-labor. Among the areas in which statutes have been passed are picketing, boycotts, sitdown strikes, injunctions, and the arbitration and mediation of labor disputes. Perhaps the most extreme example of an anti-labor measure that one might cite is the anti-strike law which Kansas passed in 1920, an act which followed in the wake of the nation-wide coal strike of the previous year. This statute made illegal strikes in industries that were affected with a public interest, referring labor disputes to an Industrial Court; when a group of miners resisted, the government clamped their leaders in jail. In 1923 and 1925, however, the United States Supreme Court held the Kansas law void in the *Wolff Packing Company Cases*. It is highly doubtful, of course, that such a measure could have been passed in a more unionized state, even in the reactionary atmosphere of the post-World War I period.

As for acts directed against picketing at the state level, our highest tribunal dealt these a severe blow in its decision in the Thornhill Case in 1940 when it declared an Alabama measure embodying this principle unconstitutional. Prior to this date, Nebraska and Oregon both had adopted anti-picketing statutes via the referendum route; Utah also had passed an anti-picketing law, but this applied only to boycotts. An open-port act which Texas had enacted in 1920, though, had been held void by the courts in 1926. Ordinances had likewise received a mixed reaction judicially, as the California, Missouri, and Oklahoma courts had declared these unconstitutional, while the Maryland Court of Appeals had affirmed their legality. Despite the decision in the Thornhill Case, the United States Supreme Court has by no means given pickets complete license, as in the Meadowmoor Case (1940) and the Ritter Case (1942) it sustained certain state court injunctions against picketing when the latter was directed to an unlawful end. Decisions in the Giboney Case (1949) and the Hanke and Cline cases (1950) brought further modifications to the Thornhill doctrine. It should be added that several states (including Massachusetts, New Hampshire, New Jersey, Texas, and Wisconsin) had legalized peaceful picketing long before the Thornhill decision outlawed anti-picketing measures.

Statutes prohibiting boycotts at the state level likewise have enjoyed a rather checkered career. Illinois, Wisconsin, Colorado, Utah, Minnesota, and Texas have passed measures of this nature, although none of these has been used other than on infrequent occasions. Prohibitions against secondary boycotts, of course, are much more common than those against primary ones. It is true that the United States Supreme Court in 1908 did affirm that secondary boycotts were conspiracies in restraint of trade in *Loewe v. Lawler,* better known as the Danbury Hatter's Case, but the Norris-La Guardia Act of 1932 permitted workers to engage in secondary as well as primary boycotts. Seventeen years later, however, the Taft-Hartley Act declared secondary boycotts to be an unfair union practice.

The fact that the so-called sitdown strike did not originate until 1936 explains the absence of legislation directed against this phenomenon from the statute books of the fifty states. After the United States Senate had condemned this technique, Tennessee and Vermont passed special measures outlawing the sitdown strike, while Massachusetts, Minnesota, and Pennsylvania all incorporated anti-sitdown strike provisions into their labor relations legislation. Its foes attempted to have the courts hold the sitdown strike illegal, but in *Apex Hosiery Co. v. Leader* (1940) our highest tribunal stated that sitdown strikes were not covered under the Sherman Anti-Trust Act, thus leaving the enforcement of legislation against the sitdown strike to the states. Delaware, Florida, Louisiana, and South Dakota have enacted anti-sitdown strike laws in more recent years. Since its earliest days, though, the sitdown strike has been used only rarely, so that it no longer constitutes the problem that it once did.

Measures designed to protect labor's rights during a strike currently enjoy a more favorable reception in the courts than do their anti-labor counterparts, but in an earlier era the judiciary regarded them with a rather jaundiced eye. This is especially true of anti-injunction statutes. After the United States Supreme Court in 1921 had held in *Truax v. Corrigan* that the state of Arizona in failing to give an injunction to one Truax had unreasonably taken property rights from him without the due process of law, the state courts thenceforth interpreted in a narrow manner the anti-injunction legislation of Kansas, Minnesota, Utah, North Dakota, Oregon, Washington, Wisconsin, Illinois, and New Jersey. There was no new development of any importance until 1932, when Congress passed the Norris-La Guardia Act which, among other things, discouraged the issuance of injunctions by federal courts in labor disputes; since that date seventeen states have adopted "baby" Norris-La Guardia Acts embodying the same principle at the state level. Injunctions, one might add, are still promulgated on occasion, but on a much more discriminate basis than they once were.

At one time or another, most states have enacted statutes providing for arbitration and mediation in labor disputes. These, in fact, date back to the 1880's and 1890's, with legislatures creating boards of arbitration and mediation in New York and Massachusetts during the peak year of 1886. State labor departments, moreover, on occasion undertook mediation and recommended arbitration. But the first really important piece of legislation of this nature was the measure which the Colorado legislature passed providing for the compulsory investigation of labor disputes in coal and related industries; along with the company union, this was a by-product of the Colorado coal strike of 1913–1914. Under this law, the state labor commission was to propose a settlement, and there was to be a thirty-day cooling-off period in which there was to be no strike. This measure has acted as a deterrent against a number of strikes in the state, although a later court decision restricted the scope of the act to public utilities. In more recent years, states in general have begun to assume a more prominent role vis-a-vis arbitration and mediation in labor disputes, but it is invariably the National Labor Relations Board which catches the public eye, as it concerns itself with the major strikes.

On a broader plane, one might point to the emergence of state labor relations acts. Massachusetts, New York, Pennsylvania, Utah, and Wisconsin adopted the first of these in 1937, two years after Congress had passed the National Labor Relations Act. Unfortunately, these initial measures were attacked on the grounds that they regulated only employer activities, leaving the unions free to act without interference; the latter three states eventually modified their laws in order to strike a more even balance between management and labor. Other states soon began to follow suit in enacting legislation of this type, such as Minnesota and Michigan in 1939, Colorado and Kansas in 1943, and Hawaii in 1945. A recent study has concluded that, in eight of the twelve states currently having laws of this type, the acts are of the Taft-Hartley variety (i.e., primarily regulating unions), while in four they are of the Wagner sort (i.e., primarily regulating management). Curiously, from the geographic point of view, such measures are found only in the middle Great Plains, Great Lakes, Middle Atlantic, and lower New England states (not counting Hawaii). The reason for this is not clear.

Every state, of course, has passed some sort of legislation dealing with strikes, but the truth remains that about three-fourths of these take place in the industrial area north of the Ohio River and east of the Mississippi River. Two-thirds of all strikes occur in the eight states of New York, Pennsylvania, New Jersey, Michigan, Ohio, Massachusetts, Illinois, and California; half, in fact, originate in New York, New Jersey, Massachusetts, and Pennsylvania alone, although these four states have only a third or so of the wage earners of the nation. Quite naturally, the large industrial cities of these and other states are often the site of strikes. Some of the famous walkouts of state history, as was pointed out earlier, have occurred elsewhere, but this fact in no way impairs the validity of our generalization. Among the important *national* strikes between the end of Reconstruction and the termination of World War II have been the railway (1877), the iron and steel (1882), the railway (1884–1885), the abortive general (1886), the bituminous coal (1897), the steel (1901), the packing houses (1904), the Great Lakes seamen (1908), the steel (1909), the steel (1919), the textiles (1934), and the coal (1943).

Focusing our attention on the more limited phenomenon of governmental intervention, one finds instances of this relative to walkouts at the state as well as the national level; generally speaking, prior to the New Deal era such intervention benefited management more than it did labor. In 1892, for example, the state militia crushed the strikers at the Homestead, Pennsylvania steel mills after the latter had run off several hundred Pinkerton detectives. The long-range effect of this series of events was to break the power of the union in the Pittsburgh district until the 1930's. Even more disastrous for the cause of labor was the Pullman walkout of 1894, which took place in Illinois. Alarmed by the impending transportation paralysis, the Cleveland Administration ordered troops to Chicago over the protests of Governor John P. Altgeld, while Attorney General Richard Olney obtained an injunction against the strikers. The latter action established a precedent which the foes of labor employed down to 1932. One prominent exception to governmental apathy or hostility toward strikes was Cripple Creek, Colorado, where miners discovered gold in 1893 and where a strike occurred during the following year. Governor Davis Waite, who earned his nickname "Bloody Bridles" during this controversy, ordered out the state militia so as to prevent bloodshed; Waite, moreover, represented the miners in peace negotiations which led to a three dollar daily wage for eight hours of work. More typical were developments around Coeur d'Alene, Idaho, the previous year (1892), where gold, silver, and lead miners struck upon being confronted with a cut in wages only to be reduced to impotence by a federal court order, a gubernatorial proclamation, the entire state militia, and General Carlin and the War Department.

It was not until the Progressive era, though, that labor was to win even the partial support of the national government during a strike. When a walkout occurred in the anthracite coal fields of Pennsylvania in 1902, the operators led by President George Baer of the Reading Railroad refused even to negotiate with the miners, but President Theodore Roosevelt eventually secured an agreement with both management and labor to accept the terms that an anthracite coal commission would set forth. Under this settlement, the miners obtained many of their goals, although they did not win union recognition. Unfortunately for the cause of labor, T. R.'s friendly gesture did not establish a precedent of pro-labor governmental intervention. The following year at Cripple Creek a sympathy strike occurred when the

Standard mill manager refused a demand by the Western Federation of Miners that he institute an eight hour day; here the governor sent in Brigadier General Chase and the state militia, arrested labor union leaders, and suspended *habeas corpus.* Following a temporary lull in the violence a train loaded with strikebreakers was blown up and the union hall at Victor was destroyed, whereupon martial law was restored under General Bell and 225 miners were deported to other states. These events marked the death knell of the W. F. M. local there. A number of Cripple Creek miners emigrated to Goldfield, Nevada, where in 1907 the governor asked for federal troops and broke a strike after the W. F. M. local walked out in protest against being paid in scrip.

Labor fared little better during the Taft and Wilson administrations in obtaining its goals through walkouts. When a strike broke out in 1912 among the coal miners of Paint Creek, West Virginia, Governor Glasscock declared martial law three times, while military courts tried and sentenced approximately one hundred persons, including "Mother" Jones. Admittedly in 1913 newly elected Governor Hatfield did order the release of imprisoned miners and suggested terms favorable to labor to end the strike, but in conducting an investigation of those events the United States Senate Committee on Education and Labor concluded that peonage was not present in the area. Labor violence also erupted again in Colorado in 1914, at Ludlow. Here the United Mine Workers ran into opposition when they tried to organize the workers, and in a skirmish the strikers' tent village was set afire and eleven people smothered to death in a cave. (This was the famous Ludlow Massacre.) After both state militia and federal troops had gone into action the victorious mine operators refused an offer of arbitration from President Woodrow Wilson, eventually establishing a company union there. Finally, there was the Boston, Massachusetts police strike of 1919; by stifling this walkout Governor Calvin Coolidge so enhanced his reputation that he won the Republican Vice Presidential nomination in 1920. In refusing to reinstate the policemen, Coolidge uttered his famous dictum that "there is no right to strike against the public safety by anybody, anywhere, any time."

The twelve years of Normalcy (1920-1932), as we know, brought to the White House and to many state capitols administrations that were pro-business rather than pro-labor in orientation. For this reason, one finds not only few instances of governmental intervention on the side of labor during this period, but also few strikes. When one did occur, as in Mingo and Logan counties, West Virginia, in 1921, federal troops appeared on the scene after unionized miners from the Paint and Cabin Creek fields had invaded the area. The inevitable result was the termination of the strike the following year and the temporary enfeeblement of the U. M. W. in West Virginia.

With the coming of the New Deal, though, the political atmosphere changed markedly. President Franklin D. Roosevelt openly courted labor, while the newly formed Congress of Industrial Organizations threw its support to him; such federal legislation as the Wagner Act of 1935 set up a protective blanket over unions which previously they had lacked. Thus, during the Harlan County, Kentucky coal strikes of 1931–1938, the La Follette Civil Liberties Committee conducted an inquiry into laboring conditions there, while the new National Labor Relations Board issued a "cease and desist" order against the operators' association. On this occasion, it was the mine owners who went on trial on charges of conspiracy, and though they escaped conviction thanks to a hung jury, they did give in reluctantly to most of the miners' demands. Then there was the 1937 Memorial Day Massacre in Chicago, Illinois. Here ten persons were killed and seventy were hospitalized when a crowd of demonstrators at a Republic Steel plant were dispersed by the police. Despite the fact that the coroner's jury found the killings to be justifiable homicide, and sixty-one marchers pleaded guilty to a charge of unlawful assembly, the La Follette Civil Liberties Committee asserted that the police had not allowed peaceful picketing, while the National Labor Relations Board condemned the Republic Steel company for improper interference, requesting the reinstatement of several thousand strikers. In contrast, gubernatorial acquiescence in high-handed labor practices was a significant aspect of the 1936 United Auto Workers' walkout in Flint, Michigan, the first sitdown strike in American history. On this occasion, the company refused to bargain with the Chevrolet strikers until they had vacated the plants, but Governor Frank Murphy refrained from using state troops to eject the workers; as a result, labor won a number of concessions from management, not only here, but also at the General Motors and the Chrysler plants. Since this date, labor has been a potent force in Michigan.

In the years following the termination of World War II, there has been a decrease in localized strikes of national importance, as the growth of unionization has led to industry-wide walkouts. One, moreover, evaluates strikes today in terms of the disastrous impact of a work stoppage on the total economy, instead of in terms of damage to property and casualties among workers. Prominent walkouts during the past quarter century have included the 1946 coal strike, the 1946 General Motors strike, the 1946 railway strike, the 1956 Westinghouse strike, and the 1959 steel strike. The 1950's did witness the local Kohler Company-United Auto Workers imbroglio in Wisconsin, a conflict which dragged on for the better part of a decade (1954–1960) to the accompaniment of barricades, machine guns, strike breakers, and mass firings. This, though, is no longer the common pattern, since both management and labor in general have adopted a more enlightened approach toward the settlement of disputes.

Doubtless one reason why labor has become more peaceful in recent years is that it has gained in political power. As early as 1878 a Greenback Labor Party elected fourteen of its candidates in Congress, polling a total of one million votes, but two years later its Presidential candidate, James Weaver, did poorly. Following World War I, National Labor and Farmer-Labor parties were organized, but both collapsed shortly thereafter, thanks in part to the opposition of both the Socialists and the American Federation of Labor. Perhaps the most noteworthy venture of the A.F.L. into politics prior to 1952 occurred in 1924, when it openly supported the Progressive Party candidate, Robert La Follette, for President; La Follette did reasonably well at the polls, amassing nearly five million votes, but he carried only one state, his native Wisconsin. Labor's first extended involvement in national politics did not take place until the coming of the New Deal and the founding of the Congress of Industrial Organizations. Thus, in 1940, President John L. Lewis of the C.I.O. opposed a third term for Franklin Roosevelt, but in 1944 the Political Action Committee of that organization strongly supported F.D.R. The American Federation of Labor finally broke precedent by backing Adlai Stevenson for the Presidency in 1952, while the successful candidate, Dwight Eisenhower, surprised many observers by appointing Martin Durkin of the plumbers' union as Secretary of Labor. The

merger of the A.F.L. and the C.I.O. in 1955 further strengthened the political position of labor nationally.

Since Reconstruction, there have been only a handful of instances where labor unions have dominated a state politically.
Such a situation (at least up to the 1962 gubernatorial election)
existed in Michigan following World War II, where the U.A.W.-
C.I.O. backed multi-millionaire Democrat G. Mennen Williams
served an unprecedented six terms as chief executive between
1948 and 1960. Williams, however, had to weather the opposition of the Hoffa-led Teamsters and a Republican legislature
more friendly to the Big Three automobile makers than to organized labor, and the eventual outcome of this conflict was the
recent debt problem.

A similar trend seems to be taking place in Hawaii. Although
at one time that economic oligarchy known as the Big Five
politically controlled this territory, the I.L.W.U. has come to
play a key role in its government in recent years. (There was a
major sugar plantation strike there in 1946 and a major longshoremen's strike in 1949, both manifesting the growing power
of labor.) This left-wing labor organization not only was the
dominant element at the Democratic conventions of 1948 and
1950, it also was a prominent force in the legislature of 1954–
1955; by 1959, though, the I.L.W.U. was teaming up with the
Republican minority so as to elect a speaker and organize the
house of representatives. What its future role in Hawaiian politics will be remains to be seen, but its ties with the Communists
was one factor which held up statehood for Hawaii.

On the other hand, labor was not at all successful when it
attempted to set up an American Labor Party in New York in
1936. This organization, the brain child of the leaders of the
garment trades, eventually gave way to the more effective Liberal Party, founded in 1944. An even worse blow psycho-
logically was the failure of labor to defeat Senator Robert A.
Taft of Ohio for re-election in 1950. At that time, the Taft-
Hartley Act of 1947 had not won the widespread acceptance it
enjoys today; many of its critics then referred to it as a slave
labor measure because it restricted the power of the unions.
Taft, however, won re-election by over four hundred thousand
votes. Perhaps the outstanding example of a victory for labor at
the polls during recent years was the defeat of a number of right-
to-work referendums in 1958. At this time, Senate Majority

Leader William Knowland lost his bid for the governorship of California, but Senator Barry Goldwater, who was running for re-election in neighboring Arizona, won a smashing victory while baiting the unions. (In Arizona, of course, labor constitutes only 8 per cent of the voting population.) The most obvious conclusion that one might draw from this analysis is that labor will vote as a bloc only when it is on the defensive.

Apart from isolated political action there have been instances at the state level where labor has joined forces politically with other interest groups, sometimes with considerable success. One of the most prominent examples was the Farmer-Labor Party of Minnesota. This organization offered its first candidate for state office as early as 1920, but it did not reach the peak of its influence until 1930, when it elected Floyd B. Olson governor. The Farmer-Labor Party also captured both United States Senate seats and carried a majority of the Congressional districts in 1936. Unlike the Progressives of Wisconsin (who finally merged with the Republicans), the Farmer-Labor Party eventually fused with the Democrats in 1944, although Senator Henrik Shipstead had earlier cast his lot with the G. O. P.

State constitutions furnish still another proof of the relatively minor role that labor has played in state politics down to the last generation. Among the few where it has left its impact are those of California and Arizona. As for the former, the Workingmen's Party had grown so powerful in the state by 1878 that it forced the legislature to call a constitutional convention; a third of the representatives that attended this gathering were members of it. Perhaps the most relevant provision of the fundamental law of 1878 was the one that no native of China was ever to exercise the privileges of an elector. The following year Republicans and Democrats fused to drive the Workingmen's Party out of existence, but it nevertheless succeeded prior to its demise in obtaining a popular majority of one hundred and fifty-four thousand to one thousand against further immigration from China. In the case of Arizona, when several labor unions formed a labor party in 1910, the Democrats agreed to accept their program rather than allow the new party to siphon off Democratic votes. At the statehood convention that met later that year George W. P. Hunt, a Democrat friendly to labor, won election as president; despite the fact that labor failed to curb court injunctions and the employment of Mexicans, it still wrote the new state's fundamental law to a large extent.

American labor has rarely successfully supported radical candidates for public office, a prominent exception being the triumph of Socialist Victor Berger at the polls in a Wisconsin congressional district in 1910. During the "Great Red Scare," however, Berger was expelled from Congress and imprisoned (1919), while in New York the following year five Socialists were deprived of their seats in the lower house of the state legislature. As for the more moderate political activities of labor, the trend has been—at least in several states—to restrict financial contributions rather than free speech. The first such measures were passed by Pennsylvania and Texas, but they were so limited in scope that one must reckon the one passed by Indiana in 1945 as the first really adequate piece of legislation of this nature; the next such law of consequence was adopted by Wisconsin in 1955. Both the Indiana and Wisconsin acts prohibit direct as well as indirect contributions on the part of labor for political activity. As for the question of constitutionality, the Texas measure was upheld by the state court of appeals in 1945 in *AFL v. Mann*, but the others have been slow in coming before the courts.

In glancing over the panorama of American labor, one encounters many oddities, but the great morphological truth is that the pattern of unionization, legislation, and strikes varies from state to state, frequently in a pronounced manner. From the total perspective, of course, labor organizing is becoming more extensive and labor legislation more progressive, while strikes have lost much of their original violence. Nevertheless, there is little, if any, similarity between the histories of any two states laborwise. As we have just pointed out, labor has become so powerful in a few states that it is in a position to dominate them politically; it is obvious, though, that this is possible only in the more heavily industrialized states, such as Michigan. Perhaps the biggest issue involving labor at the state level today is that of right-to-work laws. It would appear that the opponents have the upper hand at the moment, since today few if any states are adopting measures of this type, but quite a few are continuing statutes enacted at an earlier date. Still, as we shall demonstrate in the conclusion, labor occupies a rather paradoxical position in this country, since it is powerful enough to influence national elections and national legislation, yet is so weak in a number of states that it has little effect on either there.

Chapter 5

Graft, Scandal, and Corruption

Observers both here and abroad often comment on the corrupt nature of American government; one theory which they frequently offer is that the lofty democratic ideals which we profess are actually unattainable, and that we use them as a cover for political behavior as dirty as, if not dirtier than, that which takes place in any other country. While scandals have occurred in a number of national administrations, especially those of Grant and Harding, similar developments have taken place at the state level, and we shall examine these so as to determine whether they have been as flagrant as their national counterparts. Commentators, though, sometimes minimize these when writing histories of their own state, as they usually desire to picture it in as favorable a light as possible. Quite naturally, they face libel suits if they do not back up their accusations with documented evidence, and this fact in part explains their frequent restraint in writing about scandals. As a result, the objective researcher must not only separate rumor from fact, but also must determine where evidence has been suppressed; it is not surprising, therefore, that the assembling of material on this topic is a highly difficult task.

Continuing these general remarks, the relatively scandal-free history of such a state as Idaho, where the two major political parties have been fairly equally matched in strength over the years, has led many observers to claim that a healthy two-party system is the best safeguard against corruption at the state level. On the other hand, there has been little graft and dishonesty in Vermont, where one party predominates. One might also debate

whether the executive or the legislative branch of state government has been more corrupt over the years; the brand of men
who have inhabited each has been the same, but it appears that
the former offers more instances of really lucrative wrong-
doing. At least two governors have gone to jail, as we shall see.
Harold Zink, however, writes that the "Indiana General Assembly of 1937 had enough grafters among its members that a
regular scale of prices was drafted for quotation to those who
sought improper favors." Thus, he takes a position diametri-
cally opposite to Richard Neuberger, whose experience in the
Oregon legislature led him to observe that "the bulk of our
members are financially honest," adding that "bribes are rare."

As a specific example of Republican corruption statewise,
one might cite the unethical practices of certain members of the
administration of J. Frank Healy, who served as governor of
Indiana from 1905 to 1909. In this particular case, investigators discovered that several state officials were pocketing some
of the funds that had been entrusted to them. Not only were the
state adjutant general and the secretary of state forced to resign
because of monetary deficiencies, but also the auditor was pres-
sured out of office, tried, convicted, and sentenced for embez-
zlement. (He was freed, though, after he appealed to the state
supreme court.) Shortages were uncovered in a number of other
funds as well, and as a result state depositories for public
money were set up; the direct primary system was extended
shortly thereafter in another move to prevent future corruption.
This series of events, moreover, was not the last such blemish
on the Indiana gubernatorial office, as Warren McCray was sent
to Atlanta in 1922 for using the mails to defraud, the first chief
executive at the state level to pay such a penalty. (Ed Jackson,
while still a candidate for governor, was accused of offering a
bribe and immunity to McCray; Jackson, however, was able to
escape prison by pleading the statute of limitations.)

There have, of course, been instances of Democratic wrong-
doing at the state level as well, such as the notorious "Louisiana
Scandals." Unlike the Indiana fiasco, these took place in a one-
party state. The key figure here was Richard W. Leche, a member of the Long political machine, who was elected chief executive of that state in 1936; in the summer of 1939 Leche was
forced to resign his position when it was discovered that numerous political leaders were using their positions or connections
for financial gain. As is frequently the case, this episode was not

a cut-and-dried case of stealing, since some of the supposedly
illicit money-making was within the law. But there was open
dishonesty as well, and Governor Leche and a group of his
associates were sentenced to prison terms. President James
Smith of the State University also pleaded guilty to mishandling
school funds totaling one million dollars. One possible explanation for this phenomenon was that a power vacuum developed
in Louisiana on the death of Huey Long, and those lesser figures who moved in to take over lacked the *savoir faire* to
manipulate the state government in the way that "the Kingfish"
did.

At least three other chief executives have had the misfortune
of facing trial, two while they were still occupying the governor's chair, although none of them was found guilty of the
crimes they allegedly committed. One of these, Lee Russell of
Mississippi (another one-party state), was named in a suit filed
by Miss Frances Birkhead in 1922, who charged that Russell
had seduced her repeatedly under promise of marriage, and that
he had also arranged for an abortion to be performed on her
which had left her an invalid for life. Russell, who served as
chief executive from 1920 to 1924, maintained that certain fire
insurance companies against which he had brought anti-trust
suits the previous year, and which had consequently withdrawn
from the state, had masterminded Miss Birkhead's allegations.
The trial, which took place in Russell's home town of Oxford
after having been moved there from Jackson because of a lack
of jurisdiction, resulted in a speedy acquittal for the chief executive.

A tendency to abuse the use of the pardoning power resulted
in widespread criticism of Len Small, a Republican governor of
Illinois (1921–1929), who freed eight thousand criminals while
serving in this capacity. But it was Small's alleged misdeeds
while acting as state treasurer at an earlier date which almost
brought about his downfall; his foes, seeking a means of removing him from office, charged that he had embezzled one hundred
thousand dollars of public funds. A trial took place during his
second term as chief executive (he had been re-elected in 1924)
at which Small did win acquittal from a jury, but he paid back
six hundred fifty thousand dollars to the state in a civil action.
His reputation thus tainted, the incumbent chief executive was
unable to win his party's nomination for a third term as gover-

nor in 1928. Small, though, also had aroused disfavor politically through his employment of machine methods. Equally fortunate was a later Republican governor, William Stratton (1953–1961), who lost his bid for a third term in 1960 but who also won acquittal at his 1965 trial for evading payment of part of his federal income tax.

More accidental was the trial of Governor Jonathan Davis of Kansas (1923–1925), who like Russell was a Democrat. In January of 1925, George H. Wark, a federal prohibition officer, went to a Topeka hotel in search of a bootlegger, but instead encountered Davis' son, who was supposedly accepting twelve hundred fifty dollars from a paroled forger for a pardon. Both the father and the son were taken into custody, and an investigation was conducted into charges that pardons were being sold on a wholesale basis. The evidence which was uncovered, however, did not place either in a compromising position. As a result, both were acquitted late in May, by which time Davis' term as governor had drawn to a close.

One might cite a few instances, too, in which a chief executive has been guilty of a serious crime and has escaped indictment for it. This was the happy fate of Republican Harold Hoffman, a roly-poly extrovert who left a sealed letter at his death, revealing that he had stolen three hundred thousand dollars while serving as motor vehicles commissioner and later as governor of New Jersey (1935–1938). Hoffman, who held the position of executive director of the state's six hundred million dollar employment security division from shortly after the expiration of his term as chief executive until shortly before his death in 1954, managed to escape detection through a series of complicated maneuvers highlighted by the transference of the "milked" Disability Fund to a bank of which he was president. Supposed irregularities in the Employment Security Division led to his suspension from its executive directorship, but prior to his own admission of guilt no one had ever exposed the secret which he took with him to the grave.

It is perhaps not surprising that the post-Reconstruction era in the South would witness numerous examples of graft and corruption, as a flowering of unethical practices had been one of the fruits of the Reconstruction period. In Georgia, for example, in 1879 the state treasurer and the comptroller general were both impeached (the latter was convicted), while a series

of scandals was discovered in the convict lease system. As for
Virginia, an investigation in 1877 revealed that embezzlements
had occurred relative to canceled bonds which had been illegally refunded. While the state treasurer of Georgia did escape
punishment by restoring misappropriated funds, his counterpart, Marshall Polk of Tennessee, received a twenty-year sentence and a fine of $366,540 in 1883 after stealing more than
$400,000 from the state treasury, while another state treasurer,
Isaac Vincent of Alabama, went to prison in 1887 for fifteen
years after absconding with $232,980 in public funds. More
fortunate was Governor Thomas Churchill of Arkansas, who
successfully attributed to faulty bookkeeping a shortage of
$294,876 that had accumulated during his six years as state
treasurer (1874–1880); his successor, Major William Wood-
ruff, "misplaced" $138,789 during his ten years in that office
(1880–1890) despite an aroused public. Two more cases that
one might cite in this connection are those of James "Uncle
Dick" Tate, ten-term state treasurer of Kentucky, who disap-
peared in 1888, leaving $229,000 missing, and William Hem-
ingway of Mississippi, his counterpart, who stayed to face a five-
year sentence after accumulating a shortage of $315,612. (An-
other Mississippi state treasurer was exposed as an embezzler in
1902.) Perhaps the most notorious episode of all involved
Major E. A. Burke, state treasurer of Louisiana, who stole
$1,177,000 between 1880 and 1889, and then escaped punish-
ment since he was in Europe when his fraudulent activities
became known; while remaining a fugitive from justice, Burke
exploited various territorial concessions which he had previously obtained in Honduras.

We might analyze many other instances of corruption in the
executive branch here, but we will cite as our final example the
notorious South Carolina dispensary system, the group of state-
controlled liquor stores which was established during the administration of Benjamin Tillman. The stench generated by this
operation was so intense that an investigation (the Lyons-Chris-
tensen) was held as a result; following this, a number of true
bills were returned and several convictions were obtained. The
culprits, though, were pardoned to the last man, despite the fact
that one individual was sent to jail. During the fourteen years
that it operated in this one-party state, the State Dispensary
accumulated aggregate profits of over six million dollars, most

of which went to county and town treasuries. The so-called Darlington War of 1894 (which we shall examine in a later chapter) sprang from resentment against this agency, although it had no immediate effect vis-a-vis its abolishment.

Hardly a session of a state legislature passes without charges of dishonesty and graft being raised, yet members of this branch of government have probably gone to jail less often than those in the executive arm. This may be for the reason that their sins are often of a rather petty character. There are a few rare instances, however, when legislative crookedness has been so flagrant as to ensure that body a place in the annals of a state. This was true of the predominantly Democratic New Jersey legislature of 1893, which was one of the most corrupt sessions in American history; since its main accomplishment was the legalization of gambling at race tracks, this body came to be known as the "Jockey Legislature." A later investigation headed by Senator Foster M. Voorhees of Union County brought to light the fact that Bernard J. Ford, Democratic-appointed Custodian of the State House, had played host at a rather elaborate bar which had been built and maintained at state expense ("Barney's State House Bar"). It was also revealed that most of the culprits imprisoned for their part in the Hudson County election scandals of 1889 and race track crookedness had bought pardons. Nevertheless, there was no series of trials following these revelations, although by this time the Republicans, who certainly had everything to gain from prosecuting these cases, were back in office.

Yet, the possibility does exist that even legislators will pay for their sins, and it is such wholesale although infrequent clean-ups as that effected in Michigan in 1943 which keep wayward solons from straying too far from the straight and narrow path. Rumors circulated at that time charging that lobbyists were purchasing the votes of legislators were so persistent that a special investigation was held. The key figure in this unsavory episode was one Charles F. Hamans, a lobbyist-briber who turned state's evidence; Hamans presented proof of payments to legislators from bankers, loan-company officers, race-track promoters, slot-machine owners, and others. Not only were there numerous convictions, but also the political careers of many legislators were ruined and the reputations of many businessmen were injured. Although this series of events perhaps has not received the attention that it should, it reveals that while a legislator may get away with petty graft, there is a point beyond which he may not steal with impunity.

It is perhaps symbolic of the corruption which is so characteristic of state government that a scandal would break out in regard to the outfitting of a capitol building. Such an occurrence took place in Pennsylvania shortly after the turn of the century. Here the new state treasurer discovered upon assuming office in May of 1906 that funds were missing from the treasury; a commission set up by the legislature the next year uncovered evidence of further wrong-doing. The consequent trial, which occurred in 1908, led to the conviction of all the defendants, but appeals to the courts delayed the execution of their sentences. In 1910, moreover, the individuals involved in the fraud agreed to a restitution of one million, five hundred thousand dollars to cover the amount stolen from the treasury. Lest one assume that this episode was an isolated case, we might also mention the bizarre events surrounding the construction of the New York state capitol at Albany; here there was so much graft that the budget had to be voted twice so as to obtain enough funds with which to finish the building.

Regardless of the fact that there are stiff federal laws against election frauds, state elections often feature vote-buying and ballot-box stuffing. Of all the aspects of political corruption at the state level, it is perhaps this one which is the most likely to go unpunished (even if it is detected), mainly for the reason that such practices are so widespread that they are more or less tacitly accepted. Unquestionably, one of the most original approaches to halting unethical actions of this sort was employed in Ohio in 1911, where those who allegedly sold their votes were brought to trial along with those who supposedly bought them; evidence was produced revealing that between ten and twenty-five thousand dollars had been distributed in elections held in Adams and Scioto counties over the years. No less than one-third of the voters of Adams county were indicted, and nearly two thousand of them were fined and given a suspended sentence of one year. This drastic expedient, though, by no means stamped out corruption in the state.

Wrong-doing at the state level, of course, is often attributable to the existence of political machines. As these are often extremely powerful, it is significant that the only large-scale crackdown on one was made possible through the efforts of the federal government; this was in 1938, when more than one hundred members of the Pendergast organization were indicted for vote frauds and for income tax evasion. There were numerous convictions in the months that followed, including that of Pendergast himself. Reforms, moreover, were shortly forthcoming, as Kansas City repudiated the political machine at the next election, while the state legislature authorized state control of the Kansas City police department in 1939. Opponents of then Senator and later President Truman have often charged that ties existed between the President and this political boss; these accusations are doubtless exaggerated, but Truman did see to it that Pendergast, who died shortly thereafter, was released from prison in 1945 prior to the expiration of his sentence.

As a final point, we might note that a number of governors have partly won election to office on the basis of their record as uncoverers of corruption. Theodore Roosevelt, for example, served as police commissioner of New York City before becoming chief executive of that state, while Charles Evans Hughes led an investigation of utilities and insurance companies. A more recent example was District Attorney Thomas E. Dewey, who terrorized criminals during the 1930's. Outside of New York state, perhaps the most notable cases were Joseph Folk of Missouri, who exposed graft in St. Louis prior to becoming governor, and Earl Warren of California, who cleaned up Oakland while serving as district attorney. Less prominent governors who were also crime busters include Dwight Green (Illinois, 1941–1949), who prosecuted Al Capone for income tax evasion; Kim Sigler (Michigan, 1947-1949), who attacked legislative graft; and Frank Lausche (Ohio, 1945–1947, 1951–1957), who raided Cleveland gambling houses while serving as municipal judge. Being on the side of law and order, of course, is one of the surest ways of attracting votes when running for office, unless the "bad guys" are powerful enough to purchase a victory.

If one were to summarize this material on corrupt practices in state politics, he might suggest that the phenomenon is universal and has resisted the attempts of well-meaning reformers to destroy it through the direct primary and civil service. Despite the claim by the noted political scientist, V. O. Key, that corruption at the state level is abating, only a few years ago Orville Hodge, Auditor of Public Accounts of the state of Illinois, went to prison after pocketing one and a half million dollars from the state treasury. (In the aftermath of this disaster, the 1957 Illinois legislature established the office of auditor-general for the purpose of rooting out possible future corruption and waste.) As for the question of whether state politics are more corrupt than their national counterpart, one hesitates at making a blanket generalization; it would appear, however, that the public is more tolerant toward unethical practices at the state level, although they do elect crime-busters to office on occasion. We shall examine this subject at greater length in the conclusion.

Chapter 6

Taxation and Indebtedness

There are perhaps few aspects of state political history which have inspired less perceptive analysis than taxation. All too frequently accounts treating this subject restrict themselves to a detailed description of legislation, totally ignoring those factors which were responsible for the adoption of a specific tax at a specific time and at a specific place. We have already touched upon taxation in the chapter on business, so that one might supplement the material presented in this section with that set forth there. Here we will attempt to outline the political dynamics of taxation at the state level, keeping in mind that party labels have little relevance in this connection. Despite the fact that nationally the Democrats generally favor increased governmental services more so than the Republicans, and thus must support higher taxes, there does not seem to be a meaningful correlation between the two at the state level. Income taxes tend to penalize the rich and sales taxes tend to penalize the poor, but states where the more mass-oriented Democrats are in the ascendancy do not always favor the former, and states where the more elite-oriented Republicans are in the ascendancy do not always favor the latter. It is true that in the historically Democratic South poll taxes are more common than elsewhere in the country, but there they are employed basically as a regulatory device to limit voting instead of as a source of revenue.

Nationally the pattern of taxation has differed markedly from that statewise. Aside from the Civil War, most of the revenue that Washington obtained in the first century of its existence came from the tariff, supplemented by various excise taxes.

During that conflict the national government imposed an income tax which lapsed shortly after the end of the fighting; on the other hand, when it enacted another such measure in 1894, the United States Supreme Court declared this unconstitutional in *Pollock v. Farmers Loan and Trust Co.* It was not until 1913 that federal authorities received legal sanction under the Sixteenth Amendment to levy an income tax. As late as 1942 the revenue that Washington obtained from corporate income taxes exceeded that from individual income taxes, but in more recent years the latter has become its chief source of revenue, furnishing roughly fifty cents out of every dollar. Of lesser importance nationally are excise taxes on such items as liquor, tobacco, automobiles, gasoline, furs, jewelry, and amusements. The tariff still yields a half-billion dollars annually, but proceeds from this tax have remained constant, while those from the others have increased by leaps and bounds.

At the beginning of the period covered by this volume (1876) the most important tax at the state level was the general property tax, a device which weighed most heavily on the farmers and from which to this date the latter have attempted to escape. During the latter part of the Nineteenth Century governmental expenditures statewise were quite limited; the business interests that dominated many state governments, such as Anaconda Copper in Montana and the railroads in general, saw to it that their tax burden was light, if indeed they were not exempted from taxation. Two instances of this that we previously cited were the moratoriums on mining taxes in Colorado and on industrial taxes in Mississippi. By the turn of the century, though, Progressives had begun to challenge business domination of political affairs, and as governmental expenditures for schools, roads, and other services increased sharply, it was only natural that a search for new revenues would take place. (One exception to this rule was Alaska, which did not adopt a comprehensive tax program until 1949, many industries being free from taxation up to that time.) This search for new sources of revenue accelerated during the New Deal, and has reached frantic proportions today, as state governments are seemingly scraping the bottom of the barrel taxwise.

The first state to adopt an income tax was Wisconsin, in 1911. Under the leadership of Robert La Follette this state had assumed a position near the front, if not at the very front, of the Progressive movement; its action antedated the ratification of the constitutional amendment permitting a federal income tax by two years. The two groups most in favor of this type of measure were the agrarian elements and the labor unions. But not every state was as enthusiastic about the income tax as Wisconsin, for the Florida legislature successfully proposed an amendment to that state's constitution in 1923 which forbade the levying of such a tax there. By the time of World War II almost every state that employs the income tax as a major source of revenue had adopted it, six in 1933 alone. In recent years perhaps the most important addition to the ranks has been Michigan, where Governor George Romney successfully led the movement for the ratification of a new constitution in 1963 which authorized, among many other things, income tax legislation. Fiscal liberals have long favored measures of this type, as the more wealthy must bear a disproportionately heavy share of the tax load. Thanks to the steep federal income tax rates of today, however, resistance is growing vis-a-vis the extension of this device into states where it is currently absent from the statute books.

In contrast, the sales tax long has been a favorite of fiscal conservatives, although it imposes a disproportionately heavy tax burden upon the poor. Business groups obviously prefer it to an income tax or a corporation tax. West Virginia enacted the first such measure at the state level in 1921, but it was not until 1929 that Georgia followed suit; there then occurred one adoption after another, thirty-one states having turned to this device by 1937. In contrast, an attempt to pass a national sales tax in 1932 ended in failure. Over the years the average sales tax rate has crept steadily upward from the original one or two per cent, until today it has reached five per cent in such states as Pennsylvania; lawmakers frequently try to soften its impact by exempting various articles from its provisions. Nevertheless, it seems likely that the lower classes will wreak political vengeance upon any state administration that attempts to raise the level of taxation much higher, as it even now pinches their pocketbooks a bit too severely for their taste. It is significant that most states employ either an income tax or a sales tax as a major source of revenue, but rarely both.

States have imposed a variety of taxes on different business activities, sometimes for revenue purposes, sometimes for regulatory ones. First one should mention corporation taxes; no less than twenty states adopted measures of this type between 1929 and 1937, 1933 being the peak year. Heavy rates, though, may not only hinder the drive to attract out-of-state industry, but may also force concerns from the state that are already present there. Inheritance taxes likewise may affect the business community in an adverse manner. Florida ratified a constitutional prohibition against this variety of tax in 1923, but backtracked in 1931 in order to share in such levies with the federal government. As for severance taxes, these may retard the economic development of a state by imposing a penalty on the extraction of natural resources; among those states that rely heavily on the severance tax as a source of revenue are Louisiana, New Mexico, Oklahoma, and Texas. Then there are the anti-chain store taxes, first adopted by Georgia, Maryland, and North Carolina in 1927, which openly attempt to discourage business operations of this nature. These have met with varying success. Gasoline taxes also provide many states with varying amounts of income, as do taxes on cigarettes and liquor; quite obviously users of these commodities are not enthusiastic about these levies. Finally, one might cite the workingmen's compensation taxes that we discussed in the chapter on labor.

Historically taxation has had an impact both on constitutional developments and statehood drives. In the case of Illinois, for example, a proposed fundamental law went down to defeat at the polls in 1920 by a humiliating margin, thanks largely to an income tax provision that proved highly unpopular. Then there are Alaska and Hawaii, where various economic interests long opposed statehood on the grounds that elevation from territorial status would result in a heavier tax burden. Gubernatorial fortunes also have been built around stands on taxation. Thus Huey Long used the compromise severance tax of two cents a barrel on oil as a tool in persuading the rural masses to elect him governor of Louisiana in 1928. Once in office, Long boosted the oil tax from two to six cents and the gas tax from one to three cents, the proceeds from these furnishing him with the funds with which to embark upon a much-needed spending program. In contrast, Governor Edward Martin of Pennsylvania, unlike Long a conservative and a Republican, courted public favor through tax reductions in the mid-1940's, eventually winning several terms in the United States Senate. Among the taxes that Martin eliminated were the personal property, the municipal loans, the mercantile, the emergency corporate loan, and the emergency bank and trust company shares.

The fact that it is difficult to generalize about taxation and politics at the state level is borne out by an examination of several case studies taken from the post-World War II era. First let us look at New York, where liberal Republican Nelson Rockefeller called for an increase in personal income tax rates shortly after becoming governor in 1959. This plea was eventually approved in modified form, but many legislators and a large segment of the public was alienated in the process; as he has unfolded his tax program during the 1960's Rockefeller has continued to encounter strong opposition from these two groups. Nevertheless, Nelson Rockefeller recently won re-election to office for a third four-year term, having held office today longer than any other governor. Then there is Michigan, where six-term (1949-61) Democratic Governor G. Mennen Williams long sought enactment of a tax on corporate profits without success, while his Republican foes in the legislature countered with a constitutional amendment raising the sales tax from three to four per cent. (This was finally ratified in 1960.) Significantly, the answer of moderate Republican Governor George Romney to Michigan's financial crisis has been an income tax, a measure which Williams himself proposed at one time. Even more ironic have been recent developments in California. Here Democratic Governor Edmund Brown pushed increases in personal income, business, and luxury taxes through the legislature during his two terms (1959-67), only to retire to private life leaving behind the largest state budget in California history for his successor to finance. As a result, newly elected conservative Republican Governor Ronald Reagan, despite his sharp cuts in governmental and educational spending, had no choice but to support a record tax increase.

Despite the continuing popularity with the voters of Rockefeller, Romney, and Reagan, all of whom raised taxes, other governors have bit the dust politically in recent years, thanks largely to their raising of the level of taxation. Perhaps the most prominent case which one might point out is that of Democratic Governor Michael Di Salle of Ohio (1959-61), who successfully supported bills providing for a twenty per cent increase in tax measures to offset a one hundred million dollar deficit that he faced upon taking office. Di Salle's reward was to lose the governorship in the next election by the largest margin in Ohio history.

One might well ask the question: "Have sectional factors influenced state taxation?" since neither party lines nor ideological affiliations have held constant in this area. Not too much has been written on the subject, but James Martin and Glenn Morrow have pointed out relative to the South that tax levels there are somewhat low vis-a-vis taxable capacity; Martin and Morrow add that an usually large share of state revenues in the South is derived from consumer taxes. These facts have led V. O. Key to conclude about this traditionally Democratic region that: "The factional system simply provides no institutional mechanism for the expression of lower-bracket viewpoints." As for New England, Duane Lockard has discovered that business taxes are much lower in traditionally Republican Maine, New Hampshire, and Vermont than in politically competitive Connecticut, Massachusetts, and Rhode Island. Significantly, both Vermont and New Hampshire have levied poll taxes, as have the one-party states of the South. Before one generalizes for the nation as a whole, however, it will be necessary for political scientists to make studies of those other sections where two-party political competition is the rule rather than the exception.

Constitutionally the most significant development taxwise in recent years at the state level has been the demise of the poll tax. This device was first extensively employed in the South around the turn of the century, not only to disenfranchise Negroes, but also objectionable whites. Opportunistic politicians have turned the tax to their advantage by bloc payments of it, as in the Mexican-American counties of Texas. Since 1920 North Carolina, Louisiana, Florida, Georgia, South Carolina, Tennessee, and Arkansas have abandoned it, but the tax still remains on the statute books of Alabama, Mississippi, Texas, and Virginia. The Twenty-fourth Amendment to the United States Constitution, though, which was ratified in 1964, provides that: "The right of citizens of the United States to vote in any primary or other election for President or Vice President, for electors for President or Vice President, or for Senator or Representative in Congress, shall not be denied or abridged by the United States or any other State by reason of failure to pay any poll tax or other tax." In addition, the federal Voting Rights Act of 1965 includes a near-ban on its use for any election for any office. As for the effects of the tax, V. O. Key has found that its disenfranchising effect is greater at the trough of the business cycle, and that a cumulative tax has more severe impact than a non-cumulative one. Some people, of course, are not going to vote anyway, tax or no tax. It is probable that more whites than Negroes have been kept from voting by the poll tax; in any event, no great social upheaval has occurred in these states where it was eliminated at an earlier date.

Looking towards the future, the federal government has relied for a long time, is relying today, and in all likelihood will continue to bank on corporate and individual income taxes as its chief source of revenue. The trend at the state level is far less discernible. Aside from the funds that they receive from Washington, state governments as a whole rely most heavily (in descending order of importance) on the general sales tax, the motor fuels tax, the individual income tax, the motor vehicle licenses tax, and the corporation income tax. What the ranking of these and possibly other taxes may be a decade or two from now is a matter of conjecture. The occupation by motor fuels taxes and motor vehicle licenses taxes of the second and fourth positions on this list may surprise a few; since they are frequently earmarked for highway construction and maintenance, they arouse less controversy than do the others as a rule. Despite its former ascendancy, the general property tax is no longer an important source of revenue at the state level, nor is it likely that it will ever regain its former prominence. As for the poll tax, its end is obviously at hand. Many states in the years ahead will doubtless be forced to turn to new taxes; that business will not be excessively victimized is quite certain, as state governments dare not kill the goose that lays the golden eggs by driving business from a state or discouraging its entry from the outside.

Exposed as they have been to a generation of deficit spending, fiscal liberals show little concern that the national government is in debt three hundred billion dollars; accepting the theory that they owe this money to themselves, they pass over this sum lightly while haggling over their own petty doubts. State governments, too, frequently must solve a debt problem of some type, but as a rule they are less able to "pass the buck." The debacle of Reconstruction was responsible for the states of the old Confederacy accumulating a considerable debt, and some of these endangered their credit ratings for years to come by repudiating this either *in toto* or in part. Other states, however, also have encountered debt problems at one time or another for various reasons; an examination of some of their struggles enables the historian to place the question of the national debt in a broader perspective. State borrowing has been heaviest in the Northeast and the Southwest, being the greatest in Massachusetts. Most states have some kind of constitutional limitation on the incurrence of debt, but Nebraska is the only state that has always been on a pay-as-you-go basis, so that the other forty-nine theoretically are in danger of encountering problems of this type.

Since the end of World War II, part of the cost of state government has been borne through increased taxes. Unfortunately, there has yet to be a tax devised which does not arouse the ire of some special interest, and this is especially true at the state level. The property tax, for example, is looked on with disfavor by the rural elements, while the sales tax is regarded as anathema by the lower class; in some states, the latter has now reached the 5 per cent plateau. Despite the fact that it is often no more burdensome than the sales tax, the income tax is widely unpopular because of the high federal rates. Then there are business taxes, which run counter to the prevalent philosophy on the part of most state governments of encouraging business, as do inheritance taxes. Finally, one might cite excise taxes, which in many cases have reached or are approaching the point of diminishing return. By 1961, the national government was underwriting one-fifth of all state expenses, but, despite the supplementing of state tax receipts with federal funds, the total debt of the fifty states was almost four times as large in 1961 as it had been in 1950. Thus, an examination of state debt problems constitutes far more than an academic exercise.

The difficulties which confronted Ohio between 1885 and 1900 might be cited as a typical example of "debtitis." Various state institutions were expanding at this time, and both the Republicans and the Democrats annually sponsored irresponsible and extravagant legislative programs. Admittedly, some of the increased expenses were justified, but the law-making body failed to meet these costs through new taxes, while administrative officials in charge of state institutions neglected to employ up-to-date business methods. During this period, the Ohio government twice had to obtain loans of five hundred thousand dollars in order to meet running expenses. Ohio, of course, is by no means a poor state, and the following cases prove that the more wealthy states are just as liable to fall into debt as their less fortunate brethren are.

Somewhat similar was the situation which confronted the Connecticut government in 1891. In this instance, the state ran out of money because the legislature refused to vote sufficient appropriations; Governor Bulkeley thereupon made an agreement with the Aetna Life Insurance Company (of which he was president) whereby the latter would cash all claims against the state. The chief executive pledged his entire fortune in return as a guarantee. Aetna did advance nearly three hundred thousand dollars to Connecticut, but this sum represented less than 10 per cent of total state governmental costs during this period. In contrast, the Mississippi legislature of 1894 attempted to straighten out the tangled finances of that state via the issuance of paper money. This expedient had been employed on many occasions earlier in American history, but it was by this time illegal, so that as a result the governor, auditor, and treasurer were arrested for violating the federal counterfeit laws. Fortunately, the jury assigned to their case refused to indict them. The experience of Connecticut in 1891 was quite similar to that of Rhode Island in 1924; here, though, it was a case of no appropriation being passed rather than an inadequate one, as a Democratic filibuster and a Republican boycott stalled action in the Senate throughout 1923 and 1924. Twenty-three banks came to the rescue in this instance by making a joint loan of four hundred thousand dollars to the state. With the growth of the cost of operating a state government, this solution daily becomes less feasible, as few banks or business concerns possess the capital to make the sort of loan required today. As late as 1931, however, Governor B. M. Miller of Alabama borrowed nearly five million dollars from the First National Bank of Montgomery and the Chase National Bank of New York with which he supported the schools and eleemosynary institutions of that state.

Of a more chronic nature have been the debt problems of Arkansas. The credit rating of this state has been poor over the years due to the repudiation of its entire debt following Reconstruction; as late as 1917 the banks of New York received instructions not to handle any of its securities. Not only was the state treasury empty by 1933, but also there were outstanding unpaid warrants of one million dollars on the general revenue fund which could be cashed only at a heavy discount. Although the legislature remedied this situation within three years through the institution of a sinking fund, a bonded indebtedness remained which rose from five million dollars in 1926 to one hundred seventy-four million dollars in 1934; this increase was attributable to the issuance of bonds to accelerate the construction of roads and highways and the assumption of responsibility for the bonds issued by road improvement districts. A highway refunding act passed in 1934 restored the state's credit, but the total highway obligations twenty years later still totaled one hundred forty-four million dollars, of which one hundred eleven million dollars was the principal. This considerable sum remained unpaid despite the fact that in 1939 the legislature gave the governor and the State Debt Board the authority to fund the state highway bonded debt at a lower rate of interest. Our excerpt from Arkansas history clearly points up the dilemma with which the states are confronted today; they are expected to furnish up-to-date transportational (and educational) systems without possessing adequate financial means for carrying out such projects.

Apart from Arkansas, Tennessee perhaps had had more of a debt problem than any other state in recent years. (Neither state has a debt limit.) In the case of the former, the crux of the dilemma lay in the amount borrowed; in that of the latter, in the management of the debt. Not only was the schedule of maturities in Tennessee poorly arranged, but also provisions for debt service were defective. Two issues of "Highway Notes" and one of "Highway Bonds" dating from 1929 and 1930 matured in a single year (1939), despite the fact that they totaled thirty-five million dollars; aside from the fact that none of these was callable, it is obvious that it would be difficult, if not impossible, to raise sufficient revenues to meet the required payments at one time. In addition, there was another issue of highway bonds in 1932, still others of bridge bonds between 1927 and 1930, and an assumption of thirty-five million dollars of county expenditures in 1927. It must be admitted that the above developments made a problem inevitable, but to make matters even worse, two unscrupulous businessmen named Luke Lea and Henry Caldwell juggled the state's finances between 1927 and 1931. The legislature finally enacted a series of reforms in the mid-1930's, when it adopted a modern system of accounting, brought about improved budgetary control, and had the state debt reorganized after an investigation by a firm of financial consultants, but the results of this debacle may still be felt today.

On the other hand, South Dakota history furnishes an example of an insolvent guaranty fund. When in 1927 the legislature abolished the old bank deposit insurance system, it rewrote the original measure to provide for a separate guaranty fund for each state bank. Not only did it jettison the insurance features of the earlier enactment, it also refused to reimburse depositors as the governor had suggested. Popular sentiment for the redemption by taxpayers of the certificates of indebtedness, however, began to evaporate when the state supreme court declared the guaranty fund insolvent. One authority has estimated that thirty-nine million dollars of those bonds issued against it were left unpaid. Recent years have been happier ones in that they have seen South Dakota emerge from debt (in 1954) for the first time in forty years; the state accomplished this feat in spite of the fact that it undertook payment of a twenty-eight million dollar bonus to veterans of World War II. One might explain this paradox on the grounds that favorable economic conditions after World War II had swollen state treasury receipts to a figure more than double that which they were at the end of the global holocaust, and these excess funds were used for the purpose of debt liquidation.

Noteworthy as South Dakota's accomplishment may be, it was surpassed by that of Pennsylvania where the General State Authority bonds, totaling forty-seven million dollars, were retired during the governorship of Edward Martin (1943–1947), a conservative Republican. This is one of the largest single debt payments any state ever has made, but, even so, Martin was able to effect this retirement and build up a treasury surplus while reducing taxes. The governor was aided in the implementation of his program by increased state revenues resulting from the wartime expansion of industry, as well as by a precipitous drop in the unemployed, thus freeing funds previously earmarked for their support. In addition, consolidation in various departments of the government reduced administrative costs.

One might assume that it would be possible to cite instances of debt crises from the annals of every state; such, however, is not the case, as quite a few states have scrupulously refrained from going into debt. Virginia is a case in point, as was pointed out earlier in this chapter. Admirers of the "pay-as-you-go" approach to financing doubtless will find much to praise in the constitutional provision authorizing a mandatory one hundred thousand dollars annual reduction in the bonded debt of Georgia. Since this amounted to ten million dollars in 1877, it will have dwindled to nothing in another ten years. Georgians may have amended their constitution more than three hundred times in other particulars, but they have displayed a marked aversion to altering its provisions so as to allow any increase in the debt. Some opponents of large government have suggested that authorities in Washington adopt a similar scheme to reduce our national debt in a systematic manner, but it is unlikely that this suggestion will ever become a reality; not only are revenues today insufficient to match expenditures, but also many liberal economists consider it desirable to have a large national debt.

Even if there is a constitutional debt limitation provision, there may be ways of bypassing it. Such has been the case in Colorado. In its original form, the Colorado Constitution of 1876 provided that the state could incur debts not exceeding three mills for the construction of public buildings, subject to the approval of the electorate; it was to repay these within fifteen years, while the aggregate debts of the state were never to exceed one hundred thousand dollars. Despite these restrictions, though, the pertinent constitutional passages were ineffective because the general assembly gave state agencies corporate power. As a result, the highway department was able to create a debt of twenty-five million dollars, which the people of Colorado eventually must pay, even though it is not technically a state debt. Moreover, there is no way of remedying this abuse other than to withdraw these corporate powers from the state agencies.

Another instance of an evasion of a debt limitation involves South Carolina. In 1929, the legislature of that state, without referring the proposition to the people as the state constitution requires, launched a sixty-five million dollar road bond project on its own. The reason that this was done was that many legislators feared that the voters would not give the issue the necessary two-thirds majority. It is not surprising that the state supreme court declared this action unconstitutional, but agreement must be unanimous on constitutional questions in South Carolina, and when there is a division of opinion it is necessary to consult with the circuit court judges. The *enbanc* court then

overruled the supreme court justices, affirming the legality of
the bonds by an overwhelming majority on the grounds that
they did not come within the scope of the constitutional provi-
son forbidding an increase in the state debt without a popular
vote. Revenues from taxes connected with the use of roads had
been dedicated to paying off the issue. This decision did pave
the way for better roads in South Carolina; the courts, though,
lost a great deal of popular respect, and the decision also tied
up the state's easiest and richest source of income for a generation.

In contrast, the West Virginia treasury deficit of 1933 merits
attention in that Governor Kump wiped it out at the height of a
depression through the most unpopular of all expedients: increasing old taxes and instituting new ones. Perhaps the amount
in arrears was not stratospheric (four million dollars), but its
creditors refused to renew it; in almost every county real estate
was up for sale for non-payment of taxes. In addition, the ratification of a constitutional amendment in 1932 which limited the
tax rates on general property had made such a dent in local
revenues that the state had to furnish supplemental aid for
schools, the needy, and highways. Examining the wide variety
of rate hikes and new levies which he advocated, one wonders
how Kump was able to push such a program through the legislature. Not only was the base of the gross sales tax widened, but
the rates were also increased, and an emergency surtax was
added; the capitation tax was boosted, while diverse new taxes
were authorized. These included an emergency consumers sales
tax, a personal income tax (this was not retained), and taxes on
chain stores, horse racing, and alcoholic beverages. It is doubtful, too, whether such a program would ever have been adopted
had it not been for the wave of sentiment for drastic reforms
sweeping the country at that time.

While many of the examples presented here date back quite a
few years, one should not assume that it is impossible today for
a state to go heavily in debt. An instance of this is the recent
ninety-five million dollar Michigan deficit; this catastrophe resulted from a deadlock between the governor and the legislature
over taxes. Strangely, the state's credit rating did not suffer
much as a result. As the 1908 state constitution did not permit
borrowing beyond four hundred thousand dollars, it was apparent that additional funds had to be raised in some other manner.
In order to accomplish this, the legislature placed a constitu-

tional amendment on the ballot in 1960 which authorized the imposition of a 4 per cent sales tax, and after the voters approved this Governor G. Mennen Williams called a special session of the legislature at which that body enacted a new tax law. On the other hand, expectations were that this measure would wipe out only about half of the deficit.

Reviewing the material which we have presented in this section, it is quite apparent that state governments, which are far less well heeled financially than are their counterpart in Washington, court disaster when they plunge head over heels into debt in order to undertake projects beyond their financial resources. Arkansas and Tennessee are cases in point. Not every state has been as successful in reducing its bonded obligations as have South Dakota and Pennsylvania; one must face the fact that at times governmental spending is popular, even though it may lead to debt. There are those, of course, who feel that the states should turn to the federal government for financial assistance, but one wonders whether this would result in any real savings to the taxpayer in the long run. Actually, the crux of the matter is that politicians at the state level frequently lack the courage to adopt the pay-as-you-go philosophy necessary to finance these projects; those in such states as Colorado and South Carolina have even gone so far as to evade their state constitutions in piling up debts. Perhaps the Kumpian policy of more and higher taxes would occasionally result in political suicide, but it is the only honest answer to this thorny question. The modern concept that when the government goes into debt we owe the money to ourselves, after all, may be only a flimsy excuse for evading the issue.

Chapter 7

Schools and Roads:
Two Political Footballs

Approximately half the money that state governments spend today goes for schools and roads. Unlike legislation relative to business and labor, where often there is a sharp division between the two major political parties, with the Republicans taking the side of business and the Democrats that of labor, rarely is there such a marked cleavage relative to highways and educaion. (Pro-segregation Southern governors are an exception to this rule.) Like God and country, everyone favors highways and education, at least up to the point where they cost too much; for this reason, an examination of the political aspects of road and school legislation is not a simple matter. In the following pages, an attempt is made to point out various phases of highway and educational policy which most often arouse political controversy, stressing those that are common to states in general rather than those that are peculiar to an isolated state; two of the most important of these have been the distribution of authority and the raising of funds. The intensity of various problems, of course, has varied over the years, while certain states have pioneered in specific innovations. As for education alone, political pressures have resulted at times in restrictions on academic freedom, and in illustrating this point our narrative appropriately treats cases involving such issues as Populism, World War I, nativism, Southern demagogism and racism, and Communism.

First examining education, it is difficult to draw parallels between federal and state activity in this area for the period under consideration, as the former have been almost *nil*. It is true that the federal Smith-Hughes Act of 1917 did provide for financial assistance to those public schools that taught vocational and agricultural subjects, but the Smith-Turner bill of 1919 establishing a national Department of Education, financial assistance to the states, and uniform educational standards failed to pass Congress. As a result, in our investigation of the main trends in public education statewise since Reconstruction prior to the last few years, we are able only to make reference to the federal government in a handful of areas. These include the United States Supreme Court decisions vis-a-vis segregation in the public schools, President Theodore Roosevelt's opposition to discrimination against Japanese pupils in the schools of California, and our highest tribunal's rulings on released time and prayer in the public schools. Since the passage of the National Defense Education Act in 1958, the national government has increasingly lavished funds on the states for educational purposes.

A thorough discussion of school financing at the state level would require a volume twice the size of this one. Few states have been as fortunate as either Texas, where oil was discovered on public school lands and the proceeds from its sale were employed to develop the educational system of the state, or Delaware, where contributions from Pierre du Pont were used to construct schools for Negroes as well as whites. In regard to the matter of federal aid, it is obvious that the formulation of educational policy may well be involved here; the current struggle between the governor, the legislature, the superintendent of schools, and the board of education would be complicated even further by the national government adding its voice to the uproar. Then there is the question of the degree of freedom that a state is to allow to localities. New York, Maryland, and New Hampshire are typical of those states that exercise strict control, while Kansas, Nebraska, and the Dakotas are representative of those that hold the reins loosely. To date, Delaware is the only state that has attempted to integrate its schools into a single, centrally administered unit (1921).

Analyzing the relationship between education and politics in more detail, Nicholas L. Masters, Robert E. Salisbury, and Thomas E. Eliot have set forth a number of hypotheses that merit examination in their book *State Politics and the Public Schools* (1964). This study deals with the educational systems of Illinois, Michigan, and Missouri. First of all, the authors point out that only a handful of the policy proposals that come before the legislature are the result of widespread public enthusiasm; nevertheless, school issues do at times arouse considerable controversy, even in the absence of organized anti-school groups. This is especially true of those involving fundamental changes in the revenue structure or heavy increases in educational expenditures. The schools, too, do not suffer from a lack of spokesmen in the capital, as in each state surveyed legislators often considered the educational lobby to be more powerful than any other. Perhaps surprisingly, many political officials are of the opinion that their efforts on behalf of schooling do not bring them comparable political rewards, with the result that role specialization has occurred within the legislative branch relative to education. Admittedly, this study was based on only three states, but it would seem that many of its findings have universal validity.

One of the most obvious conclusions that one might reach from an examination of state history is that the problems which professional educators face today are not quite the same as the ones with which they had to deal fifty years ago. This is especially evident in the case of compulsory attendance. Laws dealing with this topic were passed in thirty-two states before the end of the nineteenth century, with Massachusetts the pioneer (1852), but none was enacted in Mississippi until 1918, so that the fight for this reform was prolonged over sixty-five years. (Even today, though, the age to which one must attend school varies from state to state.) Then there is the question of segregation, which is far more ancient than one might suppose. Following Reconstruction, no less than seventeen states required whites and blacks to attend different schools, while four permitted it (Kansas, Wyoming, New Mexico, and Arizona). A half century or so ago, the issue was whether Negroes were being given the separate and equal facilities to which they were entitled as a result of *Plessy v. Ferguson* (1896); today, since the decision in *Brown v. Board of Education* (1954), it is how long it will be before they are completely integrated with the whites. But the Negroes are not the only minority group which has been involved in disputes of this nature. In 1906, the San Francisco Board of Education made an attempt to segregate ninety-three Japanese, thereby bringing about a diplomatic crisis that was not resolved until the Board rescinded its original order at the request of President Theodore Roosevelt. Under the "Gentlemen's Agreement" of 1907, this nation agreed to admit Japanese children under sixteen as students in our public schools, in return for which Japan promised to restrict the emigration of laborers to the United States.

Equalization and consolidation are two other questions which have attracted increased attention at the state level in more recent years. In regard to the former, the Idaho Equalization Act of 1933 and the New York Cole-Rice Law of 1925 are typical of those measures which embody this principle, although the movement in this direction had begun before the turn of the century, as the "Barefoot Schoolboy" Law which the Washington legislature enacted in 1895 demonstrates. The crux of the matter here is the general inferiority of rural schools to urban ones and how to remedy this disparity; the standard solution is to juggle appropriations so that the former will obtain more financial assistance than they normally would receive. On the other hand, consolidation involves the construction of one large school to replace several smaller ones, or a reduction in the number of school districts. Representative examples of laws designed to implement the latter aim are the Initiated Act 1, passed in Arkansas in 1948, and the Community Unit Law, enacted in Illinois in 1947; President Herbert Hoover's Citizens' Conference on the Crisis in Education, which met in 1933, moreover, urged the states to reorganize their school districts into larger units. The movement toward consolidation is naturally allied with the general trend in this country toward centralization, and it has its critics just the same as the drive toward equalization.

Another important dilemma that schools have had to face in recent years is the matter of religion in the classroom. The question of allowing students to skip classes so that they might obtain religious instruction first reached our highest tribunal in 1949. In its decision involving the schools of Champaign, Illinois, that body reversed the ruling of the state court upholding the practice, criticizing the use of rooms in the public school buildings for religious instruction. Despite its decision in this McCollum case, the United States Supreme Court declared constitutional the New York education law of 1940 in *Zorach v. Clauson* (1941); here, however, the classes in religious instruction were not held in the school building. In 1963, our highest tribunal outlawed the use of prayer in public schools, but scattered groups apparently are violating this ruling with impunity.

This decision will doubtless prove to be much more difficult to enforce than that involving released time; the Dirksen Amendment constitutes the most serious effort to circumvent it.

Perhaps the most significant trend that has emerged relative to free public education at the state level since the end of Reconstruction has been the growing ascendancy of secondary over primary schools. It was around 1890 that the great expansion of the high school began; that this same date marked the closing of the frontier is perhaps only coincidental. This movement, though, met with resistance in some states, as Georgia did not amend her constitution to permit taxes to be levied to support high schools until 1910. Unfortunately, despite the work of such groups as the Commission on the Reorganization of Secondary Education, the secondary schools of the nation even today vary widely in quality. Agricultural high schools (the University of Minnesota set up the first one in 1888) and manual high schools (Baltimore established the first of these in 1883) likewise have become more numerous, and regular high schools over the years have grown less academic and more vocational. Another key development has been the rise of the junior high school. This innovation first took root between 1910 and 1920, with Berkeley and Los Angeles, California, along with Columbus, Ohio, the pioneers in the establishment of this new intermediary step. As a result of the growth of high schools and junior high schools, primary schools no longer occupy the limelight, as they once did before the demands of an increasingly complex society made mandatory long years of schooling.

With the growth of schools, it was only natural that a group of professional educators would emerge who regard themselves just as capable, if not more so, of guiding the educational system of their states as the professional politicians. This has led to numerous clashes. One area where this has been unusually evident is in the implementation of the recommendations arising from the great school system investigations that have taken place in a number of states. Among these have been Vermont (1912), Wyoming (1915), Texas (1923), Alabama (1940), Idaho (1946), and Maine (1955). Two investigations have occurred in West Virginia (1929 and 1945) and three in South Dakota (1918, 1954, and 1959–1960), so that, as is the case with the studies of state government, sometimes there have been more than one. It is noteworthy that analysts from outside the state sometimes conduct the survey, as reformers may fear that individuals connected with the state educational system are incapable of making an objective study. In any event, the quality of the survey or lack thereof is not always reflected in the measures passed to remedy the alleged deficiencies, as legislators are notoriously unsympathetic when experts in any field offer grandiose programs for their unprotesting approval.

In conclusion, there is no question but that in the years to come federal assistance to the school systems of the fifty states will increase progressively, but it probably never will amount to a total subsidy covering every expense. Integration likewise seems destined to proceed, although opposition to it has been used as a vehicle to public office by segregationist politicians in Southern states. The Little Rock crisis of 1957 and the Oxford crisis of 1962 are analyzed in the chapter on domestic insurrections.) The differences in salaries, length of terms, standards, and percentage of dropouts indicate that state educational systems are not of uniform excellence. Nevertheless, Americans were concerned about their schools prior to the Space Age; such omnibus state measures as the Edmonds Act (Pennsylvania, 1921) and the "6-0-1" law (South Carolina, 1924) constitute proof of this truth. Fifty years ago, there was no such thing as an integration problem (except for the Japanese in California), but the people of that day were preoccupied with such educational issues as compulsory attendance, which they regarded as critical, despite the fact that many of the issues of those times are no longer of vital concern. Perhaps the states have not been totally successful in developing and implementing their school programs, but such trends as the movement toward equalization and consolidation demonstrate that educators are aware of what needs to be done, even though they many not always be able to carry their reforms to completion.

Turning to a related topic, the question of academic freedom in America is one which has been with us ever since the colonial period. Careful study reveals that, prior to the emergence of the issue of Communism in recent years, the main sources of contention were evolution, Populism, and World War I. Regardless of the Scopes Case of 1925, the agitation over evolution was greatest during the 1860's, 1870's, and 1880's; a decline in the number of ministers serving as trustees and presidents of colleges and universities later accompanied the growth in respectability of evolution as a doctrine. During the Populist era of the

1890's, there were a number of purges, but (significantly) conservatives were fired in the West just as reformers were fired in the East. Thus, the Bryanite J. Allen Smith lost his position at Marietta College only to be offered another at the University of Missouri, where the Populist president was to make a place for Smith by dismissing a gold-standard professor. (Smith declined this job.)

In 1900, the American Economic Association made the first professional inquiry into an academic freedom case—that of the firing of Edward A. Ross at Stanford because of his advocacy of municipal ownership of utilities and a ban on oriental immigration. This intervention admittedly ended in failure, but it did set a precedent for the creation of the American Association of University Professors. With the outbreak of World War I, anyone suspected of being pro-German or pacifistic was placed in a shaky position; in some schools, the study of German history and culture and even the German language was prohibited. Perhaps the most famous protest in the name of academic freedom was that of Charles A. Beard, who handed in his resignation at Columbia when that university not only instituted a general investigation, but also suspended academic freedom for the duration of the war. With the defeat of Germany, however, the new Communist government in Russia became the focal point of hatred.

One of the most important phenomena of the 1920's was the resurgence of American nativism, along with that of the Ku Klux Klan. White Anglo-Saxon domination has been a political football throughout American history, from the days of the Know-Nothing Party during the 1850's to the Kennedy-Nixon Presidential campaign over a century later. In 1919, the Nebraska legislature passed a law requiring all children to attend public school; this measure in effect abolished private and parochial institutions. Since many of the latter were sponsored by the Lutheran denomination, this religious group naturally was affected by the act, but this piece of legislation was directed primarily against the Catholics. The United States Supreme Court, though, threw out this law in the famous Meyer Case (1923), also invalidating at this time an Oregon statute sponsored by the revived Ku Klux Klan which contained similar provisions. A quite different example of thought control was the Buchanan-Clark Bible Bill, a measure passed by the Ohio legislature in 1925. This act not only required that teachers read ten verses of the Holy Scriptures to their pupils every day, but also prescribed that all students above the fourth grade memorize the Ten Commandments. Nativists and Ku Kluxers quite naturally exploded in rage when Governor "Veto Vic" Donahey refused to sign this piece of legislation; the recent United States Supreme Court decision relative to prayer prevents the future enactment of such a law.

Sometimes sheer politics may be the factor underlying large-scale educational purges. In 1930, for example, Governor Theodore Bilbo forced out of office the presidents of the University of Mississippi, the A. and M. College, the State College for Women, and the State Teachers College for opposing him, while he also initiated the dismissal of hundreds of faculty members. As a result, the Southern Association of Colleges and Secondary Schools suspended the institutions which Bilbo had purged; the students thereupon rioted and burned Bilbo in effigy. It was not until 1932 that these schools gained reinstatement, and then not before the Conner administration had made provision for the appointment of a collegiate board of trustees with staggered terms. Another flagrant violation of academic freedom took place in Georgia a decade later during the governorship of Eugene Talmadge, a man in many ways similar to Bilbo. In 1942, this demagogue came to the conclusion that the University of Georgia was on the verge of allowing Negro students to enroll; he thereupon demanded that the Board of Regents fire certain faculty members whom he regarded as the conspirators. When the board refused to act as he requested, he remade it so that it would comply with his wishes. Talmadge's action naturally attracted widespread attention, and after the various accrediting agencies and educational associations had investigated the matter and threatened to take action, he backed down from his extremist position. One of the most significant reforms of the Arnall administration that took office the following year was the removal of the governor from the Board of Regents and the increasing of the length of the terms of its members. Other Southern firings of note include the ouster of President J. William Fulbright from the University of Arkansas and of President Homer Rainey from the University of Texas, both during World War II.

In more recent years, the focal point of many academic freedom cases has been the issue of Communism, yet a number of these also arose following World War I. One representative episode was the attempt made in 1922 to shut down the Rand School for Social Science in New York City; this move ultimately failed when the legislature repealed the message under which this action was taken. As for the post-World War II period, there are literally dozens of incidents that one might cite, including the suspension of eight suspected Communists from the New York public school system in 1950, but we shall restrict ourselves to a brief examination of the loyalty oath crisis at the University of California.

In 1949, that institution promulgated a decree requiring that every faculty member sign such a pledge; after considerable bickering it dismissed twenty-six professors because they refused to sign. Admittedly, this pledge was declared invalid by the state supreme court in 1952, but the state loyalty oath was upheld, becoming a part of the California Constitution via the amendment route in that same year. The reasoning employed by the drafters of the University of California loyalty oath, of course, was that a Communist would refuse to sign such a pledge and thus expose himself, although in practice matters did not work out so simply.

Taking a look at the future, it would seem that cases involving academic freedom will continue to occur most frequently relative to Communists and alleged Communists. Nevertheless, one must recall that the Populists were once just as much in disfavor as the Communists are at present, and today there are few, if any, objections when a professor advocates Populist doctrines in his classroom. Episodes such as the Meyer Case, the Buchanan-Clark Bible Bill, and the Scopes Case also reveal that religious leaders sometimes use political pressure to dictate educational policy, even though such interference seemingly has been on the decline in recent years. Of course educational purges have occurred on strictly political grounds, as the Talmadge firings attest, while the interplay of education and politics has manifested itself recently in the firing of President Clark Kerr of the University of California following the inauguration of Ronald Reagan as governor. One may only hope that such organizations as the American Association of University Professors will be able to keep violations of free speech at a minimum in the years ahead.

Unlike schooling, in which area there has been considerable opposition to federal aid to the states, there has been extensive assistance forthcoming from Washington for highway construction since 1916, when Congress passed the Federal Aid Road Act. The United States government, though, has been building roads on its own since the early days of the republic; it financed in part the National (Cumberland) Road, a hard-surface highway extending from Cumberland, Maryland, to Wheeling, West Virginia, that was completed in 1818. Another road, the Natchez Trace, led from Nashville, Tennessee, to Natchez, Mississippi. But in 1830 President Andrew Jackson vetoed a bill providing for construction of a road between Maysville and Lexington, Kentucky, and when later in his administration he turned the National Road over to the states, the federal government withdrew from this field until 1916. As Washington possesses financial resources which the states lack, it has sponsored most of the major highway building projects of recent years, many of them under the Federal Highway Act of 1956. In 1936, the state of Vermont did decline an offer from the federal government to spend eighteen million dollars in constructing a motor highway, a bridle path, and a foot trail, as well as to establish a national park running the entire length of the state, but the rejection of this Green Mountain Parkway scheme is a rare exception to the rule that the states are greedy for handouts from Washington to finance the construction of roads.

If only because of the large quantities of money involved, it is only natural that state highway financing would become a political football at times. As the chapter on debts points out, Arkansas and Tennessee nearly brought financial ruin upon themselves by their issuance of large quantities of road bonds. One dilemma which was more of a problem a half-century ago than it is today is that of removing legal road blocks which obstruct highway building; at one time, for example, the Wisconsin Constitution prohibited the use of state funds for internal improvements of this type, and it was necessary to adopt a constitutional amendment in 1908 to remedy the situation. We have shown in the chapter on debts how South Carolina circumvented a constitutional provision requiring that road bond issues be submitted to the people for approval. As a rule, states finance highway construction with bonds rather than with taxes, Massachusetts having initiated this practice in 1893. The only significant exception has been Virginia; the voters of this state approved a referendum in 1923 which committed its government to the "pay-as-you-go" principle. Since that date, this concept has become linked with the name of Harry Byrd, whose chief executiveship during the days of the depression will be discussed in the chapter on the governors, but in recent years Virginia has shown signs of abandoning, at least in part, its reluctance to incur debts in road building. Another problem which faces every state is the distribution of expenses for highway construction between the state government and the local governments. For any state to take upon itself the management and maintenance of all roads outside cities will only increase the financial burden; North Carolina assumed such control in 1931, with Delaware, Virginia, and West Virginia following suit.

As for some other aspects of the highway scene, in his chapter "State Politics and Highways" in the book *Politics in the American States,* Robert S. Friedman lists four major focal points of controversy: (1) disputes involving competition between automotive transportation and other forms of transportation, (2) disputes involving other interests aided or hindered by the construction or abandonment of particular roads, (3) disputes involving producers of highway materials and equipment and builders of highways, and (4) disputes concerning partisan and local needs. Friedman finds that the automobile industry has won out over its competitors in the majority of cases, while rural roads generally have received priority over urban roads. He also concludes that standards have become increasingly rigorous relative to highway location, the purchase of rights-of-way, the purchase of equipment and materials, and construction contracts, although he does admit that one still finds corruption now and then.

There have been innumerable instances of the interaction of politics and highways in state history, but a series of events which took place in Georgia between the two world wars constitute an unusually vivid example of the unfortunate consequences which may result from their mingling. In 1925, Governor Clifford Walker attempted to remove John Holder, the chairman of the State Highway Board. After the other two members refused to recognize his authority, Holder unsuccessfully sought a writ of *mandamus* in the Macon superior court; the state supreme court, however, later decided in his favor. Holder, in fact, served eighteen months beyond the legal expiration of his term on January 1, 1928, as the Georgia senate refused to confirm any of the nominees for the position whose names the new chief executive, Lamartine Hodges, had set before it. During the first governorship of Eugene Talmadge, though, this demagogue dismissed the chairman of the State Highway Board along with other members, declaring martial law in a restricted area. As a result, the federal government temporarily withdrew financial assistance for roads from Georgia. Just prior to World War II, a new clash developed between Governor Eurith Rivers and the State Highway Board when the chief executive attempted to divert money from the highway fund in order to reduce certain deficits. As the board refused to cooperate with him, Rivers countered by removing its chairman. The purge victim stubbornly refused to accept his firing, whereupon the governor declared martial law in a restricted area and placed state troops in charge. This controversy eventually reached the federal courts, where a judge found Rivers in contempt and had him arrested; Rivers did clear himself at length and obtain the funds that he desired, but he nevertheless failed in his attempt to replace the chairman.

The cry for good roads has been an incessant one at the state level since the turn of the century, despite long-time rural opposition to spending money for highway improvements. Over the years, the movement has taken such forms as the Minnesota good roads convention of 1893, where a speaker noted that "a perfect highway is a thing of beauty and a joy forever," the Colorado Good Roads Association set up in 1905, and the "Help Pull West Virginia Out of the Mud" campaign staged under the auspices of the West Virginia Good Roads Federation in 1919. Eleven states attended the first national good roads conference in 1894. With the decline of the railroads and the rise of the automobile, it was only natural that emphasis on an expanded system of highways would increase, and it is unlikely that even the present movement toward air transportation will in any way lessen this trend. By 1917, every state had a motor vehicle registration law; by 1924, a competently organized highway department. In an era of increased economic competition, moreover, a state with second-rate highways is in danger of cutting itself off from the mainstream of economic life.

When one begins singling out states that have been leaders in highway innovations, one must turn first to Michigan. That this state has been a pioneer should not surprise anyone, as it long has been the center of the automobile industry. Not only was the first rural concrete road in this country built in Wayne

County in 1909, but Woodward Avenue (which extends from Detroit to Pontiac) is generally regarded as the nation's first super-highway; by-passes in the Flint area were among the earliest attempts to divert traffic away from congested areas. Other pioneering efforts for which this state has been responsible were the adoption of one hundred feet or more as the standard width for a right-of-way, the designation of twenty feet as the accepted breadth for pavements, the evolution of the technique of snow removal from the roads, and the use of oil and chemicals for laying dust. One might cite various other highway firsts, however, which originated in states other than Michigan. State aid for road construction to counties apparently had its inception in New Jersey in 1891, while a state commissioner of public roads first took office in the same state in 1894. On the other hand, the Connecticut legislature enacted the earliest state speed law in 1901; this measure provided for a maximum of eight miles per hour in cities and twelve in the country. The Bronx River Parkway in New York, built between 1916 and 1923, was the first modern highway of parkway design in this country. Admittedly, these states are all in the North, but one does find innovations elsewhere. South Carolina, for example, has developed three different types of road surfacing—sand-clay, bituminous, and cotton fabric.

Perhaps the most significant innovation relative to state highways that has won widespread acceptance during the past quarter-century has been the reintroduction of the turnpike concept. The first of these to be built was the Pennsylvania Turnpike; opened to traffic in 1940, its original length was approximately 160 miles. Recent years have witnessed the construction of a number of significant new ones. Among the most noteworthy of these was the 427-mile throughway between New York City and Buffalo, finished in 1956 at a cost of $675 million. Yet, turnpike mileage is by no means evenly distributed; such states as New York, Pennsylvania, Ohio, Indiana, and Texas have far outstripped the others in the construction of this type of road. As for the future, the growing number of automobiles probably will dictate a corresponding increase in turnpike mileage, although it is quite likely that the day will come when there is a more equitable balance among the states.

Another aspect of highway history which aroused considerable controversy during a by-gone era is privately constructed roads. One of the most noted of these is the Coleman du Pont

Road in Delaware; built at about the time of World War I, this highway was presented to the state as a gift by Du Pont. Another is the W. J. Connors Highway in Florida. Originally, this thoroughfare, which extends from "twenty mile bend" on the West Palm Beach canal to Lake Okeechobee and along its shore to Okeechobee City, was a toll road; finished in 1924, its admirers toasted it the following year at a giant barbecue. It, too, eventually became the property of the state. The record of privately constructed roads, though, has not been a uniformly happy one. This is especially true in the case of Kentucky, where private companies built many of the turnpikes of the state; under their charters, these enterprises enjoyed the privilege of collecting tolls with which to finance and maintain these thoroughfares. But a lawless element destroyed the toll-gates when their keepers ignored various threats and kept collecting the tolls, with the result that Governor William Bradley eventually authorized the state to purchase the turnpikes and place them under Kentucky ownership. We shall have more to say about lawlessness in Kentucky around this time in the discussion of the tobacco night riders in the chapter on domestic insurrections.

Viewing the highway scene as a whole, the objective analyst has little choice but to be slightly pessimistic. One could cite quite a few examples of states with inadequate highways, including some outside the South, all of which are suffering economically as a result. In general, it is an undisputed fact that the efforts of the states vis-a-vis road construction have been far inferior to those of the federal government in recent years, certain turnpikes aside. The basic problem, of course, is financial. What the ultimate solution is remains to be seen, but it is apparent that state governments will either have to increase taxes or float new bond issues to meet future needs, as the cost of improving and extending present state systems is constantly on the rise. It is highly questionable whether a Virginia-type "pay-as-you-go" policy is feasible today; on the other hand, a number of states have constitutional limits on the incurring of debt. Thus, the trend toward seeking federal assistance is almost inevitable.

Chapter 8

Constitutional Comparisons
and Contrasts

The circumstances surrounding the writing of the Constitution of the United States are among the most analyzed events in all of American history. Although at one time scholars regarded this document as the epitome of liberalism, this stereotype has lost favor since Charles A. Beard published *An Economic Interpretation of the Constitution* in 1913. On the other hand, most national historians have neglected the constitutional conventions which various states have held over the years, as they have left these to local writers who themselves have not given these gatherings the attention that they merit. State government texts, too, place little stress on state constitutions as separate entities. This shortcoming will be remedied in the following pages, as not only those conventions whose product became fundamental law will be examined, but also those whose creation suffered defeat. We, moreover, will demonstrate that there were many differences both as to philosophical orientation and types of issues considered. The resulting documents, of course, likewise vary as to length, the time lag between their formulation and that of the prior fundamental law, provisions, and the extent to which they have been amended. There is not much point in analyzing in detail every state constitution drawn up since Reconstruction, as some of the southern and western ones are similar to certain others; we shall, however, discuss at length all of the more recent ones, as well as a half-dozen that the voters rejected.

Following the close of Reconstruction, four Southern states drew up new constitutions in response to the changed political conditions of that era. The Republican Party largely collapsed when the federal government withdrew its troops, while the Bourbons or conservative Democrats seized the initiative. The first of these documents was the Texas fundamental law of 1876, which reduced the term of office for the governor from four to two years, making judgeships and administrative officials elective except for the secretary of state. The Georgia Constitution of 1877 and the Louisiana Constitution of 1879, on the other hand, provided that judges of the state supreme court were to be approved by the legislature, while the Florida Constitution of 1887 authorized that some judges be elected, some appointed. All four documents gave the chief executive the power of veto, and made provision for separate school facilities for whites and blacks, although (as we have seen) their provisions relative to the selection of judges differed markedly. Among the other distinctive features of these fundamental laws were the regulation of insurance companies by Georgia and the termination of the Louisiana Lottery charter by that state in 1895.

In contrast, the attempts by Southern Populists to ally themselves politically with the Negro resulted in Southern conservatives sponsoring the ratification of the most reactionary group of constitutions in American history. These documents were adopted by Mississippi in 1890, by South Carolina in 1895, by Louisiana in 1898, by Alabama in 1901, and by Virginia in 1902; their most noteworthy characteristic was their disenfranchisement of the black man through various means. That of Louisiana increased the powers of parish and local governments, while that of Virginia provided for the political separation of cities and counties. Another reactionary feature of the Alabama fundamental law was that it placed severe restrictions on internal improvements such as public roads and public schools; a progressive feature of the Mississippi fundamental law was its encouragement of new industry. Both documents also provided for quadrennial meetings of the legislature, while that of Mississippi set up an electoral college system for governors and other administrative officers. Significantly, there was a marked reluctance on the part of all of these constitutional conventions that met between 1890 and 1902 to submit their work to the people for approval.

The eight Western statehood constitutions that date from the period 1876–1896 are a more diverse lot. The Populist Presidential candidate, James Weaver, did exceptionally well in two of these states in 1892, demonstrating uneven strength in three others, while William Jennings Bryan, the Democrat and Populist candidate in 1896, carried all but North Dakota. Consequently, it is not surprising that the provisions of these documents were consistently liberal; there was no Negro problem in these states to wreck reform as was the case in the South. Turning to specific documents, the Colorado Constitution of 1876 is particularly noteworthy for abrogating the law of riparian rights along streams as well as for vesting all political power in the people, who have the right to initiate both statutory laws and constitutional amendments. Then there are the four statehood constitutions of 1889. That of Wyoming gave women the right to vote; schools were declared to be the responsibility of local communities, while all water was made the property of the state. Just compensation for work and reasonable working conditions were also provided for. More conservative in character was that of Montana. With William Clark of Clark-Daly feud fame as chairman, the constitutional convention here placed limits on mine taxation which the electorate did not abolish until 1924, Anaconda having held the state in its iron grip, as was pointed out in the chapter on business and government.

In the case of South Dakota, fundamental laws drawn up here in 1883 and 1885 had not won the approval of Congress; when that body did pass an Enabling Act in 1889, it demanded a new document which would provide for an equitable division of the territorial debt and records, and a reapportionment of the legislative and judicial districts. The new constitution of 1889 was otherwise similar to the 1885 version, which had altered and expanded the section on corporations. As for neighboring North Dakota, it established a rather orthodox governmental framework while imitating a model drawn up by Professor James Bradley Thayer of Harvard Law School; this may surprise those who are acquainted with the trend in the state after World War I toward experimental legislation of the Nonpartisan League variety. The first of the two fundamental laws of 1890, that of Washington, won approval at the polls by a large margin, but two independent articles providing for woman suffrage and prohibition did not carry. Its Idaho counterpart of the same year has won a place on the liberal blacklist because of its section disenfranchising the Mormon population on the grounds of polygamy. Finally, there is the Utah document of 1896; as is the case with Louisiana, this Western state has had a number of constitutions, but all the others were of a territorial nature. The most important feature of the last in this series was its ban on polygamy, since Congress had long held up statehood for Utah because of this tenet of the Mormon faith.

Four other fundamental laws from this quarter-century await analysis. Rather moderate in character was the California Constitution of 1879, a document which received a narrow vote of confidence at the polls. Aside from those clauses directed against the Chinese, this document also set up a State Board of Equalization to guarantee equitable taxation, created a more uniform scheme of land assessment, forbade combinations or agreements which hindered competition, and established a State Board of Railroad Commissioners. This was the period when the Workingmen's Party was at the peak of its strength in the state. In Kentucky, on the other hand, there had been a clampdown on out-of-state financial groups just prior to the drawing up of a new fundamental law during 1891. Perhaps its most significant feature was its embodiment of the principle of centralization; not only was local government placed entirely under the control of the legislature, but also matters relating to railroads, commerce, and corporations were dealt with in a similar manner. More complex in conception was the New York Constitution of 1894, which was not written to implement a single basic objective. The term of the governor was reduced from four to two years, while various courts were consolidated, abolished, and set up, but the over-representation of the rural counties in the legislature was maintained. One of the more unusual characteristics of this fundamental law was its divorce of state and local politics; state elections now take place in even years and municipal in the odd. Finally, the document that Delaware drew up in 1897 reflected the sectional struggle between Wilmington and the remainder of the state. Among its more important features were the general corporation and divorce provisions, Delaware being a haven for the chartering of business. This constitution also reduced the eligibility of the chief executive to two terms while giving him a very limited removal power and the right to veto items in appropriation bills; by requiring a two-thirds affirmative vote it set up an almost insurmountable obstacle against future reapportionment.

Analyzing the entire group of state constitutions adopted between the end of Reconstruction and the beginning of the Progressive era, one must conclude relative to these documents that:

1. Nearly half, or ten, of these fundamental laws were drawn up in Western states, and only one in an Eastern one (New York). Two were produced in border states (Kentucky and Delaware), seven in Southern ones.

2. Eight constitutions, all Western, were the consequence of a shift from territorial to state government. Five were the result of a desire on the part of many white Southerners to disenfranchise the Negro, four a reaction on the part of Southerners in general to the Reconstruction era there.

3. Nearly three-fourths, or fifteen, were written in the thirteen-year period between 1889 and 1902, an unprecedented concentration. These years roughly coincide with the terminal dates of the Populist era. Every statehood constitution of this quarter-century but one (Colorado) was a product of this thirteen-year period, as was every anti-Negro one.

4. The Western statehood fundamental laws were the most liberal in character, the Southern anti-Negro ones the most conservative.

5. The four constitutions not relating to Western statehood or to Reconstruction and the Negro have little in common relative to geography or purpose.

In terms of quantity, the two decades of the Progressive era were fairly productive constitutionwise, but three of the five documents dating from this period were the consequence of statehood. That of Oklahoma (1907) followed the wishes of the Enabling Act by prohibiting polygamous marriages and excluding intoxicants from the Indian areas for twenty-one years. As we have noted in the chapter on sectionalism, the attempt to keep the capital at Guthrie until 1913 ended in failure. Despite the restrictions that the Enabling Act placed on the deliberations, liberals were successful in writing initiative and referendum provisions into the new fundamental law. President Theodore Roosevelt was not pleased with the finished product, which was of unprecedented length, but he did not attempt to sabotage it. As for the Arizona Constitution of 1912, this document, too, contained initiative and referendum clauses. In fact, the recall of judges section was so unpalatable to President William Howard Taft that he held up Arizona statehood until the people removed it; having obtained statehood, they later put it back in.

Other progressive features of this fundamental law included the direct primary and municipal home rule. More conservative in character was the New Mexico document of 1912, which did include the referendum, but hamstrung it with various limitations. Here the amending process was unsatisfactory to the federal government. In addition, the rights of Spanish-Americans were guaranteed, much to the displeasure of many Anglo-Americans.

The only Northern constitution ratified during the Progressive era was that of Michigan, in 1909. Many liberal ideas were incorporated in this new fundamental law; home rule, for example, was provided for villages and cities. Corporate franchises were limited to thirty years, trust companies were placed under the banking laws, and the legislature was given the authority to set up regulatory commissions. There also was an emphasis on conservation and improved accounting techniques in state government; women taxpayers were allowed to vote on questions concerning the issuance of bonds or the expenditure of money, but not otherwise. As we shall see, Michigan later was to adopt a new constitution in 1963. Shifting our attention to the South, during this period Louisiana ratified two new fundamental laws, thus equalling its performance during the last quarter of the nineteenth century. One important feature of the 1913 document was a thousand-word article relating to the funding of the state debt. Curiously, it also contained the provision that the omission of any clause found in its predecessor of 1898 did not constitute the repeal of such a clause, unless it was inconsistent with it. The final fundamental law in this series, which is still in effect, was drawn up in 1921. By this time, the attention of the electorate had shifted from such issues as legislative powers and Negro rights to taxation, education, and highways; this metamorphosis is reflected in the 1921 document, which is the longest in the history of the country. One might well debate the role which the bizarre constitutional tradition of this state played in the later emergence of Huey Long.

With the advent of the great depression and the approach of a global conflict, the focus of attention at the state level temporarily shifted away from constitutional reform. Finally, during World War II, Georgia took the quite unusual step of delegating the responsibility for amending the old fundamental law of 1877 or creating a new one to a commission of twenty-three. This state, in fact, actually established a precedent when the voters approved the new constitution in 1945, since prior to that date no similar creation anywhere had ever become fundamental law; the new document to a large extent perpetuated the old one, but it did make a few notable changes which aroused some controversy. Not only did it authorize a merit system, but it also allowed home rule for counties and cities under certain conditions. In addition, it raised the salary of both the governor and the legislature, and provided for the creation of the office of lieutenant governor. Another striking feature of this fundamental law was that it failed to include any reference to primary elections, an omission designed to circumvent the Supreme Court if that body attempted to rule in regard to the denial of voting rights to Negroes. This constitution also was the first one in forty years to add elective officers to the state list. Generally speaking, however, the document was much more progressive than most of its Southern counterparts, and must stand as one of the shining glories of the Arnall era.

Another wartime product was the Missouri Constitution of 1945. There had been an attempt at constitutional revision here some twenty years previously, but the voters adopted only six of the twenty-one amendments which a constitutional convention that met in 1922 and 1923 proposed. The new gathering, which first convened in September, 1943, was almost evenly divided between the two major political parties, a welcome change from some of the lopsided political imbalances in similar conventions elsewhere in former years. This body remained in session a little over a year, and produced a new fundamental law two-thirds the length of the old one; among the major changes it wrought were the reduction of seventy-odd departments, boards, and commissions to not more than fourteen, the granting of greater powers to local government, and the abandonment of the general property tax. A merit system for state eleemosynary and penal institutions was also set up, while women were given the right to sit on juries. The new document enjoyed widespread support, especially among the newspapers, and won ratification at the polls by a five to three margin. A separate proposal for a unicameral legislature narrowly met defeat at this time.

Turning to New Jersey, a noteworthy program of administrative reorganization was instituted here in the years following World War II; this series of reforms, moreover, was accompanied by constitutional revision. Prior to 1948, the government of New Jersey had been creaking under the burden of the out-of-date Constitution of 1844. This fundamental law had escaped any basic alteration except for a series of amendments passed in 1875. The main feature of the 1948 document was the abandonment of the principle of a weak executive, an obstacle which a chief executive of outstanding ability (such as Woodrow Wilson) had occasionally overcome in the past; apart from this, it provided for a complete reorganization of the court system, a streamlining of the administrative branch, and an expansion of the Bill of Rights. It might be added that New Jersey has pioneered in the utilization of constitutional commissions, although the people rejected the work of those which met in 1881, 1894, 1905, and 1942.

The 1950's witnessed the formulation of new constitutions in two territories which soon thereafter became states, Hawaii and Alaska. The convention which drew up the former in 1950 was plagued by charges that some of its members had Communist ties, and one delegate, F. S. Silva, was ousted by that body after he had refused to testify before a House committee. The fundamental law which it drew up, though, was somewhat on the conservative side; among its more noteworthy features were a $60 million limit on the state debt, a provision that the legislature was to elect the state auditor, and a guarantee of the right to homestead. An attempt was made to include the "law of the splintered paddle" of King Hamehameha the Great in the preamble (an affirmation that the government was to protect the people), but this proved to be unsuccessful. Voters ratified this constitution by a three-to-one margin in November, 1950, and it went into effect in August, 1959, following the addition of four amendments.

In contrast, the fundamental law written by the constitutional convention which met at the University of Alaska in 1955–1956 "adopts to a remarkable degree the most advanced thinking in political science and public administration to the situation in Alaska." This document, which was formulated by a diverse group including thirteen lawyers, nine merchants, four fishermen, four miners, three housewives, two trucking operators and two bush pilots, was not based on regional or group interests. Under it, the governor and the secretary of state were to be the only elected officials, while there was also a strong emphasis on local self-government. (One finds boroughs rather than counties in Alaska.) In addition, there is a provision that the question of calling a new constitutional convention must be placed before the voters every ten years. Like its Hawaiian counterpart, this fundamental law went into effect in 1959, three years after it had won overwhelming approval at the polls.

The most recent state to adopt a new constitution is Michigan, the only one aside from Louisiana to draw up more than one fundamental law in the present century. Demand for reform here was not universal, and newly elected Republican governor George Romney had to maneuver the document that he was sponsoring to a narrow victory at the polls in 1963 over the combined opposition of the United Auto Workers and the Justices of the Peace Association. This constitution contains such controversial features as an income tax clause, a raised debt limit, and legislative reapportionment; the first two of these was partly the result of the financial problems which the state encountered during the final years that G. Mennen Williams was chief executive. It is noteworthy that since ratification Governor Romney has won re-election twice by progressively larger margins, and if he does indeed capture the Presidency, he may attribute this triumph largely to his record in Michigan, the cornerstone of which is this fundamental law.

Analyzing the entire group of state constitutions adopted since the beginning of the Progressive era, one might conclude relative to these documents that:

1. Nearly half, or five, of these fundamental laws were drawn up in Western states. Three were produced in Northern states, one in a border state, and three in Southern states.

2. Five constitutions, all Western, were the consequence of a shift from territorial to state government.

3. No document was written in the period between 1921 and 1945, an unprecedented hiatus. These years roughly coincide with Normalcy and the New Deal. Three date from the three-year span 1945–1948, three from the four-year span 1959–1963, and four from the six-year span 1907–1913.

4. These fundamental laws were consistently liberal in character. Even one of the more conservative ones, that of New Mexico, was hardly reactionary in orientation.

5. The seven constitutions not relating to statehood have little in common relative to geography or purpose, although three date from the three-year period 1945–1948.

A comparison of the era from the end of Reconstruction to the beginning of the Progressive era with that just examined reveals that:

1. The ratio of Western documents to the total number decreased moderately, while that of Northern ones increased sharply and that of Southern ones fell somewhat.

2. A slightly larger percentage of fundamental laws during the more recent period were a consequence of statehood.

3. The concentration of new constitutions between 1889 and 1902 was balanced off by an absence of new ones between 1921 and 1945.

4. The earlier group of documents covers the entire length of the political spectrum, while the latter group falls more consistently in the liberal sector.

Having examined a number of proposed constitutions which did become fundamental laws, we now shift our attention to an analysis of several which for some reason or other failed to attain this status. The first of these is the Arizona Territory Constitution of 1891; despite the fact that it was the work of a nonpartisan body containing many of the most able political leaders of the territory, it was not entirely practical and was also distasteful to many Easterners. An examination of Congressional sentiment reveals that the provisions most widely regarded as offensive were those authorizing the use of silver as legal currency for the payment of state debts and declaring all rivers to be state property. It may be true that many Arizonians thought that these controversial features were necessary, but Congress wasted no time in rejecting the document.

As for the discarded Connecticut Constitution of 1902, in examining the record of the convention which drew up this document we catch a glimpse of the struggle between the small towns and the large cities which characterized the history of the state. The small towns, moreover, were sufficiently represented and had the political leadership to block major changes; what did emerge was a compromise measure, the Bissell Plan. Aside from inadequately resolving the problem of reapportionment, this proposed fundamental law included a simplified amendment process, a minor salary hike for legislators, and an extension of the time allowed a governor to act upon a bill. Not only did the work of this convention stir up political animosity, it also failed to capture popular enthusiasm; as a result, the document met defeat by a two-to-one margin at the polls.

One of the above fundamental laws was given the death blow by Congress; the other, by the people. In the case of the Indiana Constitution of 1911, the judiciary was the executioner; this document's most curious feature did not lie in any of its provisions, but in the fact that the legislature drew it up. Thus, it is not surprising that many of its provisions favored the law-making body. Not only was the legislature given the power to pass acts instituting the initiative, referendum, and recall, it was also authorized to adopt measures implementing workmen's compensation and granting special charters to cities. Under this new fundamental law, too, the size of the house might be enlarged and the length of the regular session of the assembly increased. On the other hand, a three-fifths majority was required to pass bills over the governor's veto, while the chief executive was also given the item veto vis-a-vis appropriation bills. Critics of the document took their case to the courts, charging in *Ellingham v. Dye* that the legislature lacked the authority to frame a constitution; the courts upheld this claim, ruling that the law-making body not only had exceeded its powers, but also had deviated from the proper legal procedure. The legislature did pass twenty-one amendments in 1913 embodying the main provisions of the invalidated document, but thanks in part to the opposition of the liquor interests, the electorate rejected the calling of a constitutional convention in 1914, with the result that the legislature refused to pass the twenty-one amendments a second time.

Although New York did adopt a new fundamental law in 1894, a convention headed by Elihu Root which met in the same state in 1915 produced a document designed to create an efficiently centralized government with responsible officials. This fundamental law gave the chief executive practically unlimited power of appointment and removal, while it also grouped one hundred sixty boards and commissions into seventeen departments; the document, moreover, established the executive budget and made the tax system more uniform. Despite the desirability of these reforms, this constitution failed to win total acceptance from any of the major pressure groups of the state, and the three groups of amendments which the convention placed before the voters embodying the suggested alterations all went down to a resounding defeat. Administrative reform, however, was effected in New York a decade later, while the executive budget eventually was adopted, too.

A constitutional convention which met during wartime was that of Arkansas. The delegates to this gathering were selected in June of 1917, while the first session was held in November of that year. Instead of the new fundamental law being thrashed out on the floor of the convention, authority was given instead to a number of committees to draft the various articles. Then the gathering met again in July, 1918. It was the general opinion of those qualified to speak that the new constitution was modern, progressive, and democratic; still, the voters rejected it at the polls that November by a vote of 38,000 to 23,000. Here there probably was no specific provision or provisions that doomed the proposed fundamental law, but rather an attachment on the part of the voters to the existing Constitution of 1874.

Still another example of a rejected constitution is that of the Illinois fundamental law of 1920. In 1922, this document went down to a humiliating defeat of 921,398 to 185,298 at the polls after the electorate had endorsed the calling of a constitutional convention in 1918 by a vote of 562,012 to 162,206. Meeting in early January, 1920, the delegates to this gathering drew up a document which abolished cumulative voting, imposed a general income tax on all net incomes, provided Chicago with a measure of home rule, and altered the procedure and organization of the judiciary. It was perhaps the income tax provision more than any other which was responsible for the disastrous reception that this fundamental law met at balloting time, although Cook County voters were incensed because they felt that it did not allot them sufficient representation in the legislature. Twelve years later, the electorate rejected another proposal for a second constitutional convention, and as of this writing Illinois has yet to adopt a new document.

If the above material lends itself to one generalization, it is that state constitutions (as well as the conventions) exhibit a variety which equals, if not outweighs, their common features. Not only have the delegations which drew up these fundamental laws differed in number from state to state, but so have the types of individuals who have served as members; the amount of time spent in deliberation also has varied considerably. A number of gatherings have been basically conservative (New Mexico, 1911), while others have been fundamentally liberal (Arizona, same year). Some conventions have dealt with a multiplicity of issues, while others have concentrated on a single one; administrative reform was the basic concern of the gathering which drew up the rejected New York Constitution of 1915, adoption of measures dictated by Congress that of the convention which formulated the South Dakota Constitution of 1889. In some instances, only a short period had elapsed since the last constitution was adopted (eight years, Louisiana, 1921), in others, decades upon decades (one hundred four years, New Jersey, 1948). As for contents, the Wyoming fundamental law of 1889 contained liberal suffrage provisions, although that which South Carolina formulated six years later embodied restrictive ones; on the other hand, the New Jersey Constitution of 1948 increased the power of the governor, while that of Texas of 1876 decreased it. Some documents have been amended innumerable times, despite the fact that others have been amended scarcely at all. Those who maintain, therefore, that state constitutions are basically similar are making a totally false assumption. What the future will bring remains to be seen, but it is likely that there will be a trend toward the use of commissions rather than conventions for the purpose of drawing up new fundamental laws at the state level, as rising costs have more and more made the calling of the latter prohibitive.

Chapter 9

Statehood Drives:
An Essay in Procrastination

Although state politics obviously are the basic factor that one must consider in tracing a state's evolution, national politics are also of consequence at times. In fact, there have been occasions when national politics have been the sole determining factor as to whether a territory became a state or not. Since the election of 1876, no less than thirteen states have joined the Union, thus completing the present total of fifty: Colorado (August 1, 1876), South Dakota (November 2, 1889), North Dakota (November 2, 1889), Montana (November 8, 1889), Washington (November 11, 1889), Idaho (July 3, 1890), Wyoming (July 10, 1890), Utah (January 4, 1896), Oklahoma (November 16, 1907), New Mexico (January 6, 1912), Arizona (February 14, 1912), Alaska (January 3, 1959), and Hawaii (August 21, 1959). All of these states experienced a period of frustrated waiting while in pursuit of their ultimate status, and the struggles they underwent constitute one of the most fascinating phases of state history. Because of the polygamy issue, the question of Utah statehood perhaps attracted the most attention at that time, but some other statehood candidacies also pivoted on explosive issues.

Like Nevada, Colorado was nominated as a candidate for statehood during the Civil War, perhaps being as deserving of this honor as its more western neighbor. Unfortunately, the Colorado measure expired in congressional committee following its introduction in 1863, but in March of the next year Congress did pass an enabling act for this purpose. After a small majority of Colorado voters had approved a new constitution, our national legislature gave its blessings to an act of admission, but President Andrew Johnson vetoed this scheme both in 1866 and 1867, being at the time hostile to congressional legislation of almost any sort. It was impossible, though, to restrict Colorado to territorial status for long; thus, in December of 1875 a convention met in Denver for the purpose of drafting another fundamental law. This time, both Congress and President approved the statehood measure (U. S. Grant now being chief executive), and Colorado joined the Union as a state on August 1, 1876, receiving the designation of Centennial State because its statehood occurred on the one hundredth anniversary of American independence.

Next we might consider the history of Dakotan statehood; here simplification rather than elaboration is in order, as these events were quite complex in nature. Bills were introduced into the United States Congress as early as 1882 providing for the immediate admission of the southern counties of Dakota Territory into the Union as a state, while maintaining the territorial status of the less populous northern ones, but agitation for the division of this entity into two separate parts had been started a decade earlier. (There also had been talk of creating an East Dakota and a West Dakota.) Political conditions seemed favorable for Congressional action in 1882, as the Republicans were in control of both houses of that legislative body and were, in general, inclined positively toward statehood. Congress, however, did not vote on the proposal at this time, and the Democrats regained their earlier dominance in the House of Representatives at the next election. The Democrats, fearing that four Republican Senators might win election if Congress created two Dakotas, lined themselves up with the single state enthusiasts, and this action temporarily blocked the dual statehood scheme. Several years later, in 1887, a referendum in the Dakotas resulted in a two-to-one vote in favor of division in the south and a slightly larger majority against it in the north; encouraged by these rather indecisive election returns, the single state faction called a territorial convention at Aberdeen in December. A group of South Dakotans, perceiving that the single staters were not to be dissuaded easily, announced that they would support a move for the immediate admission of the northern section as a state. This magnanimous gesture calmed the fears of those North Dakotans who had thought that their territory might suffer relegation to a second-rate status, and the Republican victory in the Presidential election of 1888 paved the way for the admission of separate Dakotan states. This party apparently felt that the northern plains and mountain territories would be favorable to its cause. Such names as Pembina, Lincoln, and Algonquin were offered at various times for the less populous half, but it eventually was admitted into the Union as North Dakota.

Montana perhaps experienced less difficulty than the Dakotas did in pressing its candidacy for statehood, yet even this territory made an unsuccessful bid in 1884 before it finally obtained its ultimate goal. At this time, a constitution was framed at Helena and ratified by the people. The Montanans' sense of urgency was quickened soon thereafter by a Congressional law prohibiting aliens from owning real estate in the territories, as a result of which measure the investment of foreign capital there and elsewhere was blocked. By 1889, though, a Republican was in the Presidential chair again so that Montana was able to obtain its coveted goal at that time. As was the case with the three other territories which became states that year, it was necessary for Montana to call a constitutional convention; the fundamental law which this body produced easily won acceptance at the polls shortly thereafter.

In regard to the fourth state admitted into the Union in 1889, Washington, its struggle differs somewhat from those of the above three, in that a Washington statehood bill actually passed Congress in 1886. This measure, which established a state including the northern counties, or panhandle, of Idaho Territory, was vetoed by President Grover Cleveland. Being a West Coast territory, Washington felt that it was more entitled to statehood status than its neighbors in the less populous interior, and it was highly incensed because its immediate southern neighbor, Oregon, had reached this goal as early as 1859. Congressional agitation for Washington statehood actually arose within two years after Oregon had become a state, but that body took no action until 1889 despite the fact that a constitutional convention had met in Washington in 1878. One factor that retarded Congressional action was the outbreak of anti-Chinese riots there in 1885, an episode which gave the territory a bad name in the east. The Republican victories in the election of 1888, as was the case with the other three states, paved the way for the realization of Washington's dream in this year.

As for Idaho, this territory became a state in the summer of 1890, being one of two territories (Wyoming was the other) which obtained this status at that time. Opposition to the admission of Idaho as a state centered around three focal points. The first of these was the belief that the Mormon Test Oath, which Idaho required of all Mormons before they could vote, violated the United States Constitution; the second was the theory that the constitutional convention which met in that territory had not legally convened. A final argument against Idaho being accorded statehood status was that the area was not populous enough to justify the election of two United States Senators. Despite these objections, though, Idaho was swept in on the statehood tide with the five other states that were admitted in 1889 and 1890.

In the case of Wyoming, there was considerable Congressional sentiment against the admission of this territory into the Union as a state, but for different reasons than in the case of Idaho. The woman suffrage clause of the Wyoming Constitution, to cite one objection, was widely regarded as too liberal, while the compulsory education clause was similarly offensive to the more conservative minded. In addition, that section in the Wyoming Declaration of Rights giving alien property holders the same privileges as other property owners aroused disfavor, as did the educational and literary requirements for voting which this fundamental law specified. In light of these criticisms, Congress might have compelled Wyoming to alter its constitution before it was granted statehood, as it forced Arizona to do later, but such was not the case.

The Idaho and Wyoming controversies, however, were minor squabbles in comparison with the furor which resulted from the admission of Utah, a goal finally achieved in 1896. The Mormons had a bad reputation in most quarters at this time because of their espousal of polygamy, and this custom delayed Utah statehood for approximately a half-century. When a constitutional convention met at Salt Lake City in 1895 to prepare a new fundamental law, it marked the seventh such gathering in the history of the territory. One unusual feature of the document it drew up was its extension of suffrage to women, but of much greater importance was the provision forever forbidding polygamous or plural marriages in the state. The absence of national politics from Utah Territory until the 1890's was another factor which militated against statehood; the two main parties were the People's Party (pro-Mormon) and the Liberal Party (anti-Mormon).

We have pointed out that, in the case of certain states, Democratic opposition in Congress delayed statehood for more than a few years. On the other hand, the candidacy of Oklahoma was temporarily blocked by the Republicans. The main argument against the entrance of Oklahoma as a state was that it had not been open to white settlement long enough (only since 1889), although the whites did stream in once they were given an opportunity. In Oklahoma, moreover, one encountered the same ticklish question—whether there was to be one state or two—which had plagued the Dakotas. The whites held two single state conventions, one in 1900 at McAlester and another in 1902 at Oklahoma City, while various Indian leaders met at Eufala in the latter year and passed a resolution opposing union with Oklahoma Territory. (The first of these conventions had taken place as early as 1896 in both sections.) The climax of the separate states movement was reached in 1905 when a constitutional convention was held by the Indians at Muskogee to which white citizens of Indian Territory were invited) the proposed new Indian state was to be called Sequoyah. Probably the major reason why the dual state scheme failed here (while it succeeded in the case of the Dakotas) was the assumption on the part of most whites that the Indians were not capable of governing themselves, although Republican politicians doubtless shuddered at the possibility of four Democratic Senators. In 1907, Oklahoma Territory and Indian Territory were joined and admitted to the Union as a single state.

As for New Mexico, a bill providing for statehood for this territory passed Congress as early as 1876, but non-concurrence in an amendment to this measure following a personal blunder by the territorial delegate Stephen Elkins (later a Senator from West Virginia) dealt a death blow to New Mexico's prospects at this time. A debate on the Force Bill (which would have turned over the supervision of elections to federal officials) was then in progress, and Elkins had the poor taste to congratulate a Congressman who had made an anti-Southern speech. This action quite naturally turned the South against the statehood scheme. The next concerted effort to have the territory admitted as a state was made in 1889, but this attempt was sabotaged by the voters of New Mexico, who were unwilling to ratify a new constitution that had just been drawn up. Many factors were responsible for the defeat of this measure, but perhaps the three most important were the electorate's fear of being dominated by the Mexican population there, its discontent with the provisions favoring the large landowners, and Roman Catholic opposition to the clause prohibiting taxation for the support of parochial schools. Only one Democrat won election to the constitutional convention; that party had refrained from voting for delegates since it was critical of the method that had been adopted of apportioning them. Over the years, moreover, the mining interests, the large merchants, and the railroads fought for a continuance of territorial status, as this would maintain taxes at a low level.

The New Mexico statehood drive took a new turn in 1904. At this time, a bill proposing the union of New Mexico and Arizona was introduced into Congress together with a similar measure joining Oklahoma Territory and Indian Territory. The former scheme passed the House of Representatives by a margin of three-to-two; its formulators drew up the bill on the assumption that New Mexico-Arizona would become a Republican state and Oklahoma Territory—Indian Territory a Democratic one. Republican Senator Joseph Foraker of Ohio, however, suggested that a vote be taken on this proposal in each of the two territories (New Mexico and Arizona), and that the single state plan be dropped unless each approved it. As events turned out, the single state bill met a resounding defeat in an election held in 1906, largely because Arizonians did not relish the location of the capital of the proposed new state at Santa Fe.

This vote revealed that a majority of the inhabitants of Arizona were in favor of separate statehood. Not only were the railways and mining companies of this territory opposed to union with the largely agrarian population of New Mexico, but also Arizona lawyers were hostile to the single state scheme. As a result, each territory went its own way thereafter in its quest for statehood, with New Mexico being the first to attain this goal. Arizona experienced more difficulty, since many members of Congress who were advocates of the gold standard feared that Arizona's two Senators would be strongly in favor of the unlimited coinage of silver. Thus, they temporarily blocked its candidacy, but Arizona, still became a state only a month after New Mexico did. By the time that Arizona obtained statehood, though, silver was being mined with less profit in the territory than it once had been, so the "gold-bugs" had less reason to be uneasy. Another stumbling block which Arizona had to overcome was the provision in its constitution establishing machinery for the recall of judges; President Taft forced a special election to be held in the territory late in 1911 for the purpose of removing this offensive feature from the fundamental law. Arizona's submission to Presidential authority proved to be deceitful, as the voters restored the recall of judges provision to the constitution at the first opportunity.

Once Arizona was granted statehood, nearly half a century passed before another state was admitted into the Union. There was talk by the end of World War I in regard to the elevation of both Alaska and Hawaii from territorial status to this rank, but in both cases this movement did not make much headway until after the end of World War II. (The first Hawaiian statehood bill was introduced in Congress in 1919, the first Alaskan in 1916.) The main argument against the candidacies of these two territories was that they were non-contiguous; some critics regarded Alaska as being too thinly settled and Hawaii too prone to Communist influence in the labor movement. (The latter is a post-World War II criticism.) A considerable minority in each territory, of course, opposed statehood because it would mean higher taxes. The Big Five (the economic oligarchy which has long played a dominant role in Hawaiian life) were also hostile to it on the grounds that it would tend to diminish their monopolistic control over the Islands, while some leaders of the Alaska salmon industry and the Alaska Steamship Line opposed it because of the federal commercial regulation which would be a consequence of such a change in status. By 1935, however, the sugar interests of Hawaii had become convinced of the desirability of statehood and were supporting it. From about 1946, the feeling grew in Washington that Alaska was likely to send Democrats to Congress and Hawaii, Republicans; a Hawaiian statehood bill passed the House of Representatives in 1947, an Alaskan one in 1950, but obstructionists in the Senate temporarily blocked final action. Considering the fact that both parties had come out for statehood for both Alaska and Hawaii by 1952, it is rather surprising that they were thwarted so long in obtaining their objective (1959). A recitation of all the Congressional bills and committees relating to this subject would take up an entire chapter.

One might draw numerous conclusions from the above material, but the most obvious truth is that Congress has played politics with the granting of statehood status from the earliest days of the Republic, and that it has not done so solely in the cases of Alaska and Hawaii (as ill-informed people or those with short memories frequently maintain). There doubtless have been many good reasons why each of the above-mentioned territories should have been admitted into the Union as states, but there have been legitimate objections as well, as we have gone to great lengths to demonstrate. Proponents of statehood have in many cases been the victims of double-dealing on the part of Congress, yet these crusaders occasionally have been guilty of questionable actions, too; one flagrant example was the hypocritical acquiescence of the Arizona electorate in President Taft's ultimatum vis-a-vis the recall of judges provision in that territory's constitution. Indications are, though, that statehood struggles are a thing of the past, since it is unlikely that any additional states will be added to the present fifty.

Chapter 10

Gubernatorial Triumphs
and Tragedies

Like our Presidents on the national scene, it is the governors at the state level whom posterity remembers; some of the latter have been outstanding, some have been mediocre, and some have been poor. Here, however, it is the middle ground which is the surest road to oblivion, as a terrible chief executive, unlike a third-rate writer or artist or composer, makes his mark on history. The first part of this chapter is devoted to an analysis of twenty outstanding governors who have served since the end of Reconstruction; admittedly, their selection is a highly subjective process, and for this reason the following presentation is doomed to raise a storm of controversy. We have included six chief executives from New York and fourteen more from outside that state, regretfully omitting several figures from both the Progressive and the New Deal eras in order to maintain a proper balance. In the conclusion, we shall compare the records of outstanding governors and Presidents, pointing out those issues which most frequently have played a vital role in each; here we will concentrate on the similarities and differences among the outstanding gubernatorial administrations of each era of state political history, demonstrating that issues have changed over the years.

Before proceeding with a discussion of the top-flight chief executives at the state level, though, we might offer a few general observations. First of all, there have been gubernatorial families just as there have been Presidential ones, among whom one might cite the Clarks of Idaho, the Proctors of Vermont, and the Tylers of Virginia. (In 1886, Robert Taylor, a Democrat, defeated Alfred Taylor, a Republican, for governor of Tennessee in the famous "War of the Roses.") Politically, the Proctors were Republicans, the Clarks and Tylers Democrats; several decades ago, two Clark brothers served closely spaced terms as governors of their state, in contrast to the four Proctors, whose terms occurred at twenty-year intervals. While no woman has served as President, there have been three women chief executives statewise, the first of whom was Nellie Tayloe Ross of Wyoming (D, 1925–1927), a capable person who applied sound business practices to government and reduced the state debt. On the other hand, "Ma" Ferguson of Texas, who twice won election as a front for her disqualified husband, "Pa," obtained notoriety by such actions as pardoning an average of five persons a day between 1925 and 1927. Another important fact is that chief executives at the state level have been successfully impeached, recalled and disqualified, while no President has. We will present case studies of each in the following section. A final point that one might make is that several governors have won election to office four or more times, thus equalling or even surpassing the record of President Franklin D. Roosevelt on the national plane. A long tenure in office, however, is no guarantee of greatness, as an examination of the administrations of the multi-term chief executives will reveal; liberals frequently point to the record of Orville Faubus as governor of Arkansas as proof of the validity of this generalization.

Despite the fact that an attempt will be made to draw examples of noteworthy governors from as many states and as many areas as possible, it is inevitable that preferential treatment be given to those from New York, as this state has produced more than any other. Significantly, there is a tradition of rich men running for public office here. Of our six New York case studies, all of whom were outstanding governors, no less than five were Presidential candidates, and one was a Vice Presidential nominee; two of the former were elected, as was the latter. One was also appointed Chief Justice of the United States, while another was elected United States Senator. The omission of Franklin D. Roosevelt from this list is no oversight, as he had difficulties with his basically Republican legislature, with the result that a large percentage of his program did not become law. Actually, upstate Republican control of the legislature persists regardless of who is governor; Alfred Smith and

Herbert Lehman, though, were able to build up outstanding records despite this handicap.

As the period from the end of Reconstruction to the beginning of the Progressive era was characterized by business domination of politics at both the national and the state levels, there was little demand for independent leadership on the part of state governors. In addition, the federal occupation of the South during Reconstruction turned the people of that region against dictation from above. Perhaps the only chief executive at the state level to attract national attention during the 1880's was Grover Cleveland of New York, a conservative who later served two non-concurrent terms as President. The following decade, Populism swept the West and the South. The most famous chief executive of this period, though, was a Democrat, John Peter Altgeld of Illinois. Altgeld aroused the ire of conservatives by pardoning some of the convicted Haymarket rioters and by opposing the use of federal troops during the Pullman Strike. Benjamin Tillman of South Carolina was a prominent Southern governor, but he ranks among the great demagogues rather than the great governors. The Spanish-American War, of course, had more of an impact nationally than statewise. Yet, it did lead to the election of an important chief executive at the state level, Theodore Roosevelt of New York, who like Grover Cleveland eventually rose to the Presidency.

While serving as chief executive of his state between 1883 and 1885, Grover Cleveland exhibited many of the traits which characterized his Presidency. Using his veto power freely, Cleveland axed numerous pieces of special legislation (both private and local), dealing a death blow to the Five Cent Fare Bill. Not only did he make appointments of high caliber, but he also reduced the number of office-holders, signing a civil service bill in the process. Honest, efficient, and relatively nonpartisan, Cleveland likewise approved measures establishing a state reservation at Niagara Falls, making inspection of financial institutions mandatory, centering the appointive power for cities in the mayors, and transferring various county officials from a fee to a salary basis. He doubtless would have served more than the two years that he did had he not been elected President, but his administration is still noteworthy despite its relative brevity.

Regardless of his numerous achievements, John Altgeld, a Democrat who served as governor of Illinois between 1893 and 1897, must be listed among the more controversial chief executives. It is true that his foreign origin was a political handicap to him, but conservatives shuddered in horror at his stand during the Pullman Strike, an episode that we have analyzed in the chapter on labor. While serving as governor, Altgeld not only had corporation taxes revised, but he also started an investigation of the state whiskey trust; this action led to a series of laws outlawing railroad rebates and price fixing. As for labor, Altgeld brought about the creation of a state labor arbitration board, and he also sponsored the first Illinois collective bargaining act. (The state courts invalidated a child and female labor law.) A start was also made toward the establishment of civil service at the city level, while many improvements were brought about in the prison and welfare system, as well as in the state university. As a whole, Altgeld probably had more of the Populist program enacted into law than any other Midwestern governor prior to 1900. Yet, like Joseph Folk of Missouri, Altgeld went down to defeat when he sought public office again, as the enemies that he made were so numerous that they crushed him at the polls.

Although he may have exaggerated his accomplishments when he claimed that he was "the best governor within my time, better than either Cleveland or Tilden," Theodore Roosevelt nevertheless was one of the outstanding chief executives in the history of New York (1899–1901). Continuing his earlier work on behalf of civil service, Roosevelt supported an 1899 act which brought about the unification of the state system; in addition, he also backed a number of labor measures, one of which was designed to safeguard women and children in industry. Perhaps the most important act passed while he was chief executive was the Franchise Tax Bill of 1899, under which public service corporations, up until then exempted from taxes on franchises for the streets they used, were subjected to taxation. During both his governorship and his Presidency, however, Roosevelt was not so much of a reformer as he claimed to be, although he constantly flaunted his progressivism.

Perhaps no period in American history produced more outstanding chief executives at the state level than did the Progressive era. Governmental activity during this period expanded both quantitatively and qualitatively. Among the most noteworthy governors were Robert La Follette (Wisconsin), Joseph Folk (Missouri), Charles Evans Hughes (New York), Woodrow Wilson (New Jersey), Hiram Johnson (California), and James

Cox (Ohio). Three were Republicans, three Democrats; four sought the Presidency, but only one successfully. It is interesting to compare the records of their administrations, as there are marked similarities regardless of party or region, demonstrating that reform sentiment was universal. This is not to say that the period was one Progressive triumph after another; such demagogues as James K. Vardaman and Theodore Bilbo of Mississippi also held office during this era. Nevertheless, conditions during these two decades were highly favorable for an able leader to make his mark as a chief executive, both statewise and nationally. Noting some of the more bizarre episodes, one might add that two governors, William Sulzer of New York and James "Pa" Ferguson of Texas, were impeached, while another, former governor Frank Steuenberg of Idaho, was assassinated.

No survey of state governors would be complete without reference to Robert La Follette, Sr. (R, 1901-1905), as La Follette while serving as chief executive of his state sponsored a program known as "the Wisconsin Idea" which has become the epitome of liberalism and reform. La Follette did have trouble with his first legislature (the predominantly stalwart senate opposed him), but when he obtained a cooperative body in 1903 he achieved quite a few important reforms. One such measure was the primary election law, which the voters approved in a referendum after the legislature had enacted it; other were an ad valorem tax on railroads and an inheritance tax. Perhaps La Follette's most famous accomplishment was the creation of the Wisconsin Legislative Reference Library, but a state civil service act was written onto the books as well. Though governors oher than La Follette have had a greater number of their proposals rendered into law than he did, nevertheless he stands as a (or, perhaps, *the*) symbol of reform.

Reform movements, of course, rarely flower unless a certain amount of corruption exists. Both graft and bribery existed in San Francisco in the period just before Hiram Johnson became governor of California, and unethical practices appeared in St. Louis prior to the elevation of Joseph Folk to the highest office of Missouri. While serving as chief executive of his state (1905–1909), this outstanding Democrat successfully sponsored anti-lobby, anti-trust, child labor, public utility, and factory inspection laws. Like Jefferson Davis of Arkansas, Folk opposed the trusts; he had his attorney general (Herbert S. Hadley) conduct a prosecution of the Standard Oil Company, as well as of other illegal combinations. In addition, a statewide primary law was enacted during his administration, while freight and passenger rates for the railroads were established. But Folk, who was the only member of his state ticket to win office in 1904, made so many enemies during his chief executiveship that he failed in his attempt to gain a Senate seat in 1908.

In view of his work in connection with various legislative investigations, it is not surprising that Charles Evans Hughes during his two terms as chief executive of New York (1907–1911) successfully proposed a scheme providing for a wholesale reorganization of the state's program for supervising public utilities. Hughes, moreover, backed a law which limited campaign expenditures, as well as another which reapportioned the senate and assembly seats. Significant as these bills were, the fifty-six acts that Hughes signed assisting and protecting workers overshadowed them; New York passed the country's first workmen's compensation law in 1910, although the court of appeals later invalidated this. Admittedly, Hughes did not have the most attractive political personality imaginable, and there were times when he alienated the professionals, but his ability was such that he could surmount these handicaps.

Upon assuming office in 1911, Woodrow Wilson had the reputation in many quarters of being little more than a scholar, but he compiled such a noteworthy record as governor of New Jersey that it catapulted him into consideration for the Presidency. While a Republican Senate made his first legislative session more difficult, Wilson still was able to get most of his program enacted, using his veto power to block those bills he found distasteful. As for specific measures, election reforms were achieved through the passage of the Geran Act (direct primary) and the Corrupt Practices Act, while municipalities were given the right to introduce the commission form of government under the Walsh Act. In addition, a measure establishing employer's liability was written onto the statute books. The most controversial feature of Wilson's governorship, though, was the "Seven Sisters Acts" of 1913. Although these measures (which were never vigorously enforced) were designed to eliminate certain corporate excesses, numerous companies which were contemplating chartering in New Jersey were frightened away by them. Upon entering the Presidency, Wilson continued his crusade for reform under the banner of the New Freedom, but the outbreak of World War I placed a damper on further domestic reforms.

It is perhaps an exaggeration to maintain that Hiram Johnson was the only outstanding chief executive that California has ever had, but the state has yet to produce his equal. Elected to office as the candidate of the Lincoln-Roosevelt League during the crest of the Progressive tidal wave, Johnson served as governor for six years (1911–1917) before moving on to the United States Senate. During Johnson's chief executiveship, a body of legislation was passed which was without precedent in the history of the state. Not only were the initiative, referendum, and recall adopted, but an effective direct primary law was also passed; a non-partisan judiciary, too, was created, while civil service was extended through the state government. Other innovations attributable to Johnson included a series of acts embodying employer's liability, a minimum wage, and an eight-hour day for women, while there were also laws of a humanitarian and social character, measures providing for additional internal improvements, and various types of legislation of a regulatory nature. Those who view the early days of the New Deal as the epitome of revolutionary change might well examine the deluge of reforms which inundated California during the second decade of this century.

Another Democratic Presidential candidate who compiled an outstanding record as chief executive of his state was James Cox of Ohio, who served as governor from 1913 to 1915 and 1917 to 1921. Much of his first administration was devoted to the passing of measures designed to implement the Constitution of 1912; some of the acts written into law included ones regulating labor, instituting an executive budget, creating a Public Utilities Commission, and reforming the school system. Despite these achievements, Cox lost his bid for re-election, but he won office again in 1916. Among the accomplishments of his final four years as governor were a series of laws establishing or reorganizing a number of commissions and boards, imposing an inheritance tax, recodifying and revising the state banking laws, and setting up a retirement system for teachers. A few bills, however, were also passed which reflected post-war anti-radical hysteria. In recognition of his achievements, the Democratic Party nominated Cox for the highest office of the land in 1920, but he lost out in the general election to Warren G. Harding, another Ohioan.

It is not surprising that the dozen years of Normalcy would produce fewer governors of the first rank than the Progressive era, although it did witness the ascension to power of the most notorious demagogue in American history, Huey Long. A representative governor of the period was Albert Ritchie of Maryland, a conservative states' rights Democrat who served four four-year terms as chief executive between 1919 and 1935. If one, then, is to point out an outstanding chief executive at the state level, he must turn to Alfred Smith of New York, a colorful reformer who unsuccessfully sought the Presidency against Herbert Hoover in 1928. Perhaps the most important Republican governor during these years was Gifford Pinchot of Pennsylvania; Pinchot's administration, however, constitutes an extension of the Progressive era rather than the beginning of a new age. Even more interesting is the record of Harry Byrd, one of the most progressive chief executives that Virginia has ever produced, yet whose sentiments ran counter to the course of American history after 1933 to the extent that he came to stand as a symbol of conservatism.

In many ways, more characteristic of the period were its gubernatorial disasters. Thus, in 1921, Governor Lynn Frazier of North Dakota was recalled, the only chief executive ever to suffer this fate, while two Oklahoma governors, John Walton and Henry Johnston, were both impeached during the 1920's. Governor Warren McCray of Indiana, moreover, went to jail in 1922, while several other chief executives escaped conviction despite trials.

Regardless of the fact that he served as governor of New York for eight years (1919–1921, 1923–1929), Alfred Smith had a long record of membership in the legislature when he was first inaugurated which ideally prepared him for the chief executiveship. Not only did his work on administrative reform in New York state government represent a milestone, but also his efforts to improve the school system were of fundamental significance. Like Hughes, Smith was friendly toward labor; a forty-eight-hour week was established in 1927, while additional laws were passed protecting women and children in industry. During his administration, too, a rather grandiose program of public works was undertaken, while conservation measures were adopted which were unprecedented in scope. The state government also assisted the local units with grants-in-aid. Unlike his successor, though, Smith's tenure as chief executive ended with an unsuccessful run for the Presidency, and after 1932 he began to veer away from the liberal leanings of his past toward a more conservative position.

As for Pennsylvania, one might cite the rather strange spectacle of a progressive Republican chief executive during the 1920's; Gifford Pinchot served another term as governor (1931–1935), but his first administration (1923–1927) is the more significant. Pinchot had earlier attracted national attention in a famous conservation controversy which flared up while William Howard Taft was President. During his first term as chief executive of Pennsylvania, Pinchot not only sponsored a new administrative code which the legislature adopted, but he also backed a measure which, when enacted, established the budget system. Pinchot, moreover, liquidated the twenty million dollar state debt; one should compare this accomplishment with the corresponding feat of Governor Edward Martin twenty years later. Aside from these achievements, a Blue-Sky Act (which prohibits the sale of fraudulent securities) was passed that anticipated a similar New Deal reform, while a twenty-five million dollar bond issue was authorized for the development of state forests (a pet Pinchot project). Comprehensive as this body of reform was, it robs the measures passed during the "Little New Deal" administration of a Democratic chief executive of the next decade (George Earle, 1935–1939) of much of their originality.

Among the most significant of all Southern governors has been Harry Byrd of Virginia, who served as chief executive of his state from 1926 to 1930, and over the years built up a powerful political machine there. Byrd's solution to the problems of balancing the economy, providing employment, and obtaining additional revenue was to encourage new industries to locate in the state; it was and is typical of Byrd that in enlarging the state road system he adopted a "pay-as-you-go" plan rather than resort to the issuance of bonds. The governmental reorganization effected during his governorship resulted in a reduction in the number of departments, while the adoption of a short ballot eliminated all administrative officials except the governor, lieutenant governor, and attorney general from consideration by the voters. As for his more "radical" actions, Bryd not only fought the gasoline and telephone companies while reducing rates, but also sponsored the first anti-lynching bill ever passed in the South. Those analysts who picture the later Senator as an impractical theorist of economy and limited government should examine his record as chief executive of Virginia, since during this period he put into practice many of the ideas which he advocates today.

With a return to political innovation following the Depression of 1929, one might expect that there would be a number of gubernatorial administrations which would match the New Deal in significance. Yet, one has more difficulty in recalling the names of leading chief executives at the state level for these years than for the Progressive era; this is not only for the reason that Franklin D. Roosevelt's personality overshadowed theirs, but also because their programs were to a large extent imitations of the New Deal. Two prominent administrations were those of Herbert Lehman of New York and Wilbur Cross of Connecticut; the first of these served longer than any New Deal governor, while the second (like Adlai Stevenson) is an example of the intellectual in politics. Other noteworthy Democratic chief executives of this era were Paul McNutt of Indiana and Frank Murphy of Michigan. Strangely enough, such Republican governors as Alfred Landon of Kansas and Harold Stassen of Minnesota attracted more attention than their Democratic counterparts. Landon ran for President against F.D.R. in 1936 and suffered a disastrous defeat, while Stassen lost to Thomas Dewey at the Republican convention in 1948, becoming a political burnt-out case at forty. Other important developments of this period included the election of such Southern demagogues as "Alfalfa Bill" Murray of Oklahoma and Eugene Talmadge of Georgia, the imprisonment of Richard Leche of Louisiana, and the disqualification of both William Langer and Thomas Moodie of North Dakota.

Considering the fruitful decade that he spent as governor of New York (1933–1942), it is rather strange that Herbert Lehman's achievements have received less attention outside the state than those of the other Empire State chief executives analyzed here. (Perhaps a new biography by Allan Nevins will remedy this neglect.) As was the case with several other Democratic governors, Lehman instituted a "Little New Deal" which resembled the national reforms of F.D.R. to a considerable extent. During Lehman's governorship, an extended welfare program was adopted, while labor was assisted as never before; in addition, schools were continually improved, and a noteworthy public utility plan was enacted. Perhaps the most amazing

aspect of Lehman's achievement was that the cost of government was actually reduced (thanks mainly to drastic economies
in administrative expenses) at the same time that grants-in-aid
to localities and appropriations for state services were increased. Lehman, however, did not finish out his last term as
governor, as he resigned shortly before its expiration to accept a
position with the federal government.

Aside from Herbert Lehman of New York, perhaps the outstanding Democratic chief executive during the New Deal period was Wilbur Cross of Connecticut. Cross, who had been a
professor of English at Yale, Dean of the Graduate School, and
Editor of the *Yale Review,* won election to the first of four two-
year terms in 1930. His first administration did not prove to be
too eventful, partly because of the opposition of a predominantly Republican legislature, but during his second term as
governor (beginning in 1933) he steered through that body
banking reform, anti-sweatshop legislation, and a minimum
wage law. Cross's third term as chief executive was even more
fruitful; the measures that the assembly passed at this time included an old-age pension, maximum hours of labor restrictions
for women and children under eighteen, and an act increasing
the power of the Public Utilities Commission. In 1936, Cross
won re-election for a fourth term. A special session of the legislature which met in the aftermath of this triumph adopted a
system of unemployment compensation, while the regular 1937
session not only wrote a comprehensive scheme of governmental reorganization and civil service onto the statute books,
but also gave women the right to serve on juries. Unfortunately,
the Merritt Parkway scandal of 1938 (involving Highway
Commissioner John Macdonald) and the Waterbury city funds
scandal (involving Lieutenant Governor T. Frank Hayes) hurt
Cross politically, and in the fall elections he lost his bid for a
fifth two-year term to Raymond Baldwin by a narrow margin.

Historians are in general agreement that there were several
other outstanding Democratic chief executives of the 1930's
apart from Herbert Lehman, including Wilbur Cross, but our
narrative would not be complete unless we mentioned the most
noteworthy Republican governor of this period, Alfred Landon
of Kansas. Elected to office in 1932, Landon demonstrated such
progressive leadership that two years later he was able to win re-
election, the only Republican chief executive to accomplish this
feat in 1934; both the zenith and the nadir of his career oc-

curred in 1936, when the G.O.P. nominated him for President. (F.D.R., of course, crushed him several months later at the polls.) As chief executive of Kansas, Landon, while adopting a program of economy, not only helped to restore the stability of the banks of the state, but also liberalized the foreclosure laws, instituted an income tax, and consolidated some inspection departments. Actually, much of his program was rather New Dealish in nature, and it is not surprising that as governor Landon enjoyed considerable non-partisan support; those who complain that the Republican Party has nominated too many "me-too" candidates (Willkie and Dewey generally are mentioned as examples) might look back to 1936 as well when attempting to document their case.

During recent years, his failure to block Richard Nixon from the Republican Vice-Presidential nomination in 1956 and his defeats in a Pennsylvania gubernatorial primary and a Philadelphia mayoralty race have injured his political reputation, but the fact remains that Harold Stassen of Minnesota was one of the most brilliant young governors in the history of this country. Taking office at the age of thirty-one in 1939, Stassen pushed through the legislature every one of his major proposals. These included governmental reorganization, civil service, a labor relations act, an anti-loan-shark law, and the authorization of a commissioner for administration. Stassen also reduced the state debt during his first two-year term, serving as Chairman of the Governor's Conference in 1939. During the summer of 1940, the youthful chief executive captured the national spotlight by delivering the keynote address at the Republican National Convention, as well as serving as floor manager for Wendell Willkie. Re-elected as governor that fall, Stassen liberalized old-age assistance, took steps to make good rural credit losses, and strengthened the labor conciliation law as we entered World War II. Re-elected to a third term in 1942, the "boy wonder" laid plans for post-war reconstruction in highways, public buildings, and housing before resigning his position in April of 1943 to enlist in the navy. This action wrote finis to Stassen's elective office-holding at the age of thirty-five.

Since the end of World War II, two governors—Thomas Dewey of New York and Adlai Stevenson of Illinois—have been their party's Presidential candidate, the former once, the latter twice. (Dewey had also run in 1944, making him a two-time loser.) One might cite two other governors—Earl Warren of California and Ellis Arnall of Georgia—as outstanding representatives of Western and Southern liberalism. When the historian reaches the last decade or so in his analysis, it becomes increasingly difficult for him to form accurate opinions as to outstanding chief executives, but one conjectures that George Romney of Michigan appears to be as likely a candidate for immortality as any, thanks largely to his successful promotion of a new constitution. Nelson Rockefeller of New York is on his way to serving twelve years as governor, but, like Earl Warren, he is so controversial a figure that any judgment is likely to offend. This period also has witnessed the election of such Southern white supremacists as Orville Faubus of Arkansas (six times) and George Wallace of Alabama, whose wife Lurleen became the third woman chief executive in state history; Republicans won the chief executiveships of Arkansas and Florida in 1966 for the first time since the end of Reconstruction.

A Southern chief executive of outstanding accomplishments was Ellis Arnall of Georgia (D, 1943–1947), a liberal who has set forth his credo in a book entitled *The Shore Dimly Seen*. Reacting against the Talmadgian theory that educators should be silenced if they do not echo the sentiments of the governor, Arnall's legislature passed a measure which removed him from the Board of Regents and increased the terms of its members; another significant reform provided for the adoption of a system of teacher retirement. In addition, the power to pardon and parole prisoners was taken away from the chief executive and given to the newly established Board of Pardons and Paroles. The most spectacular achievement of the Arnall administration was the lowering of the voting age to eighteen years, making Georgia the first state in the Union to adopt such a law. Like his liberal counterparts elsewhere, Ellis Arnall typifies the Hyde half of the Jekyll-Hyde politics of the South, although individuals of his stripe are by no means widely popular in that region.

Thwarted twice in his ambition to become President, Thomas Dewey still fulfilled his urge to be a chief executive by serving three non-concurrent terms as governor of New York (1943–1945, 1947–1949, 1951–1953). Despite the fact that other Republicans since then have taken a much more radical stand than he (Nelson Rockefeller is a prominent example), his welfare and labor policies were a constant irritation to the Old Guard faction of the Republican Party. Unlike most of the other outstanding New York chief executives, Dewey did not always take the initiative at reform; in the case of the disputes over the anti-discrimination law and a state university, he allowed the Democrats to stir up popular sentiment, and then capitalized on this to his advantage. Through his "pre-veto" system he was able to kill any bill he did not want to take action on in a legislative committee. Perhaps he was at times guilty of "me-tooism," but few would question Dewey's exceptional administrative ability, which unfortunately projected at times as coldness.

His critics may fervently desire that he be impeached as Chief Justice of the Supreme Court, but there is little question but that Earl Warren is the most important chief executive to serve California since Hiram Johnson. Like Thomas Dewey a racket-busting district attorney, Warren used the office of attorney-general as a stepping stone to the governorship, winning the latter in the election of 1942. As chief executive, Warren put the Department of Public Welfare on the merit system and reorganized the Department of Industrial Relations; while reducing the sales tax he increased old age pensions and widened unemployment insurance coverage. In 1944, he was the keynote speaker at the Republican national convention. Thanks to the unique California cross-filing system, Warren won renomination as both a Republican and a Democrat in 1946, coasting to re-election with no major opposition. Although he did pay off the state debt, he spent heavily for schools and roads, also sponsoring prison and institutional reforms. Warren opposed the firing of a number of professors at the University of California who failed to sign a loyalty oath, but approved a law requiring a similar oath from all state, county, and local employees. In 1948, he was the Republican candidate for Vice President, while, in 1950, he won an unprecedented third term as governor by a two-to-one margin over James Roosevelt. Warren was not destined to serve this out, though, as in 1953 President Dwight D. Eisenhower appointed him to the highest tribunal.

Unlike Warren, the governmental background of Adlai Stevenson, who won election by a half-million vote margin as governor of Illinois in 1948, was not one of state and local politics, but rather one of diplomatic service at the national level. As chief executive, Stevenson placed the state police force on a merit system, later employing it to smash the organized gambling interests; in the humanitarian field, he upgraded the overcrowded and understaffed mental hospitals. Undertaking a ten-year highway modernization program, Stevenson had trucks taxed on a ton-mile basis. He also raised the salaries of qualified civil employees while abolishing some thirteen hundred super-fluous positions; the fact that he was able to get approximately two-thirds of his total program enacted into law was another factor that led to his nomination as the Democratic Presidential candiate in 1952. It is significant that as governor Stevenson operated on the principle that state administrations should solve their own problems without relying unduly on federal aid, al-though his Presidential campaigns did not place an undue amount of emphasis on states' rights.

Summarizing this section, it has been demonstrated that it is necessary for a governor to sponsor successfully a wide variety of constructive measures to be regarded as outstanding. While we have paid particular attention to the chief executives of the more important states, noteworthy governors have come from the others as well; there have been, moreover, first-rate chief executives statewise during periods other than the Progressive or New Deal eras. To seek the Presidency is obviously no infal-lible criterion of greatness, as mediocre men have lusted after the highest public office of the land, while brilliant ones have been content solely to serve their states. Nor does the projection of a charismatic television image guarantee inclusion among the elite, despite the fact that we seemingly have entered an age in which one's record in office weighs less heavily with many voters than various subjective factors. In any event, the states-men whom we have examined here deserve widespread recogni-tion just as our Presidents do, and it is hoped that this presenta-tion marks a positive step toward effecting this end.

During the course of American history, four of our Presi-dents have been assassinated, while another was almost con-victed following his impeachment. At the state level, one gov-ernor-elect (Goebel) and two ex-governors (Frank Steuenberg and Huey Long) have likewise been murdered, while a number of others have been removed from office in a more orthodox manner; not only have chief executives been impeached, but others have been recalled and disqualified as well. Considering the poor quality of many, it is perhaps unfortunate that more have not been relieved of their duties. Quite naturally, for every successful impeachment, recall, or disqualification, there have been several abortive attempts; the analysis which we offer here includes episodes of the latter sort as well as of the former. Despite the fact that this subject is one of the most fascinating aspects of state history, these episodes are not so well known as they should be, for which reason the following case studies merit particular attention.

New York has doubtless produced more first-rate governors than any other state, but even one of its chief executives has been the victim of an impeachment proceeding. In 1912, William Sulzer, a Tammany Hall candidate from New York City, was elected governor on the Democratic ticket; Sulzer had been nominated through the efforts of Charles Murphy, a political manipulator. When Sulzer showed signs of independence, however, a legislative committee which had been set up at the instigation of Murphy investigated him, and this group reported in August of 1913 that Sulzer had falsified the accounts of his campaign expenditures. The Assembly thereupon voted to impeach him the next day, and a court of impeachment consisting of members of the senate and court of appeals tried him on eight charges in September. Convicted on three of these charges, Sulzer was removed from office on October 17. Standing as he does in the procession of New York chief executives between Charles Evans Hughes and Alfred Smith, he represents a gaping void between the two towering peaks, although he perhaps was a victim of a political expediency.

Of a more justified nature was the impeachment of Governor James "Pa" Ferguson of Texas in 1917. This colorful figure posed as the champion of the downtrodden farmers, winning a smashing victory in the primaries through his advocacy of such measures calculated to benefit the latter as a maximum rent law and a state warehouse system. Unlike Sulzer, Ferguson did not meet his doom until after he had begun to serve a second term; a twenty-one-day hearing held in the house of representatives in August of that year produced twenty-one charges against him. The bill of impeachment, among other things, accused Ferguson of misappropriating state funds, falsifying records, depositing state funds in his own bank, attempting to influence state officials via personal loans, interfering with the administration of the University, and refusing to divulge the source of a large personal loan. The trial, which took place before the senate, lasted through September; that body convicted the chief executive on ten of the twenty-one charges. Regardless of whether he was guilty or not, it is unlikely that Ferguson would have been impeached if the alumni of the state university had not been alienated by his actions. Ferguson attempted to "save face" by resigning, but the legislature would not allow him to do so. In any other case, such a black mark would have meant a ruined political career, but by means of the unprecedented strategy of running his wife Miriam for office, "Pa" won election as governor again in both 1924 and 1932.

Neighboring Oklahoma, one notes, affords two instances of the successful impeachment of a chief executive, and these occurred a mere six years apart. The first involved Governor John C. Walton, a Democrat supported by the Farmer-Labor Reconstruction League, who began to skirmish with various political leaders and school executives only a few months after he took office. Using the disorder which existed in the state as an excuse, Walton proclaimed martial law in Tulsa in August, 1923; when an Oklahoma City grand jury began to investigate charges of misconduct against him and other state officers, he extended his proclamation to include the entire state. Walton, moreover, blocked a proposed meeting of the legislature on September 26, at which it was to consider an impeachment measure. His critics, however, then circulated petitions advocating an initiated measure which would allow the legislature to meet in special session without the permission of the chief executive; after they obtained enough signatures to place this measure on the ballot, the chief executive tried to stop the election, but was unsuccessful. This proposal was approved by a margin of three-to-one at the polls. Of the twenty-two charges against Walton which the house drew up at the special session that followed, the senate sustained no less than eleven by the necessary two-thirds majority, the vote on the overuse of the pardoning power being unanimous. Walton doubtless put up more of a struggle than any other governor who has suffered impeachment, but his maneuverings only delayed his fate.

In the case of Henry S. Johnston, another Oklahoma Democrat, a good deal of the opposition which developed against him was based on trivial grounds, at least in comparison with Walton. Certain key figures in the Eleventh Legislature apparently resented the power which Mrs. O. O. Hammonds, confidential secretary to the governor, exerted; as Johnston was rather elderly, he was unable to adhere to the crushing work schedule on which a younger man might thrive. An effort was made to impeach the chief executive at a special session of the legislature held without a call from Johnston, but this action was declared illegal by the state supreme court. A second, and legally valid, trial took place between January and March of 1929. After the house had impeached Johnston on eleven charges, the senate suspended him from office on January 20. Certain of his critics made an attempt at the proceedings to create a scandal out of the use of asphalt instead of concrete in highway construction, but investigators were unable to bring forth any substantial proof of corruption. The impeachment leaders eventually concentrated on the eleventh charge (incompetency), and the senate adjudged the suspended governor to be unfit to hold office on that count. There have been chief executives as old as Johnston who have served with distinction, but they are exceptions to the rule.

Attempted impeachments, of course, range all the way from a mere proposal to a full-length trial; most of the former are not worth citing, but there are instances of the latter which merit inspection. One such case was the abortive impeachment of Governor Henry Horton of Tennessee in 1931. This maneuver, which Boss Edward Crump had inspired, centered around an alleged conspiracy involving Horton to allow the use of state funds for personal profit, and official neglect of duty. Of those charges formally placed against Horton, these were the most important. A vote was held on the first article on June 5, at which time the chief executive was cleared by a vote of fifty-eight to forty-one; the remaining articles were defeated by roughly the same margin four days later. Then there was the attempted impeachment of Governor Huey Long of Louisiana one year earlier. This, too, was a failure, as it was impossible to obtain the two-thirds legislative majority necessary to convict the Kingfish; here a group of fifteen senators blocked the impeachment move. As for the post-World War II era, a special session of the Arizona legislature was held in September, 1945, at which an effort was made by various members to impeach Governor Sidney Osborn. The grounds for such a drastic action were that Osborn supposedly misused state funds in connection with the development of the Colorado River, an issue which has caused much controversy in Arizona and surrounding states over the years. These proceedings, however, led to the complete clearance of the chief executive, who went on to accomplish some notable reforms before his untimely death.

During the Progressive era, there was much agitation for the adoption of the initiative, referendum, and recall in many a state. Despite the frequency with which the first two have been employed statewise, the recall of an official, especially a governor at the state level, has been rare. All states but Oregon provide for impeachment proceedings, while only a dozen or so authorize the use of the recall. The first time that this device was exercised against a chief executive in this country was in North Dakota in 1921, when Governor Lynn Frazier, who was a member of the Nonpartisan League, was recalled. The somewhat unusual political set-up in that state has been discussed previously. A special gubernatorial election took place here later the same year in which R. A. Nestos, a Republican who was also a member of the Independent Voters Association, defeated Frazier, who was attempting to make a comeback. Attorney General William Lemke (who ran for President on the Union Party ticket in 1936) and Commissioner of Agriculture and Labor John Hagan were recalled along with Lemke, but those measures which had been initiated to halt the industrial program formulated by Frazier ironically were defeated at this time.

North Dakota also has the distinction of being the only state to have had two of its governors disqualified, both within the incredibly short span of six months. The first to lose his position was William Langer, then affiliated with the Nonpartisan League and later a Republican member of the United States Senate. Langer was removed from office on July 18, 1934, having been adjudged disqualified by the state supreme court; the grounds for this action were that he had been convicted on a federal charge of conspiracy in a case involving solicitation of contributions from governmental employees for his political newspaper, the *Leader*. As the federal courts later reversed his conviction, Langer's disqualification was perhaps unjustified, and in 1936 the people expressed their confidence in him by electing him governor while a candidate in the individual column on the ballot, the first such victory in the annals of any state. After Ole Olson, the lieutenant governor, had served out the remainder of Langer's term, Thomas H. Moodie, North Dakota's first Democratic chief executive in twenty-four years, took office in January, 1935. Moodie, however, was declared ineligible on February 2 by the same body which had disqualified Langer; the state supreme court ruled in this connection that Moodie had not resided long enough in the state to serve as governor. Walter Welford, the Nonpartisan League lieutenant governor, was then sworn in, the fourth chief executive which the state had had within a little more than half a year. This series of events quite naturally constitutes one of the strangest episodes in the history of any state.

Not all attempted disqualifications, of course, have been successful. This was true of the effort to remove Governor James Boyd of Nebraska following the election of 1890 on the grounds that he was not an American citizen. Boyd had been born in Ireland in 1834, and his foes charged that his father, who brought him to the United States ten years later, had not gone farther in the matter of naturalization than to file a declaration of intentions in 1849. Politics, though, were a consideration here, as Boyd was a Democrat and an anti-prohibitionist who had been victorious in an election in which the independents gained control of the legislature. After Governor John Thayer refused to give up his office, calling out the militia in the process, the case went to the courts; the highest tribunal of the land finally acknowledged Boyd's right to hold office on the grounds that he had attained citizenship by being both a resident and a territorial officer of Nebraska Territory. The Nebraska Supreme Court had earlier ruled against him. There is no exact national parallel to this incident, but such distinguished statesmen as Alexander Hamilton and John Altgeld were ineligible for the Presidency merely because they were born abroad. In 1871, one might add, Governor Butler had been a victim of impeachment proceedings here, ostensibly on the grounds that he had pocketed $16,000 of school-land fund money, although the real objection to him was that he had shifted the capital from Omaha to Lincoln.

As for the removal of governors by assassination, the murder of Governor-elect William Goebel of Kentucky in 1900, which was a consequence of a disputed gubernatorial election, failed to attract prolonged national attention. On the other hand, the bombing of ex-Governor Frank Steuenberg in Idaho in 1905 is an episode which had significant implications relative to the labor movement. While serving as chief executive of this state, Steuenberg had employed force in breaking up riots in the Coeur d'Alene mining region. After he had completed his second term as governor, Steuenberg returned to his home in Caldwell; here a bomb exploded one day when he opened his front gate, killing him. It was generally believed that certain members of the Industrial Workers of the World were attempting to get revenge on Steuenberg for halting the disorder around the mines, and Harry Orchard was arrested as the suspected murderer. Orchard implicated such noted labor figures as "Big Bill" Haywood, Charles H. Moyer, and George A. Pettibone in his confession; the trial was particularly significant in that Clarence Darrow conducted the defense. Orchard, who admitted that he was a professional killer, was sentenced to death but his sentence was commuted to life imprisonment because he had turned state's evidence.

Taken as a whole, these cases represent a fascinating aspect of state history, although few of the chief executives involved were particularly outstanding. Perhaps the most striking feature about the various impeachment proceedings is the number of charges which the inquisitors drew up in each case; the impeachment managers invariably "covered the waterfront," hoping to find one or two really serious accusations which would stand up before a court of inquiry. The recall, of course, is obviously a more democratic means of removing a governor, and its rare use is thus puzzling, as dozens of chief executives have incurred the electorate's wrath. In regard to disqualifications, there doubtless have been times when the supreme court of a state could have found some technicality on the basis of which it might have removed a chief executive, but such an action would require a collective daring rare among justices. Finally, as for assassinations, a governor is a far less important personage than a President, but he makes enemies, too, and one would theorize that there would have been quite a few murders of this type. But the fact is that there have not, as such killings are as rare as a recall or a disqualification. The truth of the matter is that the voters always have a chance to liquidate a chief executive at the next election, and almost without exception they have the patience to delay his execution until then.

Chapter 11

The Breakdown of Democracy:
Domestic Insurrections

The overwhelming majority of the controversies which have arisen throughout American history have ended in peaceful solutions. Our Civil War is the one great exception to this rule. Still, at the state level, domestic insurrections have occurred which are manifestations of popular discontent unable to find a satisfactory outlet via the democratic process. Among the examples of localized disorders that one might cite are Bacon's Rebellion, the Whiskey Insurrection, the Nat Turner Insurrection, and Dorr's Rebellion; since the end of Reconstruction, even uprisings as limited as those have been a rarity. A handful, however, have taken place, and the following narrative samples twenty of these, ten from west and ten from east of the Mississippi River. Although such a scheme of division is not entirely satisfactory, we have divided those treated here into three categories: economic, social, and others. As they were discussed previously, violent labor eruptions are excluded from the present listing; some of these match in extent and violence many of the episodes analyzed in the present chapter.

Among the more significant varieties of domestic insurrections have been those involving economic issues. One might cite the Lincoln County War as a typical instance of this phenomenon. This event, which took place in New Mexico Territory in the late 1870's, resulted from an attempt by the Dolan-Riley firm to block the McSween Tunstall combination from taking part in the business life of the county, although technically the vendetta stemmed from a routine move to settle an estate. Complicated as its basic motivation may have been, this war grew from a series of skirmishes into a general disorder so extensive in scope that President Rutherford Hayes dismissed Governor Samuel Axtell for incompetency and appointed Lewis Wallace as chief executive in 1878. One month after the President had signed a proclamation demanding a halt to law violation, Governor Wallace issued a declaration of amnesty for all misdemeanors and offenses committed between February of that year and then; this action proved to be an effective method of restoring order, as it removed the possibility of a series of trials. New Mexico Territory was also the site of the Colfax County War in 1885, a controversy between the new owners of the Maxwell land grant and a group of squatters which saw the latter eventually bowing to eviction notices following a skirmish at Springer.

The Southern Pacific Railroad's domination of California politics in the decades following Reconstruction has been examined in the chapter on business and government. One of the bitterest fruits of this period was the Battle of Mussel Slough, an engagement occurring on May 12, 1880, which Frank Norris later immortalized in his novel *The Octopus*. While the railway was extending its line in the 1870's, it encouraged settlers to occupy its lands with the understanding that they would be able to purchase these later at a moderate price. When the day of reckoning arrived, though, instead of offering terms in the originally mentioned range of two dollars and a half to ten dollars an acre, the Southern Pacific raised the ante into the twenty-five to forty dollar bracket. Unethical as this action was, the fact that the railway included the various improvements which the settlers had made in the sale price further enraged the homesteaders. Five farmers were killed and many others arrested while resisting eviction orders; the funeral was attended by a queue of mourners two miles long. Despite the adverse publicity arising from this incident, nevertheless, the Southern Pacific continued to maintain its iron grip on the state down into this century.

An example of a skirmish between cattlemen and homesteaders is the Johnson County War of 1892, an event which comes from the pages of Wyoming history. Many homesteaders at this time made a practice of rounding up calves owned by some absentee cattle baron and applying their own brands to them; those of Johnson County even formed an association and declared their intention to rustle. Cattlemen on the northern range naturally resented this series of developments, so they formulated a plan under which they hired regulators (men who were to kill the rustlers). An armed invasion of Johnson County took place in April, 1892; the attack began at the KC ranch, where two homesteaders perished, and ended at the TA ranch, where the invading army barricaded itself. When news of the war reached Governor A. W. Barber, this official telegraphed President Benjamin Harrison that there was an insurrection there, and the arrival of troops from Fort McKinley brought the skirmish to a close. Although the invaders were arrested, there were no convictions, perhaps because public sentiment was divided between the cattlemen and the homesteaders. One political consequence of this episode was that in the election of 1892 many Republicans in northern Wyoming shifted their allegiance to the Democrats, as they felt that the Republican Party had backed the Cheyenne cattlemen.

On several occasions in this volume we refer to the role that Amalgamated (now Anaconda) Copper has played in Montana history; at this point in the narrative we might touch on the war which broke out in 1903 between the company and Frederick Augustus Heinze, its leading rival of that day. Not only did Heinze bring suit against the Anaconda, St. Lawrence, and Neversweat mines, which were the best of the Butte properties, but he also claimed apex rights to the Leonard and Michael Davitt. Perhaps the most colorful feature of this feud was the intermittent sabotaging by one side of the other side's mines; warning, though, was usually given, so that the men working in the target area almost always were able to escape. For this reason, the number of actual deaths were few, but scores were injured in mass combat or in private fights. This conflict did not end until Heinze sold out his interests to Amalgamated in 1906 for ten million dollars, leaving that company in total control of the state's economy.

Although the 1900 assassination of Governor William Goebel was perhaps more sensational, the 1907 revolt of Kentucky tobacco farmers against the unfair marketing practices and reduced prices of that day is one of the most striking episodes in the history of this state. On the night of December 7, having reached the limit of their endurance, five hundred of these rode into the village of Hopkinsville, wrecking two hundred thousand dollars worth of property in protest. Among the techniques which these and other farmers employed to effect their ends were the destroying of tobacco beds, the burning of warehouses, and the scrapping of stored tobacco; this movement, however, affected western Kentucky more than it did the other parts of the state. As Governor J. C. W. Beckham failed to take action, there was no use of state troops against the farmers until Governor Augustus Willson took office. One sidelight to this conflict was an international dispute involving certain Italian farmers near Hopkinsville whose property was destroyed in the course of the disturbance. It is true that a crisis in state morale was precipitated by this struggle, but a burley pool was formed soon afterward and a new type of tobacco was introduced in an attempt to lessen agrarian discontent.

Because of the general discontent which characterized Alaskan history for a number of years, one would surmise that this area would have been the site of numerous riots and insurrections over the years. Such, though, has not been the case. Perhaps that episode in Alaskan history which most nearly fits in with the material being presented here is the Cordova Coal Party of 1911; in the course of this incident, three hundred citizens from Cordova marched on the Alaska Steamship Company's dock and dumped several hundred tons of coal from British Columbia in the ocean. These vandals were protesting the Copper River and Northwestern Railway's failure to use steam coal from nearby mines. This episode, of course, reminds one of the Boston Tea Party, but it was a much less effective protest; only eight years later Congress passed the Jones Act which gave the Puget Sound carriers then operating a monopoly vis-a-vis trade with Alaska, further restricting that territory's economic freedom.

Shifting our attention next to Oklahoma, 1917 witnessed an episode known as the Green Corn Rebellion, an incident which was entirely different in character from the Snake Rebellion of the previous decade. In 1914, a secret organization advocating the abolition of rent, interest, and profit sprang up in Arkansas and spread to Oklahoma; this group, the Working Class Union, proposed to use revolutionary means to effect its ends. By 1917, it had enrolled thirty-four thousand members, and upon the passage of the Draft Act, it turned to violence, cutting telephone wires, destroying pipe lines, and dynamiting water mains and sewers. Two thousand farmers, including some Negroes and Indians, took part in this rebellion, the several "armies" subsisting on barbecued beef and roasting ears. The episode came to an end in August, when citizen-police arrested four hundred fifty rebels.

The depression of 1929 provided the background for the colorful Battle of Booneville, an incident which took place north of Utica in New York in 1933. Here the Class I price of milk had plummeted downward from an earlier peak of $2.90 per hundred pounds, and by August of this year producers were averaging less than $1.00 at the marketplace. Understandably dissatisfied with their lot, they precipitated a general strike, setting up blockades on highways, dumping milk, and threatening to sabotage milk plants and milk trains. The actual "battle" was a rather one-sided affair; state troopers employed tear-gas bombs and riot sticks, beating four hundred strikers unconscious. It took a general economic recovery, of course, to solve the milk producers' dilemmas.

Turning for our final example to Louisiana, the Long era witnessed the famous Battle of the Airport, an event which took place in January, 1935, a few months before the assassination of the Kingfish. Just previously, the legislature had enacted a favorite Long measure providing for a tax of five cents a barrel on refined oil; Standard Oil, which at this time was employing three thousand eight hundred workers, thereupon dismissed nearly a thousand of these in an economy move. Some of these discharged employees, together with some state workers that Long had fired, now formed the Square Deal organization, threatening violence. When this group did revolt, Long called out the state militia to deal with them, and in a clash at the Baton Rouge airport the Long forces easily routed the Square Dealers. Such an episode demonstrates the ruthlessness with which Long sometimes dealt with his political critics.

Perhaps the most important conclusion which one might reach from an analysis of these cases is that economic dissatisfaction in American life has violently manifested itself over a number of issues. Business rivalry, railroad domination, cattlemen v. homesteaders, mining rights, tobacco marketing conditions, coal imports, milk prices, and oil taxes have been the focal points of the episodes just covered. It is tempting to attribute these particular domestic insurrections to Western lawlessness, but only New Mexico and Alaska were still territories at the moment in question, while three incidents took place east of the Mississippi. In terms of results, such occurrences as the Battle of Mussel Slough and the Battle of Booneville brought only disaster to the rioters; nevertheless, the Kentucky night riders did pressure the adoption of some reforms, while the Lincoln County War and the Johnson County War raged beyond the control of local authorities. Yet despite the violence employed, only the Green Corn Rebellion was truly the work of philosophic radicals.

Equally volcanic at times has been racial friction. It is noteworthy that following Reconstruction the focal point of this agitation was not the Negro, but rather the Chinese; our government forbade the further immigration of this group into the United States in 1882. The first anti-Chinese riots took place in California, where in July of 1877 agitators burned twenty-five laundries to the ground, triggering off a reign of terror that lasted several months. At Truckee in November of 1878, the entire Chinese population of one thousand was expelled. When an anti-Chinese disorder broke out at Denver, Colorado in 1880, the Chinese minister appealed to our Secretary of State for compensation, but James G. Blaine took the position that local authorities had done everything that they could under the circumstances. (Other protests followed.) There also were disturbances at Rock Springs, Wyoming, where twenty-eight Chinese were murdered in 1885 for not taking part in a strike, and at Tacoma, Washington, from which the Chinese citizenry of that town were driven shortly thereafter. Fortunately, anti-Chinese feeling throughout the West began to die down after the exclusion act had been in operation for several years.

That an incident of the type which we are analyzing here which involved the Mafia would occur is not surprising, but that it would take place in Louisiana is. After 1877, many Italians, some of whom belonged to this secret society, settled in New Orleans; in 1891, the Mafia had the chief of police of this city shot to death, with the result that officials there had nineteen Italians arrested. A jury, however, freed six of the men and failed to convict the remainder, with the result that a mob broke into the prison and killed eleven of the men. Since three of the victims were Italian citizens, the lynching had international ramifications; our government eventually paid nearly twenty-five thousand dollars to the families of the slain men. Three Italians later died at Hahnville in August, 1896 in still another manifestation of local ill-feeling toward this nationality group.

Despite the fact that the 1962 incident at Oxford, Mississippi over the entrance of a Negro into the university there caused a nation-wide furor, one might point out even more violent episodes from the annals of the South. At Wilmington, North Carolina in 1898, for example, six hundred white citizens became so discontented with the Republicans and the Negroes controlling this metropolis that they rebelled; the highlight of this insurrection was the burning of the offices of the *Record,* a newspaper whose Negro editor, A. L. Manley, often printed "inflammatory editorials." Not only was the city placed under armed guard, but ten Negroes were killed, ten or more jailed, and an indefinite number forced to leave town as well. (Mayor Wright fled to New York.) A new city government eventually took over with ex-Congressman A. M. Waddell as mayor; the Raleigh *News and Observer* proudly announced on November 13 that "Negro rule is at an end in North Carolina forever."

As we know, the great wars between the Indians and the whites had come to an end by the turn of the twentieth century, but the so-called Snake Rebellion that occurred in Oklahoma Territory in 1909 affords an instance of a conflict involving both Indians and Negroes. At this time a faction of the Creeks which opposed land allotment and desired a return to old tribal ways occasionally met at Hickory Ground; a collection of houses and tents where they held their gatherings stood on this site. When a group of Negroes, some of whom allegedly had stolen meat from a smokehouse, congregated here and in the surrounding habitations, a band of officers attempted to search them. In the unfortunate melee that followed, several Negroes were killed, despite the fact that the officers eventually were driven off. Following this, another posse came with a warrant for the arrest of Crazy Snake, who supposedly had been responsible in part for the Negroes' conduct; a fight occurred at his home between the posse and a group of Indians in which two deputy sheriffs lost their lives. Crazy Snake, who was wounded, was never seen again. A subsequent investigation revealed that the Indians needed protection.

Although the previously analyzed Wilmington, North Carolina incident took place in the South, unpleasantries involving the Negro have occurred elsewhere as well. Northerners like to regard themselves as highly tolerant, but the fact remains that one of the most violent race riots in the history of America broke out in Detroit, Michigan in June of 1943. Here no less than thirty-five individuals (including twenty-eight Negroes) were killed, while the number of injured has been calculated as high as one thousand persons; two million dollars in property, moreover, was destroyed during the course of the rioting and looting. Our involvement in a world war at this time unquestionably has prevented this episode from winning the place it deserves in the history books, as with so many deaths and injuries occurring elsewhere the Detroit race riots relatively speaking were of little significance.

Racial flare-ups, however, have by no means been limited to conflicts involving the Negro. Contemporary with the Detroit incident, but of a more sporadic nature, was a series of outbreaks in Los Angeles during World War II; at this time many Mexican youths organized gangs, thereby triggering what is generally known as the Zootsuit Riots. The name which these skirmishes bear comes from the gang members' unofficial costume, which was a pair of high-waisted, baggy trousers tight at the ankles, a sport coat with padded shoulders and lengthy skirts, and a flat-crowned, broad-brimmed hat. Lives were lost and property was damaged during the course of this "war." While the Mexicans may not have been totally to blame, most people regarded them as being the instigators. These immigrants from south of the border, though, have been a problem in this part of the country for a long time, so that this series of occurrences was only the natural culmination of racial discontent which had been building up over the years. A strike among the melon pickers of the Imperial Valley of California in 1928 had focused attention on the Mexican labor issue.

Two Southern "domestic insurrections," both of which were triggered by white resentment against the Negro, close our presentation of racial disorders. The first of these took place in Little Rock, Arkansas three years after the United States Supreme Court had enunciated its desegregation ruling (1957). Here a federal district judge nullified a state court injunction which forbade the school board to integrate the high school. Although no rioting had as yet taken place, Governor Orville Faubus called out the National Guard to maintain order; after meeting with President Dwight D. Eisenhower, Faubus did not withdraw the troops until the federal court issued an injunction against his tactics, whereupon rioting broke out on September 23. The President dispatched a thousand paratroopers to Little Rock on the next day, and after Negroes had entered the school he gradually withdrew the troops. Despite the attention that it attracted, this perhaps was the least violent episode that we have analyzed here.

A bloodier incident occurred in the Fall of 1962 when James Meredith, a Negro, applied for admission to the all-white University of Mississippi. When school officials balked at accepting him, President John F. Kennedy and Attorney General Robert Kennedy placed pressure on Governor Ross Barnett to change the decision; after it had become apparent that persuasion would not work, the President sent marshals and troops to the scene. Two persons died in the ensuing melee, in which tear-gas bombs were thrown into the crowd, rioters hurling all sorts of debris at the marshals and the troops in retaliation. Soldiers afterward arrested retired General Edwin Walker, a noted advocate of right-wing causes who urged the rioters on. Despite this carnage, Meredith eventually did register as a student; he was graduated the next year after officials there had made an unsuccessful attempt to withhold his degree.

Admittedly, these eight cases do not constitute an exhaustive survey of race riots in the United States, but they do demonstrate that these occurrences are not a recent development. Furthermore, they reveal that such incidents have taken place elsewhere than in the South. It is obvious that the Negro has been the focal point of these episodes more often than not, but other minority groups also have been the object of attack; four of our eight cases deal with Chinese, Italians, Indians, and Mexicans rather than with the black man. Significantly, despite widespread criticisms in Africa of the treatment of the Negro here, it was the Chinese and the Italian governments, not some Dark Continent one, which protested the treatment of their people. Increasing federal intervention in domestic occurrences of this nature, of course, has focused additional attention on the question of racial disturbances, as has recent civil rights legislation.

It doubtless is true that, from both the quantitative and the qualitative points of view, most state insurrections have resulted from either economic or racial discontent. There have been other causes, though, of these riots and uprisings, and at this point in the narrative one might cite two cases demonstrating this fact which date from the Populist era. We first shall examine the City Hall War, an episode which took place in Colorado during the governorship of the noted Populist leader Davis Waite

(1893–1895). The preceding legislature had empowered the chief executive to appoint the police and fire board of Denver, so Waite selected several individuals to fill these positions. His appointees, however, failed to carry out his efforts to reform and control Denver and he thereupon tried to remove them; the incumbents then defied Waite by barricading themselves in the City Hall with three hundred armed men, following which he retaliated by surrounding the building with militia and cannon. Fortunately for all parties concerned, cooler heads persuaded the governor to preserve order with national troops rather than to attack the entrenched dissidents. The courts eventually handed down a decision affirming that Waite did have the right to remove the officials, but not the authority to use force to install them.

The infamous liquor dispensary system which Benjamin Tillman set up in South Carolina was a prime example of administrative corruption; here we might refer to it in connection with the Darlington War, a disorder arising out of local disenchantment with "Pitchfork Ben's" pet scheme. In May of 1894, shooting broke out at the railway station between seventeen constables and various citizens just prior to the former's departure from town, with the result that several persons died. Governor Tillman now called out the militia, but the three companies in Columbia refused to obey his orders, as did those in Charleston and in some of the smaller towns. Consequently, it became necessary to employ volunteers. Tillman now declared Darlington and Florence counties in a state of insurrection, while proclaiming a press censorship, but there was no head-on clash, despite the fact that the tension lasted for a week or so. It is true that no one went to jail for participation in this insurrection; it is also true that the Darlington War had no immediate effect vis-a-vis the elimination of the dispensary system.

Still another episode which demonstrates that domestic insurrections may spread across state boundaries was the almost legendary feud between the pro-Union McCoys of Kentucky and the pro-Confederate Hatfields of West Virginia in the days following Reconstruction. As is often the case with controversies which have deep ideological roots, this imbroglio was triggered by two relatively trivial incidents: a disagreement over the ownership of a razerback hog, and a love affair between a male Hatfield and a female McCoy. Tempers began to blaze up around 1882, at which time members of the two warring clans started killing each other indiscriminately, and the strife reached its climax when an agent of the governor of Kentucky entered West Virginia with a posse and seized certain members of the Hatfield clan. Despite the supposed illegality of this action, the courts ruled in the case of *Mahon v. Justice* that neither the Constitution nor the laws of the United States provide relief for an individual who is seized in one state, and then forcibly carried into another to stand trail for an offense which he allegedly committed against it. Ill-will smouldered for a long time afterwards, but the introduction of the railroad and industry into the Tug River Valley led to the eventual waning of this feud.

In summary, perhaps the most striking feature of the twenty incidents which we have presented here is the fact that they have occurred in all parts of this country, even in the North and the East. To identify anti-Negro riots with the South exclusively is to pay homage to a stereotype rather than to the truth; to analyze economic disorders in terms of a single section or a single issue is also to do violence to history. It is true that in more recent years these outbreaks have been characterized by fewer deaths and less damage to property, but the recent Los Angeles and Detroit race riots seemingly herald a new era of violence. From the over-all point of view, it would be rash to claim that most of these incidents are of seminal importance, yet they do constitute a throw-back to a more lawless epoch and merit at least examination if not prolonged attention. Certainly, it is essential that the historian be aware of those issues which the democratic process has not been able to resolve peacefully. We shall return to this topic in the conclusion, where we shall explain how the Civil War contributed to the development of one-party states in this nation.

Chapter 12

National History vs.
State History

At various places throughout this volume, we have made reference to developments at the national level in an attempt to place their counterparts statewise in broader perspective. Definite relationships do exist between national politics and government and state politics and government; the intellectual atmosphere of an era, for example, affects the latter as well as the former. It is a serious mistake, however, to conclude that state history is only a pale carbon copy of national history, and that what occurs at the former level is a second-rate version of the latter. Basic dissimilarities do exist between the two; these are especially apparent in the areas of politics and government, as we shall demonstrate in the following analysis, which follows the order of the table of contents. This chapter is admittedly experimental, and the generalizations set forth here are tentative rather than definitive in character, but such an approach does offer new insights. Doubtless, a key reason for the relative neglect of state political history has been the failure of scholars to employ sufficient cross-references between it and its national counterpart, especially in their surveys of American political history.

The Civil War has had many repercussions, but one of the most important has been that in approximately half the states of the Union one party dominates public office to the extent that the other plays a very minor role. Most of the one-party Democratic states are in the South, and here resentment against the North because of its suppression of the greatest of all domestic insurrections, the Civil War, has bred prejudice against that section which has led to one-party rule and an incomplete degree of intellectual freedom. On the other hand, in the case of the Republican one-party states, those in the Great Plains region were partly settled by Northern veterans after the Civil War, while those in New England were within that general area where the abolitionist movement, which was one of the causes of the Civil War, first took definite form in William Lloyd Garrison's American Antislavery Society. For this reason, it was only natural that the Democrats would be in disrepute in both places following that conflict. The fact that there is something of a trend away from one-party states at the state level today doubtless is largely attributable to the increasing cross-fertilization of ideas which is tending to tear down provincialism. In contrast, despite the stranglehold which the Republicans held on the Presidency for a score of years following the Civil War and that which the Democrats held for a score of years following the Depression of 1929, there was considerable rivalry between the major parties in Congress during those eras except for brief periods. Thus, no one party has ever dominated the country indefinitely as one party has dominated some states. There has not been, moreover, a national political boss to rival Thomas Pendergast, Edward Crump, Frank Hague, the gallery of Republican impressarios who charted the destiny of Pennsylvania for seventy-five years, or the powerful Martin-Byrd machine that has run Virginia for half a century. With the exception of that of Hague, who was in clandestine alliance with the Republicans at times, all of these political machines functioned in one-party states. At the state level, too, an individual factor such as social unrest may lead to exaggerated manifestations of radicalism such as that which occurred in California during the 1930's, or another one such as intolerance may lead to exaggerated manifestations of reaction such as that which took place in Indiana during the 1920's. Such extreme behavior rarely, if ever, characterizes national politics.

In regard to fusion, national politics in the early days of our republic were relatively fluid, as the Era of Good Feelings demonstrates, but since Reconstruction there has been no successful attempt in this direction. The Populists did unite with the Democrats in 1896 in an effort to elect William Jennings Bryan President, but this attempt did not bear fruit as did several similar coalitions at the state level during this same period. For an explanation of this phenomenon, we must turn to an economic analysis of politics. The farming elements of the Great Plains, which resented certain practices of the railroads and other economic interests, sought reforms through political action; since the Republican Party around 1890 was under the national leadership of a conservative like Benjamin Harrison and the Democratic Party under that of a conservative like Grover Cleveland, the agrarian bloc formed a third party, the Populists. In the Election of 1896, William Jennings Bryan, the fusion candidate of the Democrats and the Populists, carried twenty-two of the forty-five states thanks to his support in the South and the West, but did poorly in the more industrialized North and thus lost out in the Electoral College. In contrast, during this same decade, the Populists were able to enter into successful alliance with one of the two major parties while seeking the governorships of such states as South Dakota, Nebraska, North Dakota, and Minnesota, as well as gaining control of the legislature of North Carolina. Populism did die out following the turn of the century, but agrarian elements in conjunction with other groups such as labor organized at the state level such successful third parties as the Nonpartisan League in North Dakota and elsewhere, the Farmer-Labor Party in Minnesota, and the Progressive Party in Wisconsin. At the national level the Greenbackers of 1880, the Populists of 1892 and 1896, the Unionists of 1936, the Dixiecrats of 1948, and the Progressives of 1912, 1924, and 1948 all nominated Presidential candidates, but none of these won. This analysis leads us to conclude that economic protest has expressed itself more effectively through third parties statewise than nationally; when Franklin Roosevelt won the Presidency in 1932 as a result of the economic tragedy that accompanied the Depression of 1929, he ran not as the candidate of some third party such as the Socialists but rather as a Democrat. It is interesting to note that while national political parties are ideological catch-alls, one finds occasional instances at the state level of political divisions entirely on philosophical lines. In the case of New York, two such parties, the Liberals and the Conservatives, play an important role, even though each is able to elect candidates to office only in fusion with one of the major parties.

Although one does find sectional shifts in power in states such as Nevada and Florida similar to that which occurred nationally, and despite the fact that the sectional rivalries in states such as North Carolina and South Carolina mirror such sectional antagonisms at the national level as those between the Tidewater and the Piedmont, the manifestations of sectionalism that one finds in many states are far more pronounced than they are nationally. Prior to the admission of Hawaii and Alaska as states, for example, there was no national parallel to such extreme instances of geographical sectionalism at the state level as those which occur in Washington and Oregon (Cascade Mountains), Idaho (Salmon River), Vermont (Green Mountains), and Michigan (Great Lakes). Then in states such as Arizona Louisiana, Maryland, Delaware, Massachusetts, New York, and Illinois there exists the phenomenon of one dominant city pitted against the remainder of the state; from the national point of view, no single state is powerful enough to dominate the country. Since sectionalism may take more extreme forms at the state level, it is not surprising that separatist sentiment has been stronger there, at least since 1865. The Dakotas, Oklahoma, Idaho, Texas, and California might be cited as examples. Nationally, though, the South is not the only section which has exhibited separatist tendencies, as the holding of the Hartford Convention in New England during the War of 1812 attests. City rivalry has been stronger statewise, too, than has state rivalry at the national level; we have cited Minneapolis and St. Paul, San Francisco and Los Angeles, and Kansas City and St. Louis, as outstanding examples of the former. It is not surprising, therefore, that capital removal sentiment has been more pronounced in certain states than nationally, since this is a variation on this particular type of rivalry.

In our analysis of the role that business interests have played in state politics and government, we presented a great deal of material. This material, if anything, strengthens considerably the economic interpretation of American history which Charles A. Beard set forth in a number of volumes earlier in this century. Despite the fact that the large corporations more or less dominated the national scene from the end of Reconstruction to the assassination of President William McKinley, as well as from the inauguration of President Warren G. Harding to the coming of the New Deal, no single economic interest has ever wielded the power throughout the country as a whole that the Southern Pacific once did in California, Anaconda Copper once did in Montana, and the Big Five once did in Hawaii. (Railroads in particular have played a key role politically in a number of states.) It is rare today for a single concern to dominate the government of a state (Anaconda still remains powerful), but it is not uncommon for a group of enterprises to unite to form a lobby that effectively controls the measures that pass through the legislature. Ohio is a case in point. Admittedly, during the Populist and Progressive eras, there was a movement at both the state and the national levels to regulate business, and certainly such governors as James Vardaman in Mississippi and Jefferson Davis in Arkansas adopted measures which far exceeded in severity comparable legislation and prosecutions that the national government sponsored during the same period. Except for this interlude, however, federal authorities have never gone as far in coddling corporations as have New Jersey and Delaware. Nor have they adopted as extensive schemes of tax exemption as have a number of states, although between 1850 and 1871 the national government did make a number of land grants to the railroads, a practice in which only Texas and Florida engaged on a large scale at the state level. States, of course, are unable to pass tariffs to protect domestic goods against foreign competition as their federal counterpart does.

Unlike nationally, governmental regulation of business at the state level began with the railroad measures that Rhode Island and other New England states passed before the Civil War and Illinois and other Granger states enacted after this conflict, but the Supreme Court dealt a severe blow to state regulation in the Wabash Case (1886) and the Shreveport Case (1914). Thus the national government was forced to step into the void with the Interstate Commerce Act (1887). The federal Sherman Anti-Trust Act (1890) resulted in few convictions at first, but beginning with the Northern Securities Case (1904) and the Standard Oil and American Tobacco Cases (1911), it began a series of prosecutions which only a handful of states, such as Arkansas and Texas, attempted to match, even though eighteen states passed anti-trust legislation between 1889 and 1891. States obviously do enact laws regulating business; among the more controversial measures of the present century have been the fair-trade and loss-limitation acts and anti-chain store taxes. But they do not begin to compare in importance with such pieces of federal legislation as the Pure Food and Drug Act of 1906, the Meat Inspection Act of 1906, the Clayton Anti-Trust Act of 1914, the Federal Securities Act of 1933, the Securities Exchange Act of 1934, the Wheeler-Rayburn Public Utility Holding Company Act of 1935, and the Robinson-Patman Federal Anti-Price Discrimination Act of 1936. Because business in many cases exercises more political power at the state level than nationally, it is often political suicide to attempt to thwart it, as Joseph Dixon found out in Montana in 1924 when he lost the governorship while successfully sponsoring an initiated measure which would increase the tax on Anaconda. Sometimes state regulation does set a precedent for the federal government; the "blue-sky" securities laws that Kansas and other states passed from 1911 on are one example. On the other hand, at times various states will imitate a national measure, as has occurred with the Pure Food and Drug Act of 1906. Actual state participation in business, though, is a rarity, and the handful of experiments along this line in the Dakotas and elsewhere hardly rival in significance such mammoth federal undertakings as the Tennessee Valley Authority.

Shifting our attention to the economic role that outside capital has played, we have pointed out that this more or less ceased to be a problem nationally with the coming of World War I, since we became a creditor during this conflict, but the situation is quite different at the state level. Following the Civil War, the South and the West became economic colonies of the North, and to a large extent have retained this status over the years, as the numerous examples that we have collected demonstrate. Whether this phenomenon was desirable or not is a matter of opinion; outside capital did drain off the profits it earned as the result of economic development, but without the assistance of outside capital there well may have been no economic development at all. This is the paradox. Nevertheless, over the past generation, a number of states have set up boards, etc., not only to encourage business enterprises already present, but also to attract new ones from without. Even reactionary Mississippi, from which state Governor James Vardaman drove the big corporations, has initiated a Balance Agriculture with Industry program. In contrast, the national government has restricted itself to measures of the Reconstruction Finance Corporation type, as too enthusiastic support for the business sector of the economy would probably result in political defeat at the polls.

Despite the stranglehold which various economic interests have held on many states for varying periods, from the standpoint of legislation labor's greatest problem has not been in getting statutes passed, but rather in persuading the United

States Supreme Court that such measures are constitutional. That body long challenged the right of the states to interfere with the working conditions that business concerns imposed on their employees, just as it has resisted other forms of state regulation of business. The highest tribunal, for example, did not uphold the principle of minimum wage standards until 1937. On the other hand, the Supreme Court has given comfort to the foes of labor by such actions as approving the yellow-dog contract (1915) and the use of injunctions against labor (1921), thus hindering state measures designed to restrict both. (The federal Norris-La Guardia Act of 1932 dealt a death blow to the yellow-dog contracts and severely curtailed anti-labor injunctions.) Since the New Deal, though, there has been a change in court philosophy in the direction of upholding state labor legislation; significantly, except for the provisions incidental to the National Industrial Recovery Act (1933), the highest tribunal has never struck down a major labor statute at the national level. Some analysts like to point out that states were passing progressive labor laws such as minimum wage and maximum hours statutes long before the national government was, but it was also enacting anti-labor measures as well, such as anti-picketing and anti-boycott acts. On the whole, national legislation has tended to be more uniformly progressive; even the Taft-Hartley Act of 1947 merely struck a more equitable balance between labor and management instead of discriminating unjustly against the former. Perhaps the most obvious proof that there remains a wide divergence in philosophy among the various pieces of labor legislation that most states have passed in recent years lies in the fact that just as many states have enacted conservative right-to-work laws as have adopted progressive fair-employment practices measures. Similarly, some states have modeled their labor relations statutes after the Taft-Hartley Act, some after the pro-labor Wagner Act of 1935.

If the pattern of labor legislation varies from state to state, so does the pattern of strikes. Some states, such as Maine or Iowa, have never had a major walkout; others, like Colorado and Illinois, have had several memorable ones. The important nationwide strikes affecting a single industry have been largely restricted to those in the areas of railroads (1877 and 1946), steel (1919 and 1952), and coal (1919 and 1946), while at the state level there has been a greater variety of memorable walkouts, with those in the general category of mining apparently the most numerous. There has never been a nationwide general strike, but there have been local ones in Seattle (1919), San Francisco (1934), and Terre Haute (1935). The federal government has intervened in strikes centered within a single state as well as in those with an interstate character, with results sometimes favorable to labor (anthracite coal strike, Pennsylvania, 1902), sometimes favorable to management (Pullman car strike, Illinois, 1894), so that it is impossible to make a blanket generalization here. Like Presidential actions, gubernatorial pressures during major walkouts have sometimes favored labor, sometimes not. Governor Davis "Bloody Bridles" Waite of Colorado, for example, represented the miners in peace negotiations during the Cripple Creek Strike (1894), while Governor John Peter Altgeld of Illinois pardoned some of the 1886 Haymarket rioters and opposed federal intervention during the Pullman Strike. In contrast, Governor Calvin Coolidge of Massachusetts dismissed the striking policemen of Boston from their jobs in 1919, a rather drastic step which helped rather than hurt his political fortunes.

Labor has enjoyed some degree of power in every national Democratic administration during the present century, as well as played a key role during most Presidential elections because of its strength in the populous industrial states which dominate the Electoral College. Yet, it has assumed a really ascendant role in only two states (Michigan and Hawaii) for any protracted period of time, and this has been in the period since World War II. For this reason, it is not possible to give numerous examples of labor domination of state government, as is the case with business control; the greatest challenge to business politically at the state level, at least in most states, comes from the rural, agrarian elements which are the largest bloc in many state legislatures. The fact that it is the federal government which has established a system of price supports for farmers obscures the fact that the states, too, have enacted such pro-agrarian legislation as those measures establishing Farmers' Institutes (beginning with Massachusetts in 1863) and those appointing County Agents (beginning with Texas in 1906), as well as those maintaining agricultural experiment stations. We shall have more to say about the political role of agriculture shortly when we examine third parties at the state level, since in many cases these have been an expression of agrarian discontent. On the basis of the material that we have presented here, one is able to conclude only that there is a better political balance among labor, capital, and agriculture nationally than statewise. It is only natural, moreover, that this economic imbalance with its political consequences, together with the exaggerated manifestations of sectional tensions, intolerance, and social unrest which one finds at the state level, would produce an atmosphere in which the political responses may at times be more extreme than they ordinarily are nationally.

As for the shadier side of the political process, voters at the state level expect more corruption in the electoral process than they do nationally. Quite frankly, the average citizen has less illusions (or expectations) that a state official will exhibit qualities of statesmanship than he does that a national official will; for this reason, he more or less reconciles himself to the fact that unethical practices are going to go on in state government no matter what he does. Yet, any prospective chronicler of corruption at the state level almost immediately runs into a stone wall of silence when he starts examining state histories in search of material. One reason for this is fairly obvious. Since these histories frequently are used as textbooks in the schools, the textbook selection committees obviously desire that the author paint as idealistic a portrait of the state as possible, and he consequently sweeps the dirt under the rug. In contrast, national histories often dwell on the misdeeds of the Grant and Harding Administrations.

Comparing and contrasting corruption at both levels, it is a well-known fact that no President has gone to jail, although Governors Richard Leche of Louisiana and Warren McCray of Indiana did suffer this fate. (This record of escaping jail does not hold true, though, of members of the Presidents' cabinets.) No President, moreover, has ever gone on trial for allegedly committing a crime and won acquittal, as did Lee Russell of Mississippi, Len Small of Illinois, and Jonathan Davis of Kansas. It is impossible to determine if any chief executive at the national level ever broke the law and escaped detection, but Harold Hoffman of New Jersey successfully embezzled three hundred thousand dollars while serving as governor of his state. In any event, even Grant and Harding are generally regarded by historians as being personally honest despite the sins of their subordinates. Turning to Congress, doubtless at any given time that body has had its dishonest members, but it is questionable if in quantitative terms the corrupt practices committed during any session have rivaled those of the Jockey Legislature of New Jersey or, more recently, the activities of various members of the Michigan Legislature of 1943. Vote-buying episodes such as those which occurred in Ohio in 1911 are partly attributable to the fact that state election laws are more loosely drawn than their federal counterpart. Nevertheless, perhaps the only episode in the annals of scandal at the state level that has attracted prolonged national attention was that of vote-buying in Missouri, and this is only because of the alleged ties between political boss Thomas Pendergast and President Harry Truman. No one who has uncovered corruption on a national scope has ever won the Presidency (Estes Kefauver tried, however), while Chester A. Arthur actually had served as director of the corrupt New York Customs House before becoming chief executive. In contrast, several governors have won election largely as a result of their image as crime busters, Thomas Dewey of New York being a recent example. State government, of course, will continue to be plagued by scandal, as unethical behavior will remain a chronic problem until that day when men surrender the control of their destiny to computers.

Any study of the dissimilarities between national history and state history must necessarily involve an examination of the role that governmental financing plays in each. It would be possible to make a comparative study of the types of taxes which have furnished the bulk of the revenue at each level; the general property tax, although it has declined in significance in recent years, has been a source of income statewise which the national government has not tapped, as has the general sales tax, which has gained in importance lately. In contrast, federal income tax rates are much higher than those of any state, while tariffs are only imposed at the national level. Another difference relative to financing is that the federal government has made grants-in-aid to the states, but the states have not made grants-in-aid to the federal government. But even more important has been the fact that the national government is able to resort to deficit financing whenever necessary, while the states are not able to employ this leading device of Keynesian economies without going through the elaborate procedure of approving a bond issue. For this reason, when expenditures outrun receipts, federal officials have not had to obtain loans, as have their counterparts in Ohio, Connecticut, Rhode Island, and Alabama, nor have they had to issue money, as the government of Mississippi once did. Certainly, the national government has never suffered because of its indebtedness as have the states of Arkansas and Tennessee during the present century. Republican Andrew Mellon, who is *persona non grata* in the eyes of Keynesian economists, did effect a notable reduction in the national debt while serving as Secretary of the Treasury during the 1920's, but such a step is obviously less of a meaningful achievement for the federal government than have been the large-scale cuts which the governments of South Dakota and Pennsylvania have made in their bonded indebtedness during recent decades. Far from requiring a mandatory annual reduction in the national debt, as Georgia does at the state level, Congress has made something of a joke out of the question of indebtedness by establishing a meaningless ceiling for the national debt and then raising this whenever that body incurs a deficit which would push the actual national debt above it. Admittedly, Colorado and South Carolina have by-passed constitutional debt limitations in various ways, as have other states, so that the record at the state level is not free from hypocrisy, either. In any event, in recent years even such a state as Michigan has suffered from a debt problem, and in an era of increasing governmental activity at every level it seems unlikely that most states will be able to follow Vermont's "pay-as-you-go" policy.

Financing governmental operations, though, is only one side of the coin; what to spend the money for is the other. Here, again, there is a sharp contrast between national history and state history, as during the present century federally the bulk of governmental expenditures has been for military appropriations and for interest payments on the national debt, while statewise it has been for schools and roads. Admittedly, a President such as John Quincy Adams did call for a program of national internal improvements, but more typical was the attitude of his successor, Andrew Jackson, who desired to leave most projects of this nature to the states. Perhaps significantly, the first real involvement of the federal government in the financing of education and highways came during the Wilson Administration with the almost simultaneous passage of the Smith-Hughes Act in 1917 and the Federal Aid Road Act in 1916. Still, despite the increase in governmental activities nationally beginning with the New Deal period, the federal government did not undertake any large-scale expenditures for schools and roads until the Eisenhower Administration pushed through Congress the National

Defense Education Act of 1958 and the Federal Highway Act of 1956. Outlays for these two items, however, still play only a minor role in the national budget. Turning to the record of performance at the state level, both educational drives and the good roads movement began to flower around 1900. Obviously, all states have not achieved equally in either field; the fact that in many states the equalization movement vis-a-vis the schools and the rivalry for funds between primary and secondary roads indicates that the record of accomplishment within a state in both areas may be rather spotty. Certainly, the federal government has performed more consistently in the numerous projects in these and other areas that it has undertaken. This uneven record relative to schools and roads within a particular state is partly attributable to the fact that both education and highways generally are under the control of local authorities to some extent, depending on the division of power within that state. Still, the national government has had to contend with the division of power between itself and the states, which is the key feature of our federal system, without significantly affecting its performance. To place all the schools and roads within a state under the absolute control of the state government, moreover, doubtless would cause as much a furor locally as it would at the state level were the national government to dictate educational and highway policies to the states.

Although the federal government has made a number of encroachments in the field of education in recent years, to date it has posed few challenges to academic freedom. If this country had a national university, this might not have been the case. The anti-Communist movement spearheaded by Senator Joseph McCarthy did lead, either directly or indirectly, to the ouster of a number of professors during the early 1950's, but such issues as evolution, nativism, and even Populism did not result in any nationally directed purges. Except in time of war, it is highly difficult for federal authorities to pressure the dismissal of members of the academic profession; nevertheless, Southern demagogues like Theodore Bilbo and Eugene Talmadge have instituted mass firings at times when nothing resembling a state of emergency existed. Critics have charged that federal aid to schools will result in eventual national control of educational policies at the state level. Whether it will also lead to federal dictation in matters of academic personnel remains to be seen, as at present the intellectual climate is such that the extensive stifling of the free expression of ideas would not win popular approval.

Of all the aspects of state history, perhaps none offers more interesting material to the analyst than do the various state constitutions, since each is the end product of a bewildering variety of pressures. From a superficial point of view, many state constitutions are longer than their national counterpart; this is for the reason that the former tend to go into specific details more, while the latter restricts itself to a general framework of government. The inclusion of specific details in state constitutions has had the inevitable consequence of spawning literally dozens of constitutional amendments. (At the national level there have been only eight since 1876.) State government textbooks invariably stress features common to most state constitutions, but in reality state constitutions and the constitutional conventions that drew them up have differed in many ways from each other. Perhaps the best approach to this general subject is to divide these documents, or at least those ratified since 1876, into three classes: (1) those designed to establish white political supremacy, (2) those drawn up as a consequence of a territory becoming a state, (3) the remaining ones. Examining first sub-class number one, the federal constitution contains a provision establishing a terminal date for the slave trade as well as another stipulating that for purposes of apportionment a slave was to count three-fifths of a white person. State constitutions, too, contain racial provisions, such as those in the California Constitution of 1879 regulating the Chinese or those in the New Mexico Constitution of 1912 protecting the Spanish-Americans. But there is no national counterpart to those documents centering around the goal of establishing white political supremacy which became fundamental law in Mississippi, South Carolina, Louisiana, Alabama, and Virginia between 1890 and 1902. (One must recall that political restrictions on the Negro in the South did not become common until 1890, not 1876, as some people mistakenly assume.) These constitutions, moreover, sometimes contained provisions severely detrimental to the state, such as that of Alabama restricting governmental expenditures for such necessary internal improvements as schools and roads.

An analysis of the second sub-class of state constitutions, those that were a consequence of statehood, reveals that federal interference has manifested itself here on a number of occasions. Prominent examples are the failure of Congress to approve the 1883 and 1885 constitutions of South Dakota Territory, the holding up of Utah statehood until that territory agreed to include an anti-polygamy provision in its fundamental law, and the refusal of President William Howard Taft to accept the Arizona Territory constitution until the electorate there had removed the section providing for the recall of judges. In contrast, the states have in no way forced any changes in the federal constitution, except for the fact that when they ratified this document six states recommended amendments to specify the popular rights that the government must never violate, and this suggestion eventually led to the Bill of Rights. Resentment at the state level following the decision in *Chisholm v. Georgia* (1793) also led to the Eleventh Amendment, which restricts the initiation of legal suits against a state, but neither in this instance nor the previous one did the states compel the federal government to take action. As a class, this second group of state constitutions has been more consistently liberal in its provisions than have the other two; even so, as progressive a President as Theodore Roosevelt regarded some of the features of the Oklahoma Constitution of 1907 as being too extreme. The fact that the Idaho Constitution of 1890 discriminated against the Mormons, and that several others have a relatively conservative orientation, does not invalidate this generalization. In attempting to explain this trend toward liberalism, one might suggest that six of the thirteen state constitutions in this second subclass were drawn up at a time when Western discontent and reform sentiment were just solidifying into the Populist movement, while two others, those of Oklahoma and Arizona, were products of the Progressive period.

On the other hand, the third sub-class of state constitutions is more complex, naturally breaking down into several further subdivisions. Subdivision A consists of four documents (Texas, 1876; Georgia, 1877; Louisiana, 1879; Florida, 1887) dating from the period in Southern history before the South restricted the power of the Negro politically. But if there was a conservative reaction in the South during these years, conservative sentiment at the national level did not lead to any changes in the United States constitution. Subdivision B includes four fundamental laws (California, 1879; Kentucky, 1891; New York, 1894; Delaware, 1897) which have little in common with and do not stand in any significant relationship to national trends.

Subdivision C encompasses three constitutions of the Progressive era (Michigan, 1909; Louisiana, 1913; Louisiana, 1921). Reform sentiment during this period inspired such important changes in our national fundamental law as the income tax, direct election of Senators, prohibition, and women suffrage amendments; in contrast, only two states adopted a new constitution other than as a consequence of statehood. Louisiana, moreover, simply added two more to a long series rather than taking a much-needed step. Finally, subdivision D covers four recent fundamental laws (Georgia, 1945; Missouri, 1945; New Jersey, 1948; Michigan, 1963). Each of these documents is relatively liberal, despite the fact that the states which produced them are quite different. Since the end of World War II, reformers have added four amendments to the United States Constitution.

In examining the entire range of state constitutions, it becomes apparent that, if one places our federal constitution in the category of enlightened conservatism, a number of state constitutions will fall considerably to the left or to the right of it. The explanation for this, as we have pointed out before, lies partly in the fact that there are more elements of imbalance present at the state level than nationally, and thus the eventual compromise among these does not always manifest a middle-of-the-road character. Perhaps the most significant experimental features of state constitutions in general are the initiative, the referendum, and the recall, none of which the federal government has ever adopted. On the other hand, the most reactionary feature of state constitutions is unquestionably the white supremacy provisions of the documents which five Southern states ratified between 1890 and 1902, and the federal government has not adopted these either. Referring to the Jacob and Vines table of one-party and two-party states, one finds that seven of eight One-Party Democratic states have adopted new constitutions since 1876, but only two of eight Modified One-Party Republican states have. These two states, moreover, drew up a new constitution only because of their shift from territorial to statehood status. In between these two groups in terms of quantitative performance stand the Modified One-Party Democratic states (nine states, five constitutions) and the Two-Party states (twenty-five states, fourteen constitutions). Percentage-wise, the achievement record of these two groups differs by only 1%. Since the combination of the figures for the One-Party Democratic states, the Modified One-Party Democratic states, and the Modified One-Party Republican states results in a total of fourteen constitutions for twenty-five states, precisely the same total that the Two-Party states have amassed, it is apparent that the adoption of new constitutions has occurred at an equal pace in two-party and one-party states. As for the six rejected state constitutions that we described along with their more successful counterparts, it is somewhat risky to generalize about them other than to note that each went to its doom for a different reason. The matter of rejected state constitutions raises a final point, which is that if our founding fathers had let the people vote on the federal constitution, it might not have won ratification. One may look upon most state constitutions as second-rate products, but at least the overwhelming majority of these have received popular approval, the period from 1890 to 1902 being that era in which there were the most exceptions to this generalization.

If the impact of the federal government on various state constitutions has been considerable, it is only natural that the impact of national events as a whole on state events has been greater than the impact of state events as a whole on national events. This is one reason why national history textbooks largely ignore state history, although this neglect is hardly justified. Perhaps the most recent prominent example of a state or states attempting to impose its or their will on the federal government is the widespread Southern resistance to integration in the area of education and elsewhere; needless to say, this attempt to preserve segregation is doubtless doomed to ultimate failure, although the Negro may never attain complete equality with the white man. As for the other side of the coin, it would be possible to give numerous instances of how some development in the national capital affected one or more states. But if one were to select one specific area which best illustrates the extent of this impact, few would be so revealing as that of the struggle for statehood which various territories have gone through. An examination of those issues which in some cases helped and in others hindered the statehood candidacies of these demonstrates that they represent a cross-section of the important issues of American history. Among these are Mormonism (Utah and Idaho), woman suffrage (Utah and Wyoming), Reconstruction (Colorado and New Mexico), the free coinage of silver (Arizona), the Mexican question (New Mexico), the recall of judges (Arizona), the Indian question (Oklahoma), and Communism (Hawaii). Political rivalry, moreover, is apparent, as the Democrats desired one Dakota and two Oklahomas, while the Republicans wanted two Dakotas and one Oklahoma; in more recent years, the Republicans supported Hawaiian statehood and the Democrats Alaskan, although the subsequent political histories of these two states has not completely justified this partisan alignment. Even more important, on the question of the omnibus admission of 1889–1890 (the Dakotas, Montana, Idaho, and Washington), the Republicans took a generally favorable attitude, the Democrats, less enthusiastic. (Of the thirteen states that have joined the Union since Reconstruction, only one, Utah, attained this status during a Democratic administration.) Sometimes Congressional actions have indirectly stimulated statehood sentiment, as was the case when a law prohibiting aliens from owning real estate in the territories blocked the investment of foreign capital there, but, in general, this phenomenon has developed on its own without any stimulation from Washington. Certainly, the opposition of the latter has not constituted an ultimate deterrent. Nevertheless, it is apparent that when one analyzes state history, he must consider the role of various factors such as federal interference over which the inhabitants of a state have little, if any, control.

Thanks to the relative failure of the legislature to assert commanding political leadership in most states, the focal point of the political process at the state level, even more so than nationally, is the governor. Instead of analyzing his constitutional duties and power as do most state government textbooks, we have instead examined the records of some of the more outstanding individuals to hold this position. Using their achievements as data, it is possible to determine what sort of legislation most frequently is written onto the statute books during the regime of a great governor, and to compare this with that most likely to become law during the administration of an outstanding President. Examining the records of our governors of distinction in detail, one must conclude that measures regulating business interests in general, and the railroads in particular, along with those protecting labor very often rank among their achievements. Such acts have also played an important role nationally, especially during the Progressive and New Deal periods, but they have assumed a more perpetual significance at the state level. One obviously might substantiate this finding by referring again to some of the material in the chapters on business and labor; it holds true despite the pro-business attitude of many state governments between the Civil War and the Populist era, and between the New Deal and the present, and despite the relative political weakness of labor in the more agrarian, less industrialized states. In contrast, few leading Presidential administrations have featured important contributions in the general area of governmental reorganization, or in that of electoral law reforms, which achievements are quite characteristic of those of outstanding governors. It is noteworthy that the first national civil service law was passed during the administration of a machine politician, Chester A. Arthur, while the first national executive budget measure was enacted during the administration of our weakest President, Warren G. Harding. Despite the recent national stress on education, too, more first-class chief executives at the state level have made their mark in this field; considering the fact that states spend more money on education than anything else, it is quite appropriate that this form of expenditure is the one most characteristic of the administration of the great governor. Finally, although tax reforms have played a relatively important role in both key Presidential and gubernatorial epochs, welfare programs at least prior to 1933 were more significant statewise, while prison reforms of major consequence at the state level instituted by leading chief executives have had no national parallel.

But this is only one aspect of the total picture; the other is in what spheres of activity do outstanding governors rarely make a contribution. In the first place, despite the fact that many Presidents have won immortality through their dealings with foreign nations, not one chief executive at the state level that we analyzed won fame as a result of his interstate diplomacy. Obviously, external conflicts have far less political significance statewise than nationally. Perhaps more surprising is the fact that none contributed significantly to constitutional revision, which makes the successful sponsorship of the Michigan Constitution of 1963 by George Romney even more remarkable; few first-rate governors, moreover, have done much to further legislative reapportionment, as this is an activity which seemingly requires a goad from the United States Supreme Court to stimulate. (No President has made spectacular contributions in these two areas, either.) It is also noteworthy that debt reduction, which is more of a vital concern to state governments than to their national counterpart, did not play much of a role in our twenty gubernatorial administrations other than those of Gifford Pinchot of Pennsylvania and Herbert Lehman of New York. This is for the reason that one frequently remembers outstanding chief executives at the state level for building schools and roads, etc., and their construction requires the expenditure of more, not less, money. Nationally, although Thomas Jefferson and his Secretary of the Treasury, Albert Gallatin, did effect a notable debt reduction, such an accomplishment does not rank highly in the age of Keynesian economics, so that Andrew Mellon, the Secretary of the Treasury during the Harding-Coolidge-Hoover decade, today receives little praise for a parallel feat.

As for the question as to whether sharp competition between the two major parties, as occurs nationally most of the time, is more likely to produce leading chief executives at the state level, one finds that only four of our fourteen outstanding chief executives outside of New York made their mark in a state where one major party has predominated. These are Ellis Arnall, Harry Byrd, Robert La Follette, and Alfred Landon. (We have employed here a 1965 table drawn up by Jacob and Vines dividing states into the categories of One-Party Democratic, Modified One-Party Democratic, Two-Party, and Modified One-Party Republican.) Perhaps a more comprehensive survey would reveal a different ratio, but our sampling indicates that outstanding governors come more often from two-party states. As for demagogues, there has been no national counterpart to such figures at the state level as Huey Long, "Alfalfa Bill" Murray, Eugene Talmadge, Theodore Bilbo, or "Pa" Ferguson. Although it is the two-party states which most often produce great governors, it seems that only one-party states where the Democrats predominate spawn demagogues; this, though, perhaps is to be expected, since few Republican candidates for public office picture themselves as the champion of the common man, which is almost invariably the stamp of the demagogue.

As for removals from office, several governors have been deprived of their positions following impeachment proceedings, while no President ever has. Not only is there something sacred about the office of President which discourages this ultimate desecration, but it also is rare for Congressional sentiment against him to be so violent that two-thirds of the members of the Senate would take this irrevocable step. This generalization, although largely applicable, is not quite so valid at the state level. Examining the grounds on which their foes successfully convicted four impeached governors, one discovers such charges as falsifying accounts of campaign expenditures (Sulzer), misappropriating state funds (Ferguson), overusing the pardoning power (Walton), and incompetence (Johnston). On the other hand, the eleven charges which the managers of the impeachment of President Andrew Johnson drew up claimed that he had violated the Tenure of Office Act, had criticized and obstructed the will of Congress, and had tried to exercise authority over the army. Then there are such instances of impeachment at the state level not leading to conviction as those of Henry Horton and Sidney Osborn, who both allegedly misappropriated state funds, unlike Johnson, although they eventually won acquittal, like Johnson. Perhaps the case at the state level most reminiscent of the Johnson impeachment is that of Huey Long, whose trial was little more than a naked contest for power between the pro-Long and anti-Long factions. There had been no national parallel, though, to that period in North Dakota history which witnessed the recall of one chief executive and the disqualification of two others. (The federal Constitution does not contain a Presidential recall provision.) Finally, the assassinations of Presidents James Garfield, William McKinley, and John Kennedy contrast with those of Governors William Goebel, Frank Steuenberg, and Huey Long. A crazed Stalwart Republican murdered Garfield, an anarchist, McKinley, and an alleged Communist, Kennedy, while an unknown assassin killed Goebel, a professional gunman whom radical labor leaders had hired, Steuenberg, and a relative of an individual whom "the Kingfish" had personally wronged, Long.

Turning next to the breakdown of democracy, armed protests against the national government rarely take place in this country, despite the frequency of domestic insurrections in many of the nations of Europe, Africa, Asia, and Latin America. The one obvious exception to this generalization is the Civil War. This hesitancy to revolt is doubtless attributable to the fact that the political system in operation here effectively resolves popular grievances; since 1865, the nearest that we have come to a domestic insurrection nationally was in 1894, when Coxey's army descended on Washington, and in 1932, when unemployed veterans staged their bonus march on the same city.

Both, of course, were peaceful protests, although in each case the government broke them up. Why, then, have there been domestic insurrections at the state level? In the first place, local social violence does not constitute treason against the United States, so there is less fear of punishment on the part of the participants. Secondly, the state government, as in the case of the Hatfield-McCoy feud or similar Western feuds, is sometimes too weak to prevent the outbreak and continuance of violence. Federal intervention, solicited or otherwise, usually has taken place either during a Western civil war such as the Lincoln County War or a racial integration crisis such as those at Little Rock in 1956 and Oxford in 1962. As far as results are concerned, the rioters on infrequent occasions have been able to achieve some of their goals; the night-riding tobacco farmers of Kentucky did pressure the adoption of a few reforms, while the white citizens of Wilmington, North Carolina, did expel a number of blacks from town. In general, however, these domestic insurrections must rank with the Civil War as ultimate failures.

In closing, it is obvious that there are many dissimilarities between state political history and national political history, including a number not analyzed here. Admittedly, our account has largely ignored the similarities between the two, which are indeed as extensive as the dissimilarities, yet it is the similarities which most analysts stress to the point that their presentations are likewise one-sided. One only wishes that other scholars will initiate research projects which will expand the limits of this study, as other aspects of this relationship merit exhaustive investigation. Even more important, it is hoped that some of the material presented here, together with other data of interest, eventually will find its way into surveys of national political history, from which it is currently largely absent. Perhaps a more complex view of the past will diminish the luster of certain stereotyped conceptions presently in vogue, but it also will lead to a truer conception of how this nation has evolved politically.

An Annotated Bibliography
of Selected Books

Topical and Regional Studies

Abrahams, Lewis: *It's All Politics* (New York: Samuel Curl, Inc., 1944), pp. 306. Touches on many aspects of corruption in American politics—cartoons—short bibliography.

Allen, Robert, ed.: *Our Sovereign State* (New York: Vanguard Press, 1949), pp. 413. Covers Mass., N. Y., Pa., Ga., Ohio, Ill., Wis., La., Neb., Tex., Utah, and Calif.—written from the liberal point of view.

Book of the States, 14 vols. (Chicago: Council of State Governments, 1935–   ). Issued every two years—contains material on contemporary developments in state government.

Chafee, Zechariah: *Free Speech in the United States* (Cambridge: Harvard University Press, 1941), pp. 634. Definitive work in the field—stresses the period since 1900—relatively brief bibliographical note.

Donnelly, Thomas, ed.: *Rocky Mountain Politics* (Albuquerque: University of New Mexico Press, 1940), pp. 304. Stresses differences as well as similarities between these states (Utah, Col., Nev., Wyo., Idaho, Mont., N. M., and Ariz.) —each chapter written by a different author—short bibliography.

Dulles, Foster: *Labor in America* (New York: Thomas Y. Crowell Company, 1960), pp. 435. Generally well written —offers no really original point of view—annotated bibliography.

Faulkner, Harold: *American Economic History* (New York: Harper and Brothers, 1960), pp. 816. Eighth edition of this work—one of the best texts in the field—impressive bibliographical essay.

Fenton, John: *Politics in the Border States* (New Orleans: Hauser Press, 1957), pp. 230. Originally a doctoral dissertation—based largely on personal contacts—offers many penetrating insights into Ky., W. Va., Mo., and Md. politics.

Good, H. G.: *A History of American Education* (New York: Macmillan Company, 1956), pp. 570. Treats primary, secondary, and college level education—has some chapters on intellectual history—bibliography with infrequent annotation at the end of each chapter.

Graves, W. Brooke: *American State Government* (Boston: D. C. Heath and Company, 1953), pp. 946. Perhaps the most comprehensive text in the field—fourth edition of this work—bibliographical note at the end of every chapter.

Graves, W. Brooke, ed.: *Major Problems in State Constitutional Revision* (Chicago: Public Adminstration Service, 1960), pp. 306. Different chapters written by various authorities —sponsored by Pi Sigma Alpha, the National Political Science Honor Society—bibliography.

Gunther, John: *Inside U. S. A.* (New York: Harper and Brothers, 1947), pp. 979. Many brilliant insights, although quality of coverage varies from state to state—written with a liberal slant—bibliography.

Hesseltine, William B., and David L. Smiley: *The South in American History* (Englewood Cliffs: Prentice-Hall, Inc., 1960), pp. 630. Superbly balanced and excellently written —most valuable for material on economics and politics— neither footnotes nor bibliography.

Hudon, Edward G.: *Freedom of Speech and Press in America* (Washington: Public Affairs Press, 1963), pp. 224. Continues in the tradition of Chafee—stresses period since World War I—footnotes and bibliography.

Jacob, Herbert, and Kenneth Vines: *Politics in the American States* (Boston: Little, Brown and Company, 1965), pp. 493. Each chapter written by an authority—first state politics text with a comparative politics approach—footnotes and bibliography at the end of each chapter.

Key, V. O., Jr.: *American State Politics: An Introduction* (New

York: Alfred A. Knopf, 1956), pp. 289. Probably the best work in its field—style somewhat heavy, but many significant generalizations.

Key, V. O., Jr.: *Southern Politics in State and Nation* (New York: Alfred A. Knopf, 1949), pp. 675. Approximately first half of book on individual states—second part more detailed and analytical.

Killingsworth, Charles: *State Labor Relations Acts: A Study of Public Policy* (Chicago: University of Chicago Press, 1948), pp. 328. Concentrates on general state labor relations acts—most of the material on the period since 1935 —bibliography.

Kilpatrick, James: *The Sovereign States: Notes of a Citizen of Virginia* (Chicago: Henry Regnery Company, 1957), pp. 347. Interestingly (if journalistically) written—advocates states' rights point of view—bulk of book on period prior to the Civil War.

Knight, Edgar: *Fifty Years of American Education: A Historical and Critical Appraisal* (New York: Ronald Press Company, 1952), pp. 484. Written as a textbook—one of the better works of its type—annotated bibliography at the end of each chapter.

Koontz, Harold: *Government Control of Business* (Boston: Houghton Mifflin Company, 1941), pp. 937. Especially valuable for its treatment of the state sphere—has special section on labor—short bibliography at the end of each chapter.

Labatut, Jean, and Wheaton Lane, eds.: *Highways in Our National Life* (Princeton: Princeton University Press, 1950), pp. 506. Each chapter written by an authority—first section historical, second analytical—bibliography.

Lipson, Leslie: *The American Governor from Figurehead to Leader* (Chicago: University of Chicago Press, 1939), pp. 282. Stresses reorganization movement—focuses on a limited number of states—bibliography.

Lockard, Duane: *New England State Politics* (Princeton: Princeton University Press, 1959), pp. 348. Covers six states— seed of work contained in author's doctoral dissertation on Connecticut politics—much contemporary material, based largely on interviews.

MacIver, Robert: *Academic Freedom in Our Time* (New York:

Columbia University Press, 1955), pp. 329. Continues where Metzger leaves off—as much philosophical as it is historical—footnotes and bibliography.

Metzger, Walter P.: *Academic Freedom in the Age of the University* (New York: Columbia University Press, 1961), pp. 232. Well written and well documented—analyzes general intellectual trends as well as case studies—but only covers period to the end of World War I—extensive footnotes but no bibliography.

Nash, Howard: *Third Parties in American Politics* (Washington: Public Affairs Press, 1959), pp. 326. Main omission the Union Party movement of 1936—many unusual illustrations—bibliography.

Nye, Russel: *Midwestern Progressive Politics* (East Lansing: Michigan State College Press, 1951), pp. 422. Deals with the period 1870–1950—touches on Ohio, Ind., Ill., Mich., Wis., Minn., Iowa, N. D., S. D., Neb., and Kan.—an excellent study—bibliography.

Peel, Roy: *State Government Today* (Albuquerque: University of New Mexico Press, 1948), pp. 176. Many stimulating insights in this rather brief volume—final chapter analyzes three remedies for the ills of federalism—bibliography.

Ransone, Coleman: *The Office of Governor in the United States* (University, University of Alabama Press, 1956), pp. 417. Work began as a study of Southern governors—a thorough monograph.

Ratchford, B. U.: *American State Debts* (Durham: Duke University Press, 1941), pp. 629. About two-thirds of volume on period since Reconstruction—stress on Tennessee and Arkansas in the modern epoch—bibliography.

Reichley, James: *States in Crisis: Politics in Ten American States 1950–1962* (Chapel Hill: University of North Carolina Press, 1964), pp. 264. States analyzed are Va., Mich., Ariz., Pa., Neb., N. Y., Tex., Ohio, Mass., and Calif.—a local expert collaborated on each chapter—concludes with three over-all chapters and an epilogue.

Rohlfing, Charles, Edward Carter, Bradford West, and John Harvey: *Business and Government* (Brooklyn: Foundation Press, 1949), pp. 808. Thorough study, well written but somewhat dull—designed as a textbook—present volume the fifth edition.

Schlesinger, Joseph: *How They Became Governor: A Study of*

Comparative State Politics, 1870–1950 (East Lansing: Michigan State University Governmental Research Bureau, 1957), pp. 103. A discussion of the paths by which a chief executive reaches office—analyzes politics in Vt., Mass., Iowa, Mo., Miss., Tex., and Mont.—footnotes but no bibliography.

Stein, Emanuel: *Labor Problems in America* (New York: Farrar and Rinehart, 1940), pp. 909. Six different sections by six different authors—supplementary readings at the ends of chapters—last section on foreign labor movement.

Thiem, George: *The Hodge Scandal: A Pattern of American Political Corruption* (New York: St. Martin's Press, 1963), pp. 244. Written by the Pulitzer Prize-winning reporter for the Chicago *Daily News* who uncovered the scandal—doubtless the definitive work on the subject—does lack accompanying documents or photographs.

Thomas, Dana: *The Story of American Statehood* (New York: Wilfred Funk, 1961), pp. 275. Emphasizes ten states—most valuable for its recent coverage of Alaska and Hawaii —short bibliography.

U. S. Department of Labor: *Growth of Labor Law in the United States* (Washington: United States Government Printing Office, 1962), pp. 316. A readable, up-to-date historical summary of the various forms of state labor legislation—assigns legal cases to a secondary role—bibliography, charts, tables, maps.

Van Devander, Charles: *The Big Bosses* (New York: Howell, Soskin, Publishers, 1944), pp. 318. Deals with N. Y., N. J., Mass., Pa., Tenn., La., Ala., Mo., Ill., and Calif.—offers many interesting insights into machine politics—based on personal contacts more than on published material.

Studies of Individual States

Adams, Ben: *The Last Frontier: A Short History of Alaska* (New York: Hill and Wang, 1961), pp. 181. Stresses the important events where Gruening is encyclopedic—a bit on the elementary side—annotated bibliography.

Ambler, Charles, and Festus Summers: *West Virginia: The Mountain State* (Englewood Cliffs: Prentice-Hall, Inc., 1958), pp. 584. Extremely detailed and comprehensive coverage—one of the best state histories—relatively brief annotated bibliography.

Avery, Mary: *History and Government of the State of Washington* (Seattle: University of Washington Press, 1961), pp. 583. Used as textbook—informative but much unimportant detail—bibliography.

Bald, F. Clever: *Michigan in Four Centuries* (New York: Harper and Brothers, 1961), pp. 528. Political and economic focus—useful chronology—selected bibliography.

Ball, William: *The State That Forgot: South Carolina's Surrender to Democracy* (Indianapolis: Bobbs-Merrill Company, 1932), pp. 307. About a third of the volume on the period since Reconstruction—interesting biographical sketches—closes on a pessimistic note.

Barber, Floyd, and Dan Martin: *Idaho in the Pacific Northwest* (Caldwell: Caxton Printers, 1959), pp. 433. Designed as a textbook—thorough—up-to-date coverage—illustrated profusely—long bibliography.

Barber, Joseph: *Hawaii: Restless Rampart* (Indianapolis: Bobbs-Merrill Company, 1941), pp. 285. Well-written—stress on modern Hawaii—arranged by topics.

Barnhart, John, and Donald Carmony: *Indiana: From Frontier to Industrial Commonwealth*, 2 vols. (New York: Lewis Historical Publishing Company, 1954). Carmony wrote chapters 11–15, 17, 22–24, and 27, Barnhart the others —a full treatment with stress on economics and politics —lengthy bibliography.

Beck, Warren: *New Mexico: A History of Four Centuries* (Norman: University of Oklahoma Press, 1962), pp. 363. Recent coverage places considerable emphasis on economics —also discusses politics, culture, and urbanization—bibliography.

Bettersworth, John: *Mississippi: A History* (Austin: Steck Company, 1959), pp. 595. Well balanced, all-inclusive, up-to-date treatment—bibliography at the end of every chapter.

Blegen, Theodore: *Building Minnesota* (Boston: D. C. Heath and Company, 1938), pp. 450. Written as a textbook—comprehensive, with extended coverage of economics and politics—short bibliographical note.

Bowman, David: *Pathway of Progress: A Short History of Ohio* (New York: American Book Company, 1951), pp.

546. Written as a public school textbook—largely historical, but much biographical material—bibliographical note in preface.

Caughey, John: *California* (New York: Prentice-Hall, Inc., 1953), pp. 666. One of the better works of its type—chronologically balanced—extremely lengthy annotated bibliography.

Cherry, Thomas, and Arndt Stickles: *The Story of Kentucky* (Boston: D. C. Heath and Company, 1940), pp. 367. Written as a textbook— touches on many different topics —rudimentary bibliography.

Clark, Blake: *Hawaii: The 49th State* (Garden City: Doubleday and Company, 1947), pp. 271. Discusses various topics—majority of book on modern period.

Clark, Thomas: *A History of Kentucky* (Lexington: John Bradford Press, 1950), pp. 498. Stresses political, economic, social, and educational elements—lengthy annotated bibliography.

Cleland, Robert: *A History of California*, Glenn Dunks, ed. (New York: Alfred A. Knopf, 1959), pp. 445. One of the best written of all state histories—a condensation of an earlier two-volume work—well-balanced treatment.

Clifford, Harold: *Maine and Her People* (Freeport: Bond Wheelwright Company, 1958), pp. 327. Work rather unsophisticated in style—strong on economics but rather weak on politics—bibliography.

Cole, Cyrenus: *Iowa Through the Years* (Iowa City: State Historical Society of Iowa, 1940), pp. 547. Overemphasis on national affairs—author died before the completion of the work—thorough political coverage.

Collins, Earl, and Albert Elsea: *Missouri: Its People and Its Progress* (St. Louis: Webster Publishing Company, 1945), pp. 455. Conceived as a textbook—contains convenient listing of key events during each governorship—numerous pictures.

Conley, Phil: *West Virginia Yesterday and Today* (Charleston: West Virginia Review Press, 1931), pp. 446. Economic area given greatest emphasis—somewhat weak on recent history—includes state constitution.

Connolly, Christopher: *The Devil Learns to Vote: The Story of Montana* (New York: Covici, Friede, 1938), pp. 310.

Author a participant in Montanan life during this period —work covers era from 1880 to 1910—admirable treatment of Daly, Clark and Heinze.

Coulter, E. Merton: *Georgia: A Short History* (Chapel Hill: University of North Carolina Press, 1947), pp. 510. Main stress political—economic and social developments given secondary emphasis—bibliography.

Cross, Jack, Elizabeth Shaw, and Kathleen Scheifels, eds.: *Arizona: Its People and Resources* (Tucson: The University of Arizona Press, 1960), pp. 385. Thorough and well illustrated, although a bit technical—discusses people, land, government, economy, and culture—bibliography.

Daniels, Jonathan: *Tar Heels: A Portrait of North Carolina* (New York: Dodd, Mead and Company, 1941), pp. 347. Emphasizes the cities of the state.

Dau, Frederick: *Florida Old and New* (New York: G. P. Putnam's Sons, 1934), pp. 377. Short, topical chapters— half of work on pre-American period—bibliography.

Davis, Edwin: *Louisiana: The Pelican State* (Baton Rouge: Louisiana State University Press, 1959), pp. 356. Alternates among politics, economics, culture, and everyday life —good balance between historical periods.

Day, A. Grove: *Hawaii and Its People* (New York: Duell, Sloan and Pearce, 1955), pp. 338. Emphasizes the social complex, economic factors, and the statehood drive—derived in part from a 1948 volume written in conjunction with R. S. Kuykendall—closes with a chapter on early Hawaii.

Debo, Angie: *Oklahoma: Foot-loose and Fancy-free* (Norman: University of Oklahoma Press, 1949), pp. 258. More stress on economics than on politics—good contemporary coverage—quite a few penetrating insights.

Doan, Edward: *The La Follettes and the Wisconsin Idea* (New York: Rinehart and Company, 1947), pp. 311. Analyzes both national and state developments—pro-La Follette.

Dolan, Paul: *The Government and Administration of Delaware* (New York: Thomas Y. Crowell Company, 1956), pp. 396. Seventh volume in a projected series—based largely on constitutional and legal material—bibliography.

Dunaway, Wayland: *A History of Pennsylvania* (New York: Prentice-Hall, Inc., 1948), pp. 724. Major emphasis on politics and economics—many of the chapters have not been properly brought up-to-date—annotated bibliography at the end of each.

Ellis, David, James Frost, Harold Syrett, and Harry Carmen: *A Short History of New York State* (Ithaca: Cornell University Press, 1957), pp. 705. Published in cooperation with the New York State Historical Association—pro-New Deal—social material somewhat limited—extensive annotated bibliography.

Farber, William, Thomas Geary, and William Cape: *Government of South Dakota* (Sioux Falls: Midwest-Beach Company, 1962), pp. 211. Written for both junior and senior citizens—omits much of the uninteresting detail usually found in such a work—bibliographical note.

Ferguson, Erna: *New Mexico: A Pageant of Three Peoples* (New York: Alfred A. Knopf, 1951), pp. 408. Three main sections: Indian, Spanish, and Gringo—treatment mainly economic and social—bibliography.

Fishwick, Marshall: *Virginia: A New Look at the Old Dominion* (New York: Harper and Brothers, 1959), pp. 305. Stresses all aspects of Virginian life—noteworthy appendix and bibliographical note on historical writing in the state.

Fletcher, John, *Arkansas* (Chapel Hill: University of North Carolina Press, 1947), pp. 421. Political treatment largely stops with Jefferson Davis—good coverage of recent social and economic trends—short bibliographical note.

Folmsbee, Stanley, Robert Corlew, and Enoch Mitchell: *History of Tennessee*, 4 vols. (New York: Lewis Historical Publishing Company, 1960). The definite study of the state—work favorable to the New Deal—extensive bibliography.

Foreman, Grant: *A History of Oklahoma* (Norman: University of Oklahoma Press, 1942), pp. 384. Much material on pre-territorial period—relatively weak on last decade or so—bibliography.

Fritz, Percy: *Colorado: The Centennial State* (New York: Prentice-Hall, Inc., 1941), pp. 518. More on national than on state politics—extensive coverage of labor— annotated bibliography at the end of each chapter.

Gara, Larry: *A Short History of Wisconsin* (Madison: State Historical Society of Wisconsin, 1962), pp. 287. Generally well written although a bit brief—numerous illustrations —bibliography following every chapter.

Gist, Noel, Thomas Morelock, Clarence Tucker, and Francis English: *Missouri: Its Resources, People, and Institutions* (Columbia: Curators of the University of Missouri, 1950), pp. 605. Each chapter written by a specialist—length unfortunately not always proportionate to significance—bibliography.

Gleeson, Paul: *Rhode Island: The Development of a Democracy* (Providence: Rhode Island State Board of Education, 1957), pp. 332. Well balanced and comprehensive except for coverage of labor—simple style but many sophisticated insights—bibliography at end of every chapter.

Goodwyn, Frank: *Lone-Star Land: Twentieth-Century Texas in Perspective* (New York: Alfred A. Knopf, 1955). pp. 344. Considerable emphasis on cities—political coverage stresses O'Daniel era.

Gosnell, Cullen, and C. David Anderson: *The Government and Administration of Georgia* (New York: Thomas Y. Crowell Company, 1956), pp. 403. One of the American Commonwealth Series—highly technical and often dry—bibliography.

Gottman, Jean: *Virginia at Mid-Century* (New York: Henry Holt and Company, 1955), pp. 584. Applies procedures of the French school of geography for the first time to an American state—well written, although excessively detailed at times—bibliographical note.

Gruening, Ernest: *The State of Alaska* (New York: Random House, 1954), pp. 606. Extremely comprehensive but tends toward excessive detail—written from the pro-Alaskan and pro-Democratic viewpoint—lavishly footnoted but no bibliography *per se*.

Guyton, Pearl: *The History of Mississippi: From Indian Times to the Present Day* (Syracuse: Iroquois Publishing Company, 1935), pp. 362. Well written for a textbook—softpedals Vardaman and Bilbo—bibliographical references at the end of each chapter.

Hackett, James: *The New Jersey Citizen* (New Brunswick: Rutgers University Press, 1957), pp. 314. Contains much valuable historic and economic data—political focus.

Hafen, LeRoy: *Colorado: The Story of a Western Commonwealth* (Denver: Peerless Publishing Company, 1933), pp. 328. Generally well written, stressing essentials—illustrations—bibliography at the end of each chapter.

Hamer, Philip, ed.: *Tennessee: A History, 1673–1932*, 4 vols. (New York: American Historical Society, Inc., 1933). First two volumes historical, last two biographical—period since 1870 not as fully covered as that up to 1870—annotated bibliography.

Hanna, Kathryn Abbey: *Florida: Land of Change* (Chapel Hill: University of North Carolina Press, 1948), pp. 455. Stress on economic development in the Twentieth Century—cultural and educational factors somewhat neglected—more periodicals than usual in the bibliography.

Harlow, Victor: *Harlow's Oklahoma History* (Oklahoma City: Harlow Publishing Company, 1961), pp. 596. Written as a textbook—each gubernatorial administration the subject of a separate chapter—short bibliography.

Heilbron, Bertha, *The Thirty-Second State: A Pictorial History of Minnesota* (St. Paul: Minnesota Historical Society, 1958), pp. 306. Lavishly illustrated with a concise text—up-to-date treatment—covers most aspects of Minnesota life.

Hobbs, S. Huntington: *North Carolina: An Economic and Social Profile* (Chapel Hill: University of North Carolina Press, 1958), pp. 380. One of the first American works of its type—somewhat dull as a whole—one hundred pages of tables—some bibliographical items at the end of each chapter.

Howard, Joseph: *Montana: High, Wide, and Handsome* (New Haven: Yale University Press, 1943), pp. 347. Primarily an economic treatment—author a newspaper man—moderately long bibliography.

Howe, Charles: *This Place Called Kansas* (Norman: University of Oklahoma Press, 1952), pp. 236. Short chapters and somewhat chaotic organization—economic coverage much more complete than political.

Howe, Henry: *Massachusetts: There She Is—Behold Her* (New York: Harper and Brothers, 1960), pp. 290. One of the Regions of America series—complete chronological coverage—bibliography a bit sketchy.

Hulley, Clarence: *Alaska: Past and Present* (Portland: Binfords and Mort, 1958), pp. 422. A thorough, well-balanced treatment—two chapters on period since World War II—bibliography.

Hunter, Milton: *Utah: The Story of Her People, 1540–1947*

(Salt Lake City: Deseret News Press, 1946), pp. 431. A centennial history of the state—more stress on economics than on politics—a considerable amount of material on Mormonism.

Jones, Nard: *Evergreen Land: A Portrait of the State of Washington* (New York: Dodd, Mead and Company, 1947), pp. 276. Both analytical and anecdotal—written by a native of the state.

Kane, Harnett: *Louisiana Hayride: The American Rehearsal for Dictatorship, 1928–1940* (New York: William Morrow and Company, 1941), pp. 471. Uncovers all the dirt—author has written several books on Louisiana.

Kirwan, Albert: *Revolt of the Rednecks: Mississippi Politics, 1876–1925* (Lexington: University of Kentucky Press, 1951), pp. 328. A penetrating study which brings all the dirt to the surface—attempts to be impartial—bibliographical note.

Kofoed, Jack: *The Florida Story* (New York: Doubleday and Company, 1960), pp. 336. Journalistic in style—deals mostly with modern Florida—essentially a social treatment.

Lander, Ernest: *A History of South Carolina, 1865–1960* (Chapel Hill: University of North Carolina Press, 1960), pp. 260. Work based on Wallace plus more recent research —fine treatment of the last two decades—short bibliography.

League of Women Voters of Massachusetts: *Massachusetts State Government: A Citizens' Handbook* (Cambridge: Harvard University Press, 1956), pp. 399. Informative and not as dry as most books of this type—suggests reforms vis-a-vis the constitution, education and welfare, and civil service—bibliography.

Lefler, Hugh, and Albert Newsone: *North Carolina: The History of a Southern State* (Chapel Hill: University of North Carolina Press, 1954), pp. 676. Main focus on politics and government and economic development—also discusses intellectual trends—extensive bibliography and several useful appendices.

Leifur, Conrad: *Our State North Dakota* (New York: American Book Company, 1958), pp. 621. Contains much useful information although there is some extraneous material— written as a textbook.

Lillard, Richard: *Desert Challenge: An Interpretation of Nevada* (New York: Alfred A. Knopf, 1942), pp. 388. One of the outstanding books of its type—stresses economically subservient role that the state plays—very brief bibliographical note.

Linford, Velma: *Wyoming: Frontier State* (Denver: Old West Publishing Company, 1947), pp. 428. Economic treatment the most comprehensive—touches on politics rather lightly —standard bibliography.

Lockridge, Ross: *The Story of Indiana* (Oklahoma City: Harlow Publishing Corporation, 1956), pp. 417. Conceived as a textbook— generally well written with thorough coverage—bibliography.

McGinty, Garnie: *A History of Louisiana* (New York: Exposition Press, 1949), pp. 318. Stress on pre-Civil War period—touches on most important points in the various fields—bibliography.

McKnight, O. E., and Boyd Johnson: *The Arkansas Story* (Oklahoma City: Harlow Publishing Company, 1958), pp. 419. Concentrates on politics—good up-to-date coverage.

McReynolds, Edwin: *Missouri: A History of the Crossroads State* (Norman: University of Oklahoma Press, 1962), pp. 483. Too much on national politics—pro-Democratic, especially pro-Truman—economic and social factors underemphasized—bibliography.

McReynolds, Edwin: *Oklahoma: A History of the Sooner State* (Norman: University of Oklahoma Press, 1954), pp. 461. Treatment essentially political—attention also paid to economics—closing chapter juxtaposes Will Rogers and Parrington.

McWilliams, Carey: *California: The Great Exception* (New York: Current Books, 1949), pp. 377. Exceptionally well written—political, social, and economic coverage—too much material on water.

Mack, Effie, Idel Anderson, and Beulah Singleton: *Nevada Government* (Caldwell: Caxton Printers, 1953), pp. 384. Much worthwhile historical material—illustrations, some in color, brief bibliographical note and bibliography.

Mann, E. B., and Fred Harvey: *New Mexico: Land of Enchantment* (East Lansing: Michigan State University Press, 1955), pp. 295. One of the most attractive works of its type, both as to text and pictures—material up-to-date—bibliography.

Martin, John, *Indiana: An Interpretation* (New York: Alfred A. Knopf, 1947), pp. 300. Biographical emphasis—author displeased because Old Indiana no longer exists—work based largely on personal contacts—bibliography.

Miller, Nyle, Edgar Langsdorf, and Robert Richmond: *Kansas: A Pictorial History* (Topeka: Kansas Centennial Commission and the State Historical Society, 1961), pp. 319. Covers most aspects of Kansas life—outstanding group of photographs—no indication as to the division of the writing assignment.

Mills, Lewis: *The Story of Connecticut* (West Ridge: Richard R. Smith, 1958), pp. 497. Written as a textbook—proportionately small amount of material on the twentieth century—bibliography.

Moore, Albert: *History of Alabama* (University: University Book Store, 1934), pp. 834. Extremely comprehensive but excessively detailed—revision of 1927 work—bibliography at end of each chapter.

Moscow, Warren: *Politics in the Empire State* (New York: Alfred A. Knopf, 1948), pp. 238. Based on first-hand experience as a reporter—inside-type information rather than statistics—no documentation.

Newton, Earle: *The Vermont Story* (Montpelier: Vermont Historical Society, 1949), pp. 282. First volume in a projected series on the states—one of the best illustrated of all state histories—material arranged by topics—annotated bibliography.

Newton, Lewis, and Herbert Gambrell: *Texas: Yesterday and Today* (Dallas: Turner Company, 1949), pp. 516. Based on an earlier volume—stress on political, economic, and social and intellectual factors—selected readings and Texas Constitution appended—brief list of references at the end of every chapter.

Olson, James: *History of Nebraska* (Lincoln: University of Nebraska Press, 1955), pp. 372. Primarily a political and economic treatment—offers an excellent analysis of the relationship which exists between the two.

Owen, Marie: *The Story of Alabama: A History of the State*, 3 vols. (New York: Lewis Historical Publishing Company, 1949). Too much material on relatively inconsequential people and topics—thorough coverage on governors, industries, though—bibliography.

Patrick, Rembert: *Florida Under Five Flags* (Gainesville: University of Florida Press, 1960), pp. 158. Well written and illustrated but a bit brief—based on sources—useful appendices and bibliography.

Pease, Theodore: *The Story of Illinois* (Chicago: University of Chicago Press, 1949), pp. 284. Major stress political and economic—abnormal amount of material on the two world wars.

Peck, Anne: *The March of Arizona History* (Tucson: Arizona Silhouettes, 1962), pp. 373. More on economics than on politics—final chapter deals with "Arizona in the Space Age"—bibliography.

Quaife, M. M., and Sidney Glazer: *Michigan: From Primitive Wilderness to Industrial Commonwealth* (New York: Prentice-Hall, Inc., 1948), pp. 374. Quaife wrote Part I, Glazer, Part II—brief, topical chapters with emphasis on economics and politics—coverage since 1900 rather scanty—short bibliographical note at the end of each chapter.

Raney, William: *Wisconsin: A Story of Progress* (New York: Prentice-Hall, Inc., 1940), pp. 554. Politics given the most complete treatment—more on agriculture than on manufacturing—bibliographical essay following every chapter.

Ranney, Austin: *Illinois Politics* (New York: New York University Press, 1960), pp. 64. Much up-to-date material—well written and interesting—short annotated bibliography.

Reeve, Frank: *History of New Mexico*, 2 vols. (New York: Lewis Historical Publishing Company, 1961). Less pedantic than other volumes in this series—good modern coverage in all fields.

Richardson, Rupert: *Texas: The Lone Star State* (Englewood Cliffs: Prentice-Hall, Inc., 1958), pp. 460. Covers many topics—proportional chronological emphasis—various maps and charts—bibliographical note at the end of every chapter.

Roseboom, Eugene, and Francis Weisenburger: *A History of Ohio* (Columbus: Ohio State Archaeological and Historical Society, 1953), pp. 412. Stress on politics and culture—economics relatively neglected—extensive annotated bibliography.

Saye, Albert: *A Constitutional History of Georgia, 1732–1945*

(Athens: University of Georgia Press, 1948), pp. 521. Throws light on politics as well as on constitutional history —much technical material—bibliographical note plus bibliography.

Schacter, Harry: *Kentucky on the March* (New York: Harper and Brothers, 1949), pp. 201. Book focused on the work of the Committee on Kentucky, 1943–1950—discusses many of the problems facing modern Kentucky—somewhat controversial.

Schell, Herbert: *History of South Dakota* (Lincoln: University of Nebraska Press, 1961), pp. 424. A comprehensive but dull treatment by the leading living authority—stress on politics and economics—discriminating bibliographical essay.

Shepard, Odell: *Connecticut: Past and Present* (New York: Alfred A. Knopf, 1939), pp. 316. Shepard lieutenant governor of the state 1941–1942—a rather informal study— more on earlier than on modern period.

Simkins, Francis, Spotswood Hunnicutt, and Sidman Poole: *Virginia: History—Government—Geography* (New York: Charles Scribner's Sons, 1957), pp. 599. Written as a textbook—stress on politics, economics, education and culture —illustrations and appendices.

Sindler, Allan: *Huey Long's Louisiana: State Politics, 1920– 1952* (Baltimore: Johns Hopkins Press, 1956), pp. 316. Chapter 4 an outstanding appraisal of Huey Long—extremely detailed in spots—fine annotated bibliography.

Steed, Hal: *Georgia: Unfinished State* (New York: Alfred A. Knopf, 1942), pp. 336. "An informal historical survey, a series of sketchy impressions of Georgia's manners and customs, past and present"—neither a whitewash nor a smear.

Steen, Ralph, *The Texas Story* (Austin: Steck Company, 1960), pp. 470. Conceived both for students and the public— standard treatment.

Stevens, Sylvester, Ralph Cordier, and Florence Benjamin: *Exploring Pennsylvania: Its Geography, History and Government* (New York: Harcourt, Brace and Company, 1953), pp. 624. Designed as a textbook—numerous photographs—bibliography at the end of every chapter.

Stong, Phil: *Hawkeyes: A Biography of the State of Iowa* (New York: Dodd, Mead and Company, 1940), pp. 300. Somewhat typical of works of this type, with an occasional attempt at profundity.

Summersell, Charles: *Alabama History for Schools* (Birmingham: Colonial Press, 1961), pp. 644. Informative and thorough, but suffers from the pedantic faults generally associated with textbooks—biographical appendix—long bibliography.

Tompkins, Stuart: *Alaska: Promyahlennik and Sourdough* (Norman: University of Oklahoma Press, 1945), pp. 350. Intensive treatment of a limited number of topics—over half the book on pre-American period—bibliographical note and bibliography.

Toole, K. Ross: *Montana: An Uncommon Land* (Norman: University of Oklahoma Press, 1959), pp. 278. Relates politics to economic factors—weak on politics after 1925—well written—bibliography.

Trachsel, Herman, and Ralph Wade: *The Government and Administration of Wyoming* (New York: Thomas Y. Crowell, 1953), pp. 381. One of the American Commonwealth Series—slightly more interestingly written than many of these volumes—bibliography.

Van Dusen, Albert: *Connecticut* (New York: Random House, 1961), pp. 470. Predominant stress on politics—economic coverage given secondary treatment—bibliographical items listed in extensive footnotes.

Wallace, David: *South Carolina: A Short History, 1520–1948* (Chapel Hill: University of North Carolina Press, 1951), pp. 753. Political focus—conservative orientation—a reduction of an earlier three-volume work.

Wallace, Paul: *Pennsylvania: Seed of a Nation* (New York: Harper and Row, 1962), pp. 322. One of the better Regions of America books—much material on industry and labor—bibliography.

Weaver, Samuel: *Hawaii, U. S. A.: A Unique National Heritage* (New York: Pageant Press, 1959), pp. 263. Many chapters have a legal orientation—political treatment somewhat brief.

Whipple, Maurice: *This Is the Place: Utah* (New York: Alfred A. Knopf, 1945), pp. 222. Rather loosely organized—many interesting illustrations—book based largely on personal contacts.

Wilson, Harold: *Outline History of New Jersey* (New Brunswick: Rutgers University Press, 1950), pp. 392. Often accepts sources uncritically—extensively detailed, but sometimes on relatively unimportant topics—lengthy bibliography.

Wittke, Carl, ed.: *The History of the State of Ohio*, 6 vols. (Columbus, Ohio State Archaeological and Historical Society, 1941–1944). One of the outstanding state histories —comprehensive and detailed—bibliography in footnotes —exceptional indices.

Wyllys, Rufus: *Arizona: The History of a Frontier State* (Phoenix: Robson and Herr, 1950), pp. 408. Politics and economics given most extensive coverage—last chapter a catch-all—lengthy bibliography.

Zornow, William: *Kansas: A History of the Jayhawk State* (Norman: University of Oklahoma Press, 1957), pp. 417. Comprehensive, well-balanced, up-to-date treatment—illustrations—bibliography.

Federal Writers' Project, *Alabama: A Guide to the Deep South* (New York: Hastings House, 1949), pp. 442; *A Guide to Alaska: Last American Frontier* (New York: Macmillan Company, 1945), pp. 427; *Arizona: The Grand Canyon State—A State Guide* (New York: Hastings House, 1956), pp. 532; *Arkansas: A Guide to the State* (New York: Hastings House, 1948), pp. 447; *California: A Guide to the Golden State* (New York: Hastings House, 1941), pp. 713; *Colorado: A Guide to the Highest State* (New York: Hastings House, 1951), pp. 511; *Connecticut: A Guide to Its Roads, Lore, and People* (Boston: Houghton Mifflin Company, 1938), pp. 593; *Delaware: A Guide to the First State* (New York: Viking Press, 1938), pp. 549; *Florida: A Guide to the Southernmost State* (New York: Oxford University Press, 1956), pp. 600; *Idaho: A Guide in Word and Picture* (New York: Oxford University Press, 1950), pp. 300; *Illinois: A Descriptive and Historical Guide* (Chicago: A. C. McClurg and Company, 1939), pp. 687; *Indiana: A Guide to the Hoosier State* (New York: Oxford University Press, 1961), pp. 548; *Iowa: A Guide to the Hawkeye State* (New York: Viking Press, 1938), pp. 583; *Kansas: A Guide to the Sunflower State* (New York: Viking Press, 1939), pp. 538; *Kentucky: A Guide to the Bluegrass State* (New York: Harcourt, Brace and Company, 1939), pp. 489; *Louisiana: A Guide to the State* (New York: Hastings House, 1941), pp. 746; *Maine: A Guide "Down East"* (Boston: Houghton Mifflin Company, 1937), pp. 476; *Maryland: A Guide to the Old Line State* (New York: Oxford University Press, 1940), pp. 561; *Massachusetts: A Guide to Its Places and People* (Boston: Houghton Mifflin Company, 1937), pp. 675; *Michigan: A Guide to the Wolverine State* (New York: Oxford University Press, 1941), pp. 682; *Minnesota: A State Guide* (New York: Viking Press, 1938), pp. 523; *Mississippi: A Guide to the Magnolia State* (New York: Viking Press, 1943), pp. 545; *Missouri: A Guide to the "Show Me" State* (New York: Duell, Sloan and Pearce, 1941), pp. 652; *Montana: A State Guide Book* (New York: Hastings House, 1949), pp. 429; *Nebraska: A Guide to the Cornhusker State* (New York: Viking Press, 1939), pp. 424; *Nevada: A Guide to the Silver State* (Portland: Binfords and Mort, 1940), pp. 315; *New Hampshire: A Guide to the Granite State* (Boston: Houghton Mifflin Company, 1938), pp. 559; *New Jersey: A Guide to Its Present and Past* (New York: Viking Press, 1939), pp. 735; *New Mexico: A Guide to the Colorful State* (Albuquerque: University of New Mexico Press, 1940), pp. 458; *New York: A Guide to the Empire State* (New York: Oxford University Press, 1940), pp. 782; *The North Carolina Guide* (Chapel Hill: University of North Carolina Press, 1955), pp. 649; *North Dakota: A Guide to the Northern Prairie State* (New York: Oxford University Press, 1950), pp. 352; *The Ohio Guide* (New York: Oxford University Press, 1940), pp. 634; *Oklahoma: A Guide to the Sooner State* (Norman: University of Oklahoma Press, 1941), pp. 442; *Oregon: End of the Trail* (Portland: Binfords and Mort, 1940), pp. 549; *Pennsylvania: A Guide to the Keystone State* (New York: Oxford University Press, 1940), pp. 660; *Rhode Island: A Guide to the Smallest State* (Boston: Houghton Mifflin Company, 1937), pp. 500; *South Carolina: A Guide to the Palmetto State* (New York: Oxford University Press, 1941), pp. 514; *South Dakota: A Guide to the State* (New York: Hastings House, 1952), pp. 421; *Tennessee: A Guide to the State* (New York: Hastings House, 1949), pp. 558; *Texas: A Guide to the Lone Star State* (New

York: Hastings House, 1940), pp. 718; *Utah: A Guide to the State* (New York: Hastings House, 1941), pp. 595; *Vermont: A Guide to the Green Mountain State* (Boston: Houghton Mifflin Company, 1937), pp. 392; *Virginia: A Guide to the Old Dominion* (New York: Oxford University Press, 1947), pp. 710; *The New Washington: A Guide to the Evergreen State* (Portland: Binfords and Mort, 1950), pp. 687; *West Virginia: A Guide to the Mountain State* (New York: Oxford University Press, 1941), pp 559; *Wisconsin: A Guide to the Badger State* (New York: Duell, Sloan and Pearce, 1941), pp. 651; *Wyoming: A Guide to Its History, Highways, and People* (New York: Oxford University Press, 1941), pp. 490. Famous series of a cooperative nature—volumes vary somewhat as to both quality and quantity—first part of each contains material pertinent to this study—all have bibliographies, some of which are annotated.

Index

References to Individuals—